HIV-AIDs, NGOs and Human Rights

HIV-AIDs, NGOs and Human Rights

Rajesh Kumar

AMIGA PRESS. INC
Delhi -110051

AMIGA PRESS. INC

H.O :- 28-A, Indra Park,

Chander Nagar, Delhi :- 110051 (India)

Tel :- 011-22504028, +91-98736-57000

Email :- amigapress@gmail.com
amigaeditorial@gmail.com
amigapub@gmail.com

Website :- www.amigapress@co.in

This edition is published by Amiga Press Inc.

ISBN : 978-93-87295-44-5

First Published 2019

Printed and bound by Replika Press Pvt. Ltd.

Preface

Non-governmental organization (NGO) is a term that has become widely accepted as referring to a legally constituted, non-governmental organization created by natural or legal persons with no participation or representation of any government. In the cases in which NGOs are funded totally or partially by governments, the NGO maintains its non-governmental status and excludes government representatives from membership in the organization. Unlike the term intergovernmental organization, "non-governmental organization" is a term in general use but is not a legal definition. In many jurisdictions these types of organization are defined as "civil society organizations" or referred to by other names.

The evolution of HIV/AIDS care has resulted in a wide range of care givers who work within public and private hospital facilities, NGOs, and community-based facilities. Others are volunteers and community health and social workers based at facilities or community sites. Many care givers are family members or part of a client's close social network. Additionally, people living with HIV/AIDS (PHA) themselves engage in self-care and provide support to other PHA through support groups. One such example of cooperative community-based efforts is the advances in policy creating interventions for children in difficult circumstances in South Africa. Models addressing children suffering abuse and neglect, or HIV/AIDS show that NGOs have provided valuable solutions. These organisations have demonstrated their commitment to caring and change by investing in individuals, groups and communities.

The narrative of the human rights movement in India and its historical origins has always been contextualized in the post-colonial democratic era. The turning point with respect to human rights activism in India was undoubtedly the Emergency period during the reign of Indira Gandhi. The Emergency was a period characterized by the curtailment of civil liberties through amendments to the Constitution to clamp down on the right to enjoy the fundamental rights enshrined within it, the promulgation of ordinances that legitimized the government's actions, such as arresting people on the pretext of 'preventive detention' as well as the establishment of new intelligence outfits, such as the CBI and RAW, which assisted the government with its agenda. All the matter is just compiled and edited in nature. Taken from the various sources which are in public domain.

This is a reference book. All the matter is just compiled and edited in nature, taken from the various sources which are in public domain.

This book is a modest attempt to discuss all these issues. It intends to focus on NGO, Globalization and Tribes in India and abroad. The case studies of various NGOs reflect the initiatives, programme execution strategies, successes and challenges faced by them in combating HIV/AIDS.

—*Editor*

Contents

1

Introduction

In Namibia, the turnout for World AIDS Day, commemorated on December 1, 2001, was disheartening, passing as it has since its inception – insignificantly. HIV/AIDS continues to have a considerable impact on the people of Namibia as thousands are infected and affected by the disease. Yet, positive developments occur. A capacity building workshop for NGOs on HIV/AIDS and Sexual Rights and a seminar on Women, HIV/AIDS and Human Rights, described by participants as "informative" and "inspirational" was held in the capital (Tibinyane 2002). Organised by Sister Namibia, the capacity building workshop created an opportunity for local NGOs to learn from their South African counterparts and to exchange experiences concerning issues surrounding treatment of HIV/AIDS and sexual and reproductive rights. Representatives from two South African NGOs, the Treatment Action Campaign (TAC) and the Women's Health Project (WHP) were invited by Sister Namibia to facilitate the workshop and speak at the seminar (Tibinyane 2002).

The examples of Germany and Namibia were picked for a good reason. There is a sharp contrast between the two countries. Germany, on the one hand, is economically sound and has a strong national health care programme. Namibia, on the other hand, has a fledgling economy and a struggling health care system. In Germany, AIDS is not a major threat, and its spread is kept well under control. In Namibia, similar to other African countries, the spread of HIV/AIDS has reached a crisis level of epidemic and pandemic proportions. In spite of these stark contrasts, both Germany and Namibia have one thing in common. They both rely on non-governmental organisations (NGOs) to coordinate efficient responses for various aspects of the HIV/AIDS problem.

The evolution of HIV/AIDS care has resulted in a wide range of care givers who work within public and private hospital facilities, NGOs, and community-based facilities. Others are volunteers and community health and social workers based at facilities or community sites. Many care givers are family members or part of a client's close social network. Additionally, people living with HIV/AIDS (PHA) themselves engage in self-care and provide support to other PHA through support groups (Kalibala 1999). One such example of cooperative community-based efforts is the advances in policy creating interventions for children in difficult circumstances in South Africa. Models addressing children suffering abuse and neglect, or HIV/AIDS show that NGOs have provided valuable solutions. These organisations have demonstrated their commitment to caring and change by investing in individuals, groups and communities (Sewpaul 2001).

The purpose of this paper is to explore the efforts of non-governmental organisations in combating the global HIV/AIDS crisis. Despite of the depth of literature already in existence concerning the benefits and effectiveness of NGOs in the health field, research in developing and evaluating the full potential and effectiveness of the transfer of HIV prevention intervention models from the research arena to NGOs in developing countries with high HIV incidence is still in its infancy. NGOs working in tandem with international, national and local public health organisations will allow HIV prevention research advances to better benefit the global fight against HIV/AIDS.

HIV/AIDS: BACKGROUND AND GLOBAL IMPACT

Before studying the role of non-governmental organisations in the global response to AIDS, it is essential to review HIV/AIDS, its spread, and global impact.

Acquired Immunodeficiency Syndrome (AIDS) is a fatal transmissible disease of the immune system caused by the human immunodeficiency virus (HIV). HIV slowly attacks and destroys the immune system, the body's defence against infection, leaving an individual vulnerable to a variety of other infections. AIDS is the final stage of HIV infection.

AIDS was first reported in 1981 by investigators in New York and California. Initially, most U.S. AIDS cases were diagnosed in homosexual men, who contracted the virus primarily through sexual contact, or intravenous drug users who became infected by sharing contaminated hypodermic needles. In 1983, French and American researchers isolated the causative agent, HIV, and by 1985 serological tests to detect the virus were developed.

HIV/AIDS grew to epidemic proportions in the 1980s, particularly in Africa, where the disease may have originated. This growth was facilitated by several factors including increasing urbanization and long-distance travel in Africa, international travel, changing sexual mores, and intravenous drug use. By 2002, AIDS had claimed over 25 million lives worldwide. Approximately 40 million people throughout the world are infected with HIV. People living in sub-Saharan Africa account for more than 70 percent of all infections, and in some countries of the region the prevalence of HIV infection exceeds 10 percent of the population. Rates of infection are lower in other parts of the world, but the epidemic is spreading rapidly in Eastern Europe, India, South and Southeast Asia, Latin America, and the Caribbean. In China, the government estimated that up to 850,000 people had contracted HIV by 2000 – more than half having acquired the virus since 1997. In the United States the HIV/AIDS incidence has stabilized at about 40,000 new infections per year. One-third of all new cases are women, for whom the primary risk factor is heterosexual intercourse.

HIV is transmitted by the direct transfer of bodily fluids, such as blood and blood products, semen and other genital secretions, or breast milk, from an infected person to an uninfected person. The primary means of transmission worldwide is heterosexual intercourse with an infected individual; the virus can enter the body through the lining of the vagina, penis, rectum, or mouth. HIV frequently is spread among intravenous drug users who share needles or syringes. Prior to the development of screening procedures and heat-treating techniques that destroy HIV in blood products, transmission also occurred through contaminated blood products; many people with haemophilia contracted HIV in this way. Today, the risk of contracting HIV from a blood transfusion is extremely small. In rare cases transmission to health care workers may occur by an accidental stick with contaminated medical equipment. The virus also can be transmitted across the placenta or through the breast milk from mother to infant; administration of antiretroviral medications to both the mother and infant around the time of birth reduces the chance that the child will be infected with HIV. HIV is not spread by coughing, sneezing, or casual contact (e.g., shaking hands). HIV is fragile and cannot survive long outside of the body. Therefore, direct transfer of bodily fluids is required for transmission. Other sexually transmitted diseases, such as syphilis, genital herpes, gonorrhoea, and Chlamydia, increase the risk of contracting HIV through sexual contact, probably due to the genital lesions that they cause.

The pathology of HIV infection involves three stages: (1) primary HIV infection, (2) the asymptomatic phase, and (3) AIDS. Primary HIV infection is the first stage during which transmitted HIV replicates rapidly. Some persons may experience acute flu-like symptoms, which usually persist for one to two weeks. A variety of symptoms may manifest themselves, including fever, enlarged lymph nodes, sore throat, muscle and joint pain, rash, and malaise. Standard HIV tests measuring antibodies to the virus are initially negative. As the immune response to the virus ensues, the level of HIV in the blood decreases.

The second phase of HIV infection, the asymptomatic period, lasts an average of 10 years. During this period the virus continues to replicate concurrent to a gradual decrease in the CD4 count (the number of helper T cells). When the CD4 count falls to about 200 cells per micro-litre of blood (in an uninfected adult it is typically about 1,000 cells per micro-litre), patients begin to experience opportunistic infections. This is Acquired Immunodeficiency Syndrome.

Full blown AIDS is the final stage of HIV infection. The most common opportunistic infections include *Pneumocystis carinii, Mycobacterium tuberculosis,* herpes simplex infection, bacterial pneumonia, toxoplasmosis, and cytomegalovirus infection. In addition, patients can experience dementia and develop certain cancers, including Kaposi's sarcoma and lymphomas. Death results from the unremitting growth of opportunistic pathogens or from the body's inability to fight off malignancies.

A small proportion of individuals infected with HIV has survived longer than 10 years without developing AIDS. It may be that such individuals mount a more vigorous immune response to the virus or that they are infected with a weakened strain of the virus.

Tests for the disease identify for HIV antibodies, which accumulate after four weeks to six months after exposure. The most common test for HIV is the enzyme-linked immunosorbent assay (ELISA). The result is confirmed using more specific tests such as the Western blot. A problem with ELISA is that it produces false positive results in people who have been exposed to parasitic diseases such as malaria; this is particularly troublesome in Africa, where both AIDS and malaria are rampant. Polymerase chain reaction (PCR) tests, which screen for viral RNA and therefore allow detection of the virus after very recent exposure, and Single Use Diagnostic Screening (SUDS) are other options. Due to the high cost of these testing procedures, they are often out of reach for the majority of the at risk population. Pharmaceutical companies are developing new tests that are less expensive and that do not require refrigeration, permitting more thorough testing for the at-risk population around the world.

There is no cure or effective vaccine for HIV infection. Efforts at prevention have focused primarily on changes in sexual behaviour by promoting abstinence and increasing the availability and use of condoms. Attempts to reduce intravenous drug use and to discourage needle reuse have also led to a reduction in infection rates in some areas. To treat HIV infection, three classes of antiretroviral medications are administered.

Each drug has unique side effects, and, in addition, treatment with combinations of these drugs leads to additional side effects including a fat-redistribution condition called lipodystrophy. Since HIV rapidly builds resistance to any single antiretroviral treatment, combination treatment is necessary for effective viral suppression. Highly active antiretroviral therapy (HAART), a combination of three or more RT and protease inhibitors, has resulted in a marked drop in the mortality rate from HIV infection in the United States and other industrialized states since its introduction in 1996. Due to its high cost, HAART is generally not available in regions of the world hit hardest by the AIDS epidemic. Although HAART does not appear to eradicate HIV, it largely halts viral replication, thereby allowing the immune system to reconstitute itself. Levels of free virus in the blood become undetectable.

However, the virus is still present in reservoirs, the best-known of which is a latent reservoir in a subset of helper T cells called resting memory T cells. The virus can persist in a latent state in these cells, which have a long life span due to their role as immune memory cells to respond readily to previously encountered infections. These latently infected cells represent a major barrier to curing the infection. Patients successfully treated with HAART no longer suffer from the AIDS-associated conditions mentioned above, although severe side effects may accompany the treatment. Patients must continue to take all of the drugs without missing doses in the prescribed combination or risk developing a drug-resistant virus. Viral replication resumes if HAART is discontinued.

As with any epidemic, tragedy shadows the disease's advance. From wreaking havoc on the homosexual male community in San Francisco in the 1980s to infecting more than one-third of adults in sub-Saharan African countries like Botswana at the turn of the 21st century, AIDS has had a devastating social impact. Its collateral cultural effect is far-reaching, sparking new research in medicine, complex legal debates, and intense competition among scientists, pharmaceutical companies, and research institutions.

To raise public awareness, advocates began promoting the wearing of a loop of red ribbon to indicate their concern. Activist groups lobby governments to fund education, research, and treatment. Support groups provided a wide range of services including medical, nursing, and hospice care, housing, psychological counselling, meals, and legal services. Victims were memorialized by the more than 44,000 panels of the AIDS Memorial Quilt, which was displayed worldwide both to raise funds and to emphasize the human dimension of the tragedy. The United Nations designated December 1st as World AIDS Day.

Regarding access to the latest medical treatments for AIDS, the determining factors tend to be geographic and economic. Developing nations often lack the means and funding to support the advanced treatments available in industrialized countries. On the other hand, in many developed countries specialised health care has influenced the misconception that HIV is treatable or even manageable. This perception has fostered a lax attitude toward HIV prevention (such as safe sex practices or sterile needle distribution programs), which in turn has led to new increases in HIV infection rates.

The magnitude of the disease in Africa, and in sub-Saharan Africa in particular, has prompted the governments of this region to fight the disease in a variety of ways. Some countries have made arrangements with multinational pharmaceutical companies to make HIV drugs available in Africa at lower costs. Other countries, such as South Africa, have begun manufacturing these drugs themselves instead of importing them. Plants indigenous to Africa are also being scrutinized for their usefulness in developing various HIV treatments. In the absence of financial resources to pay for new drug therapies, many

African countries had found education to be the best defence against the disease. In Uganda, for example, songs about the disease, nationally distributed posters, and public awareness campaigns starting as early as kindergarten have all helped to stem the spread of AIDS. Prostitutes in Senegal are licensed and regularly tested for HIV, and the clergy, including Islamic religious leaders, work to inform the public about the disease. Other parts of Africa, however, have experienced little progress. For example, the practice of sexually violating very young girls has developed among some HIV-positive African men because of the misguided belief that such acts would somehow cure them of the disease. Better education and advocacy of safer practices, as encouraged and directed by NGOs working in conjunction with the United Nations system, and community leaders and members, can battle the damaging stereotypes, misinformation, and disturbing practices associated with AIDS.

Laws concerning HIV and AIDS typically fall into four categories:

(1) mandatory reporting,

(2) mandatory testing,

(3) laws against transmission, and

(4) immigration.

The mandatory reporting of newly discovered HIV infections is meant to encourage early treatment. Canada, Switzerland, Denmark, and Germany, among other countries have enacted mandatory screening laws for HIV. Countries like Estonia require mandatory testing of prison populations (in response to explosive rates of infection among the incarcerated). The United States requires some form of testing for convicted sex offenders. Other legal and international issues concern the criminalization of knowing or unknowing transmission (more prevalent in the United States and Canada) and the rights of HIV-positive individuals to immigrate to or even enter foreign countries.

In the United States, communities have fought the opening of AIDS clinics or the right of HIV-positive children to attend public schools. Countries like Thailand, India, and Brazil challenge international drug patent laws, arguing that the societal need for up-to-date treatments supersedes the rights of pharmaceutical companies protected by international patent laws. At the start of the 21st century, Western countries were also battling the reluctance of the Vatican, some Muslim nations, and other countries such as China to single out homosexuals, prostitutes, and drug dealers for special attention out of fear of appearing to condone their lifestyles. These are all only some of the examples of the obstacles HIV/AIDS related NGOs all over the globe must face and surmount regularly.

Less developed countries (LDCs) have made impressive progress in human development since the Second World War. However, those achievements are being undermined as countries lose young, productive people to HIV/AIDS. Households fall into deeper poverty, economies stumble and the impact of the epidemic is felt across society (UNAIDS 2002).

The Demographic Impact: More than 60 million people have been infected with HIV since the beginning of the epidemic almost 20 years ago. In 2001 alone, the HIV/AIDS epidemic claimed an estimated 3 million lives. In the 45 most affected countries, between 2000 and 2020 an estimated 68 million people will die due to AIDS. In many countries, AIDS is erasing decades of progress in human development by drastically reducing life expectancy (UNAIDS 2002).

The impact on households: AIDS pushes people deeper into poverty as households lose breadwinners, livelihoods are compromised and savings are consumed by the cost of health care and funerals. Women are left bearing bigger burdens as workers, care givers, educators and mothers. Yet, their legal, social and political status leaves them more vulnerable to HIV/AIDS (UNAIDS 2002).

The impact on the health sector: In all affected countries, the HIV/AIDS epidemic is putting the health sector under strain. Overall quality of health care dropped. There is a shortage of hospital beds. While demand for health services is expanding, more health care personnel are affected by HIV/AIDS. Home-care initiatives are a key coping mechanism for mitigating impact (UNAIDS 2002).

The Impact on Education: A noticeable decline in school enrolment occurs as AIDS hampers the ability of education systems to fulfil basic social mandates as teachers succumb to the disease. How well educational institutions adapt and function will influence how well societies recover from the epidemic (UNAIDS 2002).

The impact on enterprises and workplaces: The vast majority of people living with AIDS worldwide are in the prime of their working lives. AIDS weakens economic activity by squeezing productivity, adding costs, diverting resources, and depleting skills. The epidemic hits productivity through absenteeism, organisational disruption, and the loss of skills and organisational memory. Production cycles are disrupted, equipment stands idle, and temporary staff need to be recruited and trained. Loss of know-how is the most often-cited cost factor (UNAIDS 2002).

Macroeconomic impact: AIDS has a profound impact on growth, income and poverty. For countries with HIV/AIDS prevalence rates of 20% or more, the GDP growth has been estimated to drop by an average of 2.6% annually (UNAIDS 2002). The factors listed above are common to the impact of HIV/AIDS globally (UNAIDS 2002). On the one hand, they trigger solidarity to combat government, community and individual denial, and offer support and care to people living with HIV and AIDS. On the other hand, individuals suffering from HIV/AIDS are stigmatised and ostracised by their loved ones, their family and their communities, and discriminated against individually as well as institutionally (UNAIDS 2002).

HIV/AIDS-related stigma and discrimination builds upon, and reinforces, existing prejudices. They play into and strengthen existing social inequalities, especially those of gender, sexuality and race.

They also play a key role in producing and reproducing relations of power and control. They cause some groups to be devalued and others to feel that they are superior. Ultimately, stigma creates and is reinforced by social inequality. HIV/AIDS victims are denied health services and education, or may lose employment on the grounds of their HIV status. This is another issue that NGOs tackling the AIDS crisis must deal with on a regular basis. To overcome such stigma, these NGOs collabourate with UNAIDS and the UN Commission on Human Rights.

Recent UN Commission on Human Rights resolutions have unequivocally stated that "the term 'or other status' in non-discrimination provisions in international human rights texts should be interpreted to cover health status, including HIV/AIDS", and has confirmed that "discrimination on the basis of HIV/AIDS status, actual or presumed, is prohibited by existing human rights standards" (UNAIDS 2002). The human rights framework provides access to existing procedural, institutional and other monitoring mechanisms for enforcing the rights of people living with HIV/AIDS, and for countering and redressing discriminatory action. Two complementary kinds of alleviation strategies are necessary to address stigma and discrimination: (1) strategies that prevent stigma or prejudicial thoughts being formed, and (2) strategies that address or redress the situation when stigma persists and is acted upon through discriminatory action, leading to negative consequences or the denial of entitlements or services. Ultimately, it is at the community and national levels that HIV/AIDS-related stigma and discrimination are most effectively combated. Communities and community leaders must advocate for inclusiveness and equality irrespective of HIV status.

In its role as the leading advocate for worldwide action against HIV/AIDS, UNAIDS – the Joint United Nations Programme on HIV/AIDS – along with its eight co-sponsors – United Nations Children's Fund (UNICEF), United Nations Development Programme (UNDP), United Nations Population Fund (UNFPA), United Nations International Drug Control Programme (UNDCP), International Labour Organisation (ILO), United Nations Educational, Scientific and Cultural Organisation (UNESCO), World Health Organisation (WHO), and World Bank (WB) – states as its mission to "lead, strengthen, and support an expanded response to the HIV/AIDS epidemic aimed at preventing the transmission of HIV, providing care and support for those infected and affected by the disease, reducing vulnerability of individuals and communities to the HIV/AIDS epidemic aimed at preventing the transmission of HIV, providing care and support for those infected by the disease, reducing the vulnerability of individuals and communities to HIV/AIDS, and alleviating the socioeconomic and human impact of the epidemic" (UNAIDS 2002). In order to achieve this, the Global Fund to Fight AIDS, TB and Malaria was set up. The Global Fund complements the work by UNAIDS by providing finance to meet these aims (UNAIDS 2002).

HIV/AIDS programmes in developing countries and countries in transition need to spend US $10 billion annually for an adequate AIDS response. Current funds are less than a quarter of that. To reach the goal of US $10 billion annual spending on AIDS in developing countries, there must be major increases in national government allocations, greater support from the private sector and increases in international assistance through the Global Fund, bilateral funding programmes and international organisations. Two-thirds of the funding is met by international assistance.

As the epidemic of HIV/AIDS continues to expand to all corners of the globe, it is clear that every sector of society must respond. AIDS is no longer a concern just of health authorities. The potential impact of AIDS makes it a challenge in economic, political, social and religious spheres as well. Among organisations responding to the crisis, non-governmental organisations (NGOs) are emerging as a powerful force in the effort to contain the epidemic. Diverse groups at risk of HIV infection have been reached by NGOs in a wide variety of innovative programmes.

MEDICAL FACTS ABOUT HIV/AIDS

The National Institutes of Health in 2001 investigated the world scientific literature relating to the ability of condom use to reduce the risk of the transmission of sexually transmitted disease. The NIH in 2001, found that the consistent and correct use of the condom reduced the risk of HIV transmission by 85%. A 15% risk remained. A more recent study, in 2003, concluded that consistent use of the condom results in only 80% reduction in HIV transmission. Other circumstances such as rupture of a condom increase the risk. Liviana Calzavera PhD., an epidemiologist at the University of Toronto, Faculty of Medicine, has stated that imperfect condom use probably offers as high a risk of transmitting HIV as does intercourse without the use of the condom.

A key question remains. Does distribution of condoms lessen the spread or increase the transmission of HIV/AIDS? Dr. George Mulcaire-Jones, president and founder of Maternal Life International, who knows first-hand that condoms don't work because of his regular travels to Africa to work hands-on in the war against AIDS, says that condoms do little physically to prevent transmission of HIV and exacerbate the problem by promoting promiscuity where that behaviour is most deadly, Asia and Africa. Norman Hearst, professor at University of California and Sanny Chen, an epidemiologist at the South Africa Health Department state that in many sub-Saharan African countries, high HIV transmission rates have continued despite high condom use. They also said that no clear examples have immerged yet of a country that has turned back a generalized epidemic primarily by means of condom prevention, adding that the main cause of the falling incidence of HIV in Uganda was a substantial drop in the numbers of casual sexual partners and that measuring condom efficacy is nearly impossible. Botswana, Zimbabwe, Kenya, and South Africa have the highest rates of HIV and also the highest availability of condoms.

Until the late 1980s, Uganda had the highest rate of HIV/AIDS in the world. They then introduced a program to teach abstinence before marriage, and marital fidelity afterwards. They only reluctantly advised condoms for high-risk groups, like prostitutes, whom they knew would not accept the other two approaches. In 1991, the prevalence rate of HIV was 15%. By 2001, it was 5%, the biggest reduction of HIV in the world. The rate among pregnant mothers in 1991 was 21.2%; by 2001, it was 6.2% and, at the same time, it was 15% in Kenya, 32% in Zimbabwe and 38% in Botswana, countries which focus on condom distribution. Their rates are still rising. Dr. Edward C. Green, an anthropologist at the Harvard School of Public Health, who used to support condom distribution, was sent to Uganda by the U.S. Agency for International Development (USAID) to study the reasons for the success in Uganda.

He reported that reduction in the number of sexual partners was probably the single most important behavioral change that resulted in prevalence decline-Abstinence was probably the second most important change. USAID, however, shelved Dr. Green's conclusions and enlisted a well-known condom advocate to write a new report. Evidence for the success of Uganda's approach has come from USAID, The Joint United Nations Program on HIV/AIDS (UNAIDS), The World Health Organization (WHO), The Harvard Centre for Population and Developmental Studies, The Ugandan Government, and numerous independent studies. Dr. Anne Paterson, assistant administrator for global health with the USAID, gave similar evidence about the effectiveness of abstinence and faithfulness in marriage in regard to efforts to stem HIV/AIDS. She reported this to the Subcommittee on African Affairs, on May 23, 2003.10

One more question. Is it reasonable to recommend the use of the condom to a married couple where one partner has HIV infection? The condom does not abolish the risk of transmitting this horrible and ultimately fatal disease. Intercourse puts the uninfected spouse at great risk. There is therefore a doubt about taking the life of an innocent human being, a dubium facti, which as such, creates the same obligation as certainty. Self-sacrifice and abstinence are the only valid moral options. Sister Miriam Duggan (Franciscan Missionaries of Africa) and Sister Kay Lawlor (Medical Missionaries of Mary) run a major abstinence program in Uganda. Sister Duggan says that the main reason why AIDS has spread so much in Africa is because of a loss of traditional values. Polygamy was practiced, but virginity before marriage and fidelity within marriage were respected. Media and peer pressure has resulted in promiscuity. The sister's program has shown that chastity is not pie-in-the-sky, but has very real positive results. Dr. Mulcaire-Jones who once believed that it would be impossible to get African men to understand natural family planning, or to adhere to a lifestyle of abstinence and sexual faithfulness in marriage now says "I have found tremendous willingness to hear and adhere to Church teachings about sexual morality-we are having tremendous success-the Catholic Church really does have the answer to this."

Why is the Focus only on HIV/AIDS?

Was it a focus on HIV/AIDS that caused the various bishops to recommend use of the condom to prevent its spread? It is true that it is a death dealing disease. However, there are many other deadly sexually transmitted infections whose spread has not caused any Catholic clerical concern. Consider the following facts:

- Gonorrhea; reduction of infection rate by condom use was 13.7% in men and 2% in women, 62 million new cases annually, worldwide.
- Chlamydia: no proof of risk reduction, 89 million new cases annually, worldwide.
- Genital Herpes: no proof of risk reduction, 92 million new cases annually, worldwide.
- Human Papilloma Virus (HPV): no proof of risk reduction, 12 million new cases annually, worldwide.
- Syphilis: no proof of risk reduction, 12 million new cases annually, worldwide.
- Human immunodeficiency virus (HIV): risk reduction 85%, but only if the condom is consistently and correctly used. There are 5.3 million new cases annually, worldwide.
- Hepatitis B virus (HBV): no proof of risk reduction, 45 million new cases annually, worldwide.

Serious Complications of these Infections

- Gonorrhea: In women, tubal pregnancy, infertility, pelvic pain, blindness in the newborn child.
- Chlamydia: In women, tubal pregnancy, pelvic pain, eye infection and pneumonia in newborn child.

- Genital Herpes: increased risk of HIV and death of newborn baby.
- Syphilis: serious and fatal disease of the aorta, heart and brain of the adult and death or congenital syphilis of the newborn baby.
- HPV: almost all cases of carcinoma of the cervix of the uterus are caused by this virus. Carcinoma of the uterus is the third most common cancer in women, worldwide. HPV, which is transmitted by anal receptive intercourse, also causes cancer of the anus.
- HBV: causes liver failure and cancer of the liver.

Conclusion

To recommend the condom as a protection against HIV gives a false sense of security, not only in regard to HIV, but also in regard to many other serious diseases, where it provides little or no protection at all. The tendency of the clergy to cave in about the Church's teaching on the use of condoms is consistent with their failure to preach and the laity's failure to put into practice the Church's teaching on contraception. When Pope Paul VI published his encyclical Humanae Vitae in 1968, he predicted that artificial contraception would lead to an increase in conjugal infidelity, a general lowering of morality, and, as is the case in China today, mandatory and arbitrary contraceptive measures. He could not have anticipated the tragic tsunami of sexually transmitted diseases that have occurred since his time. Safer sex' is an oxymoron, and the most dangerous expression in the English language.

CAN WE FIND A SOLUTION TO THE HIV-AIDS CONTROVERSY

The assumption proposed by Gallo in 1984, that the cause of AIDS is infection with HIV viruses was founded on the correlation between the detection of antibodies to these viruses and the onset of AIDS. This view became generally accepted, and today it is still the foundation stone of HIV-virus related measures for the prevention and treatment of AIDS. Duesberg vehemently opposed this opinion. However, although his reasoning was in many respects justified, it was unanimously rejected by AIDS researchers with an interest in virology. The time for re-evaluation has come, now that methods are available for the direct detection of HIV viruses and for the detection of cellular anti-HIV immune reactions.

In this regard, the work of Bentwich and Jehuda-Cohen of Israel deserves special attention. They developed a polyclonal B-cell activation test with which they were able to demonstrate that HIV infections are common among anti-HIV-antibody-negative high-risk individuals. The disease is brought under control by cellular immune reactions and the anti-HIV antibody test remains negative. They also demonstrated that individuals with a positive anti-HIV antibody reaction as a rule showed a pre-existing activation of their immune system at the time of infection. By contrast, the majority of people whose immune system was healthy and normal at the time of infection with HIV showed only a cellular immune reaction by which the HIV viruses had been brought under control and probably partially eliminated from the body.

Strong support for this work came with the reports of Mosmann and Coffman concerning functionally opposing cytokine profiles of CD4 helper lymphocytes. They demonstrated that two groups of cells could be identified among the CD4 helper cells; these they designated Th-1 ancl Th-2 cells. The Th-1 cells secrete preferentially IL-2, IL-12 and IFN-d, which stimulate the cellular immune reactions. The Th-2 cells produce primarily IL-4, IL-6 and IL-10, by which they stimulate the humoral immune reactions. Clerici and Shearer established that displacing the lymphokine profile Th-1 to the Th-2 profile is of crucial importance for the course of HIV infection. Thus, numerous high-risk individuals who are anti-HIV antibody negative show a strong immune reaction of the Th-1 type to HIV antigens.

Moreover, these authors have recently reported that the lymphokine profiles Th-l and Th-2 are linked by hormonal equilibrium states between cortisol and dehydroiso-androsterone (DHEA): cortisol assists the formation of Th-2 cytokines, while DHEA promotes the formation of Th-1 cytokines. Important supporting evidence for the influence of the lymphocytic cytokine profile on the course of HIV infection, which was studied by Clerici and Shearer was brought to light in the investigations of "murine acquired immunodeficiency syndrome" (MAIDS), which is caused by defective mouse leukaemia viruses. IL 4-deficient mice survived infection with this virus, while IL-4 producers succumbed to the disease.

What is the relationship between the lymphocytic cytokine profiles Th-1 and Th-2 and acquired immunodeficiency states in stress reactions? As we said in our review of AIDS prevention in HIV carriers, an acquired immunodeficiency state is a component of all stress reactions.

The concept of stress first described by Selye in 1936 essentially states that the body presents a standard response to the numerous somatic and psychic stresses, in which activation of the neuroendocrine stress axis hypothalamus-pituitary-adrenals plays a central role.

The increased release of catecholamines and glucocorticoids from the adrenals centralises the metabolism on the supply of rapidly available energy sources, in particular glucose. The glucocorticoids limit the inflammatory reactions and in so doing raise the susceptibility to infection. They reduce the number of lymphocytes and eosinophils and the thymus weight, and are at the centre of suppression of the specific Iymphoplasma-cell immune reactions.

The problem of stress-related irnmunosuppression and its effect on latent viral infections was for more than a decade the area of research of Kiecolt-Glaser and Glaser. In extensive investigations they showed that psychic stress reactions raise the titre of humoral antibodies to viruses such as EBV, CMV and HSV-l, simultaneously attenuating the cellular immune reactions, which are measured in cytotoxic T-cell reactions to these viruses.

They explained their findings in terms of the release of latent viruses by the attenuation of cellular defence mechanisms and the secondary stimulation of the formation of humoral antibodies. This interpretation is supported by the observation that the titre of anti-poliomyelitis antibodies is unchanged during stress reactions.

Unlike the three herpes viruses mentioned above, poliomyelitis viruses are completely eliminated by the immune reaction after spreading through the body. During their investigations, the authors also observed that the balance between the cyclic nucleotides AMP and GMP, which play a central role in the regulation of lymphocytic metabolic functions, can also be ascribed to the general stress process.

The rise in cAMP, which is characteristic for the suppression of all specific cellular immune reactions, is linked to a reduction in cGMP and is concomitant with the decline in cellular immune reactions and the increase in humoral immune reactions.

From what has been said so far it might be supposed that HIV infection can be brought under control by cellular immune reactions in individuals with full immunocompetence, some of the viruses being eliminated and some remaining dormant within the body.

On the immunosuppressant behaviour of high-risk groups: homosexual males, drug addicts of both sexes, haemophiliacs and recipients of blood transfusions Bentwich and Wainberg have many times since 1985 pointed out that homosexual males not infected with HIV often exhibit marked activation of their immune system.

The interferon system, the subpopulations of peripheral lymphocytes, the elevated cell-bound cytotoxicity, and the formation of serum autoantibodies are involved here. Of special note was the finding that the reactivation of an Epstein-Barr viral infection prior to infection with HIV correlated significantly with the appearance of anti-HIV antibodies. The concentration of transforming growth factor in the seminal fluid is relevant in this context. This is an immunosuppressant protein whose function it is to protect the sperm in the vagina from immunological attack by the woman's body. During anal intercourse, it is evidently capable of weakening the immune system of the passive partner.

The immunosuppressant action of opiates has been most widely researched. In studies in mice, chronic administration of morphine causes severe involution of the thymus, characterised by increased apoptosis, primarily of CD4+/CD8+ thymocytes. The reason for this is probably that morphine increases the formation of corticotropin in the hypothalamus, thereby increasing the formation of ACTH in the pituitary and cortisol in the adrenal cortex. It can thus be assumed that hypercortisolism plays an important role in opiate-induced immunosuppression. To date there have been few investigations of the immunosuppressant effect of cocaine. With regard to its effect on AIDS, let us here refer simply to the animal studies of Lopez and Watson, who showed that in murine AIDS (MAIDS) cocaine dramatically increases the damaging effect of the retroviral infection on the lymphoreticular tissue of the intestinal mucosa.

The question concerning the extent to which immunosuppression in haemophiliacs is correlated with the anti-HIV-antibody status has been researched in detail. The studies of Madhok are of most significance in this regard. The first point to mention regarding this problem is that about half of haemophiliacs produced no anti-HIV antibodies in response to the repeated administration of HIV-contaminated "largepool" coagulation products during the period 1981-1986. To date, no investigations have yet been performed to ascertain whether this patient group has neutralised the HIV viruses by exclusively cellular immune reactions, and then partially eliminated them.

However, it is certain that the "large-pool" factor-VIII products in use at that time inhibited the formation of IL-2, thereby weakening the cellular immune reactions. Moreover, at a time when HIV infection was still unknown among haemophiliacs, numerous patients died of acquired immunodeficiency diseases. It must also be considered that, as a consequence of the administration of "large-pool" products manufactured from a large number of pooled plasmapheretic donations from paid donors, the large majority of haemophiliacs used to suffer from chronic hepatitis, which may be regarded as a supplementary immununosuppressant risk. Neither should one underestimate the iron overload as a result of bleeding into the joints and the blood transfusions this necessitated.

Haemophiliac immunodeficiency is characterised to particularly good effect by the following two observations. Bedall et al. made the observation that anti-HIV negative haemophiliac adolescents exposed to patients with open tuberculosis developed just as frequently as did children receiving chemotherapy for the treatment of solid tumours. Counter to expectations, in a well-studied group of Dutch haemophiliacs Rosendaal et al. observed a 2.5 times higher mortality rate from cancer. The question currently under debate is whether the genetically engineered factor-VIII products, which evidently do not stress patient's immune system, are suitable substitutes for products manufactured from human plasma.

Pathogenetic Mechanisms of Acquired Immunodeficiency States

The Th-l/Th-2 imbalance of the cytokines of CD4 lymphocytes, which has an immunosuppressant effect, and the displacement of the ratio of the cyclic lymphocytic nucleotides cAMP/cGMP are at least in part attributable to hypercortisolism within the context of stress reactions. This is due to the increased formation of corticotropin in the hypothalamus and the resulting activation of the formation of ACTH in the pituitary and cortisol in the adrenal cortex. In association with sympatheticotonic activation of the autonomic nervous system, which occurs in parallel, this is the standard physiological reaction to all inflamrnatory, toxic, psychic and nutritive stress states. In persistent subclinical stress states there is continuous slight activation of macrophages, with increased formation of monokines and oxygen radicals.

This state has a broad tolerance threshold, and can be compensated in the long term. It is manifested as a moderately increased susceptibility to infections and certain degenerative diseases. According to Bentwich and Wainberg, this group includes the many anti-HIV antibody-positive individuals in Africa, Asia and Latin America in whom endemic infections associated with HIV infections favour the humoral immune reaction and weaken the cellular immune reaction. Thus, according to WHO statistics of 1 July 1994, the number of notified AIDS cases in south-east Asia between 1979 and the end of June 1994, which amount to a total of 6739, has so far not risen above the 0.5% threshold of the estimated 2.5 million anti-HIV antibody-positive carriers of the virus.

This group of anti-HIV antibody-positive HIV carriers contrasts with the groups within North America and Europe at high risk of contracting AIDS. In these groups, intensive and continuous stresses play a considerable part in the outbreak of disease. As already mentioned, the persistent activation of macrophages with the release of inflammation mediators and oxygen radicals are prominent in these groups. This leads to increased hypercortisolism which in the lymphoid tissue reduces its most sensitive element, the immature thymocytes, by increased apoptosis, thereby appreciably reducing the number of immunological precursor cells. Gradually the other populations of CD4 helper cells are affected as well, presumably also by HIV viruses, and progressive lyrnphopenia occurs, with a corresponding displacement of the CD4/CD8 ratio. The increasing attenuation of the cellular immune reaction finally leads to activation of the infective agents latent within the body, and thus to the large number of opportunistic inflammatory diseases characteristic of AIDS.

HUMAN RIGHTS IN INDIA

The situation of human rights in India is a complex one, as a result of the country's large size and tremendous diversity, its status as a developing country and a sovereign, secular, democratic republic, and its history as a former colonial territory. The Constitution of India provides for Fundamental rights, which include freedom of religion. Clauses also provide for Freedom of Speech, as well as separation of executive and judiciary and freedom of movement within the country and abroad. It is often held, particularly by Indian human rights groups and activists, that members of the Dalit or Untouchable caste have suffered and continue to suffer substantial discrimination. Although human rights problems do exist in India, the country is generally not regarded as a human rights concern, unlike other countries in South Asia. Based on these considerations, the report Freedom in the World 2006 by Freedom House gave India a political rights rating of 2, and a civil liberties rating of 3, earning it the highest possible rating of *free.*

India claims an abiding commitment to human rights, but its record is marred by continuing violations by security forces in counterinsurgency operations and by government failure to rigorously implement laws and policies to protect marginalized communities. A vibrant media and civil society continue to press for improvements, but without tangible signs of success in 2007.

India faces serious insurgencies and armed political movements in several states. Armed groups have been responsible for attacks on civilians, killings, torture, and extortion. In response, however, Indian security forces have repeatedly engaged in abusive tactics. The government has yet to root out the policies responsible for the violations, and continues to grant virtual impunity to perpetrators. Despite signing a new United Nations treaty to combat forced disappearances in February 2007, the Indian government is yet to launch a credible independent investigation into alleged disappearances and fake "encounter killings" throughout the country. There is continuing failure to protect the rights of women, children, Dalits, tribal groups, religious minorities, and those living with HIV/AIDS. Authorities have introduced significant legal and policy reforms in many of these areas, but implementation has lagged, exacerbating popular discontent over widening economic and social disparities.

Combating Maoist Extremists

An ongoing campaign by leftwing extremists called Maoists or Naxalites has gained momentum in several Indian states. The Maoists find support among the rural poor, who feel left out by India's modernization process and surging economic growth. Unfortunately, these same vulnerable groups also suffer at the hand of the Maoists because of the latter's illegal taxes and demands for food and shelter. Succumbing to such extortion puts civilians at risk of retaliation by security forces.

According to the Ministry of Home Affairs, 950 people died in 2006 in Maoist-related violence and as of November 2007, according to data gathered by the South Asia Terrorism Portal, more than 550 people had died, including 200 civilians.

Violent attacks, whether perpetuated by the Maoists or security forces, take place in remote areas, making it difficult to independently monitor the situation.

Conflict in Jammu and Kashmir

While the violence which began in 1989 has abated slightly since talks were initiated between India, Pakistan, and some separatist groups in 2005, abuses by all parties continue. In February 2007, police investigations into a "missing persons" case in Jammu and Kashmir exposed a problem long alleged by human rights groups: people were being killed in custody by security forces who constructed fake armed encounters, staging executions to look like acts of defence. In April 2007, a working group on Jammu and Kashmir recommended the repeal of laws sanctioning impunity, such as the Armed Forces Special Powers Act, but the government has failed to act.

Armed Conflicts and Security Force Impunity

India's diverse ethnic and regional identities, coupled with deeply rooted economic and social grievances, have fueled violent insurgencies and armed campaigns.

Militants often target civilians and engage in torture and extortion. While a number of regional conflicts pose serious threats, counterinsurgency operations by Indian security forces have led to large-scale violations including arbitrary detention, torture, and extrajudicial killings. Perpetrators are rarely prosecuted and the Indian government has not acknowledged or addressed institutional shortcomings that foster such impunity.

Violence in the Northeast

Ethnic separatist tensions in some northeastern states ignited again in 2007. Based on newspaper reports, the South Asia Terrorism Portal recorded 640 deaths in 2006; as of November 2007, 880 people had already died. In Assam, alleged members of the United Liberation Front of Asom (ULFA), a militant group, attacked and killed scores of Hindi-speaking migrants, most of them from Bihar state. Over 200 civilians had been killed in the violence as of late November.

Manipur remains among the most violent states in the northeast, with militants blamed for widespread extortion and targeted killings and security forces accused of violations such as torture, arbitrary detention, and custodial killings.

Failure of Relocation and Rehabilitation Policies

Tremendous economic growth and plans for industrial development and infrastructure building have uprooted millions of traders, farmers, and landless labourers. Protests by affected groups are ignored and often brutally curbed through excessive use of force. On March 14, violence in Nandigram in West Bengal state during protests against state-sponsored land acquisition claimed at least 14 lives. In November, the ruling Communist Party of India (Marxist) (CPM) allowed its cadre to forcefully evict the Nandigram protestors.

The National Human Rights Commission, political parties, and civil society activists condemned the violence that followed. The state government, which had advance notice of the evictions, failed to deploy adequate security forces to ensure law and order. There have also been protests in several other states including Maharashtra, Uttar Pradesh, and Orissa.

Justice for Past Abuses in Punjab

In 2007 there was still no progress in investigating thousands of secret cremations in the northern state of Punjab. Following a spate of violent attacks by Sikh militants starting in the early 1980s, security forces illegally detained, tortured, executed, or "disappeared" thousands of people during counterinsurgency operations. None of the security officials who bear substantial responsibility for these violations has been brought to justice. The National Human Rights Commission in 2007 prepared for final hearings to determine compensation in a small number of cases, but the government still has not investigated how people died and who was responsible.

RIGHTS OF DALITS AND INDIGENOUS TRIBAL GROUPS

In March 2007, the Committee on the Elimination of Racial Discrimination (CERD) urged the government to take effective measures to protect Dalits and tribal groups. Dalits and indigenous peoples (known as Scheduled Tribes or adivasis) continue to face discrimination, exclusion, and acts of communal violence. Laws and policies adopted by the Indian government provide a strong basis for protection, but are not being faithfully implemented by local authorities. Instead of addressing these concerns, the Indian government insists that caste is not the same as race and therefore discrimination based on caste and tribe falls outside the mandate of CERD.

Legacy of Communal Violence

A number of attacks occurred on places of religious worship in 2007, including a bomb blast at the revered Sufi shrine in Ajmer in October. The Indian government succeeded in preventing communal riots following this and other attacks. The Indian government, however, has failed to prosecute most of those who instigate or participate in religious mob violence. Despite national and international condemnation, the Gujarat state government continues to protect those responsible for the killing of Muslims during the 2002 riots. After more than a decade of hearings, a special court convicted 100 people for their involvement in the 1993 serial bomb attacks in Mumbai. However, the individuals believed responsible for attacks upon Muslims in January 1993 which preceded the bomb blasts are yet to be prosecuted and punished. Despite promises made by the prime minister in 2005, there was also no progress in justice for victims of the 1984 anti-Sikh riots.

Death Penalty

There were no executions in 2007 but the death penalty remains on the books. Over 40 people were sentenced to death for the 1993 Mumbai bombings.

Human Rights Defenders

In Chattisgarh state, which experienced more Maoist violence than any other state in 2007, civil society organizations have come under attack in a classic example of "punishing the messenger." Prominent human rights defender Dr. Binayak Sen was detained for his alleged contact with the Maoist groups. Several journalists and other human rights activists said that they had been threatened by government officials.

Failure to Protect Children's Rights

Despite a scheme launched three years ago to provide universal education, millions of children in India still have no access to education and work long hours, many as bonded labourers.

Many children continue to be forced into becoming soldiers in areas where there are armed conflicts, or are trafficked for marriage, sex work, or employment. Others languish in substandard orphanages or detention centres. In 2007, the National Children's Commission began operations to ensure protection of children's rights.

MAKING HUMAN RIGHTS WORK: LINKING RIGHTS WITH PARTICIPATION

If human rights are to have real meaning, they must be linked to public participation. And participation must be preceded by empowerment of the people. A sense of empowerment requires a sense of dignity, self-worth and the ability to ask questions. The sense of empowerment along with a sense of legal entitlements and constitutional guarantees gives rise to a political consciousness based on rights. A process of political empowerment and a sense of rights empowers citizens to participate in the public sphere.

Most mass movements in modern India (the All India Democratic Women's Association, Ragpickers Union etc) have emphasised the process of empowerment while they also 'struggled' for rights. The notion of 'struggle' was implicit in claiming and promoting rights. Most social action groups and people's organisations started by challenging and changing oppressive power structures that perpetuate patriarchy, casteism and poverty. Thus at the core of many such organisations was political transformation through people's empowerment wherein people can assert their rights and voices and demand justice. The process of social and political empowerment encompassed a sense of conscientisation based on dignity, rights and participation. That is why the slogans of the Shramajeevi Sanghatana, the union of erstwhile bonded labourers and Adivasis (tribals) in Thane district of Maharashtra assert that "We are not animals, but human beings", "We are not here to beg, but to demand justice".

People-centred advocacy is a possible link between rights and participation. People-centred advocacy seeks to connect social development, human rights and governance. It is about creating enabling conditions for socio-political empowerment and enhancing the capability of the marginalised to advocate for themselves so that they can claim their rights, seek public accountability and participate in the process of governance. People-centred advocacy seeks to go beyond changing public policies to changing people's attitudes, behaviour and unjust power relationships.

The Community Learning Movement (CLM) promoted by the National Centre for Advocacy Studies (NCAS) is an effort to empower grassroots communities so that they can seek accountability from the institutions of governance, demand their rights and participate in the political process. CLM takes a cluster of 10-25 villages. Four volunteers from each village participate in an action-learning cycle of 18 months, in six phases of three months each. Once in three months, the volunteers meet for two to three days to share experiences, learn new topics and build strategic plans for addressing local issues. The Learning Space or Open Notice Board maintained by the CLM local unit provides information (policy, budget, local government etc) that affects the villagers and the volunteers update the Board regularly. As a result of these initiatives, the CLM group in Karnataka has come up with its own community newspaper and wall magazine. Ordinary women, who have developed a sense of their rights and responsibility, have sought accountability from local government officials and exposed corrupt forest officials involved in illegal tree-felling and smuggling of timber from the forest.

People-centred advocacy can be an effective way to link rights and participation. However, the challenge is how to transform this linkage into an emancipatory politics that would help the poor emerge from the structural inequalities that perpetuate poverty. Human rights are legtimised claims and the State has an obligation to respect, protect and fulfil these rights. However, rights become real only when people begin to realise their full potential as human beings and assert their rights in the private and public sphere.

ADDED VALUE PROVIDED BY THE HUMAN RIGHTS APPROACH TO POVERTY REDUCTION

Some poverty reduction strategies already have features that reflect international human rights norms. For example, the emphasis placed on civil society participation in the Poverty Reduction Strategy Paper approach advocated by the World Bank and the IMF reflects the right of individuals to take part in the conduct of public affairs, as well as the related rights of association, assembly and expression. The introduction of social safety nets resonates with the rights to a reasonable standard of living, food, housing, health protection, education and social security. Anti-poverty strategies that demand transparent budgetary and other governmental processes are consistent with the right to information, while the insistence that strategies are "country-owned" corresponds to the right of peoples to self-determination.

This congruence between features of existing poverty reduction strategies and the international human rights framework gives rise to two important points. First, the departure represented by the introduction of a rights-based approach to poverty reduction should not be overstated. Second, the application of human rights to poverty reduction reinforces some of the existing features of anti-poverty strategies. The value added by the human rights approach to poverty reduction consists both in the manner in which it departs from existing strategies and in the manner in which it reinforces them. The major elements of this process may be enumerated as follows.

By introducing the dimension of an international legal obligation, the human rights perspective adds legitimacy to the demand for making poverty reduction the primary goal of policy-making. The last decade has witnessed a move towards poverty reduction as the focus of international cooperation as well as of national policy-making. The human rights perspective adds strength to this movement by drawing attention to the fact that poverty signifies non-realization of human rights so that the adoption of a poverty reduction strategy is therefore not just desirable but obligatory on the part of States that have ratified international human rights instruments.

Recognition of the principles of equality and non-discrimination, which is a central premise of the human rights approach, helps to highlight the fact that a great deal of poverty originates from discriminatory practices – both overt and covert – at the international, national and local levels. This recognition calls for the reorientation of poverty reduction strategies from a tendency to focus on narrow economic issues towards a broader strategy that also addresses socio-cultural and political-legal institutions that sustain the structures of discrimination.

Recognition of complementarities between civil and political rights, on the one hand, and economic, social and cultural rights, on the other, adds impetus to the process of strengthening and broadening the scope of poverty reduction strategies. In particular, it helps dispel the misconception that civil and political rights and freedoms are luxuries and relevant only to relatively affluent societies. Accordingly, the human rights approach demands that measures be taken to ensure civil and political rights are integral components of poverty reduction strategies.

Unlike old-style approaches to poverty reduction, the human rights approach attaches as much importance to the processes whereby developmental goals are achieved as to the goals themselves. In particular, it emphasizes the importance of ensuring people's participation, especially participation by the poor and otherwise marginalized groups, in all aspects of decision-making. The importance of participation is being increasingly recognized. The human rights approach reinforces this recognition by drawing attention to the fact that participation is valuable not just as a means to other ends but also as a fundamental human right that should be realized for its own sake.

Making trade-offs among alternative goals in the light of social priorities and resource constraints is an integral part of any approach to policy-making. The human rights approach is no exception, but it offers the poor better protection by ruling out certain kinds of trade-offs that are potentially harmful to them. In particular, it rules out any trade-off that leads to retrogression of a human right from its existing level of realization or to non-achievement of certain minimum levels of realization that have been identified as core obligations.

Perhaps the most important source of added value in the human rights approach is the emphasis it places on the accountability of policy-makers and other actors whose actions have an impact on the rights of people. Rights imply duties, and duties demand accountability. It is therefore an intrinsic feature of the human rights approach that institutions and legal/administrative arrangements for ensuring accountability are built into any poverty reduction strategy.

In sum, the human rights approach has the potential to advance the goal of poverty reduction in a variety of ways: (a) by urging speedy adoption of a poverty reduction strategy, underpinned by human rights, as a matter of legal obligation; (b) by broadening the scope of poverty reduction strategies so as to address the structures of discrimination that generate and sustain poverty; (c) by urging the expansion of civil and political rights, which can play a crucial instrumental role in advancing the cause of poverty reduction; (d) by confirming that economic, social and cultural rights are binding international human rights, not just programmatic aspirations; (e) by adding legitimacy to the demand for ensuring meaningful participation of the poor in decision-making processes; (f) by cautioning against retrogression and non-fulfilment of minimum core obligations in the name of making trade-offs; and (g) by creating and strengthening the institutions through which policy-makers can be held accountable for their actions.

The word "guideline" is understood differently by different people and institutions. The set of Guidelines presented here should be seen as elaborating and clarifying certain principles that should guide the process of formulating, implementing and monitoring a poverty reduction strategy if it is to be consistent with a human rights approach. The expectation is that once the principles are understood, the actors involved in poverty reduction will be able to implement them in practice, keeping in view the specificities of their own context. In other words, this is not a manual that purports to teach in a mechanical, comprehensive and directive way how to implement human rights in the context of poverty reduction. While the principles of the rights-based approach to poverty reduction enunciated in these Guidelines are broadly applicable to both rich and poor countries, the primary focus is on poverty in poorer countries. In part, this is in recognition of the obvious fact that poverty is a much more serious problem in these countries. But it is also partly because poverty in rich countries has special features that need to be addressed separately. Perhaps these Guidelines could be expanded in the future to address those issues.

The Guidelines presented here do not address all aspects of human rights with equal emphasis, because they are formulated for the specific context of poverty reduction, which is only a part of the broader human rights agenda. The rationale of the choice of rights, of the relative emphasis placed on different rights, and of the targets, indicators and strategies to be found in these Guidelines should be understood in this context.

The choice of human rights to be addressed in these Guidelines was based on a judgement as to which rights are most relevant to the context of poverty. This judgement was in turn guided by the understanding that human rights can be relevant to poverty in different ways. Of special significance in the context of poverty reduction are rights that have either constitutive or instrumental relevance.

The idea of constitutive relevance of human rights derives from our understanding of what it means to be poor. According to a widely accepted view, a poor person is one who is deprived of basic capabilities – such as the capability to be free form hunger, to live in good health, to be literate, and so on. In the language of rights, one may say that a poor person is one for whom a number of human rights remain unfulfilled – such as the rights to food, health, education and so on. Such rights have constitutive relevance for poverty if a person's lack of command over economic resources plays a role in causing their non-realization. Some human rights are such that their fulfilment will help realize other human rights that have constitutive relevance for poverty. For example, if the right to work is realized, it will help realize the right to food. Such rights can be said to have instrumental relevance for poverty. The same human right may, of course, have both constitutive and instrumental relevance. These Guidelines address the rights that are considered to be most relevant to poverty – on either constitutive or instrumental grounds or on both.

The Guidelines are divided into three sections. Section I sets out the basic principles of a human rights approach that should inform the process of formulating a poverty reduction strategy. Section II sets out the human rights approach to determining the content of a poverty reduction strategy. It identifies, for each of the rights relevant to poverty reduction, the major elements of a strategy for realizing that right. Here the rights are classified under two broad headings – national and international – depending on the level at which action will have to be taken. Section III explains how the human rights approach can guide the monitoring and accountability aspects of poverty reduction strategies. Like the principles discussed in Section I, accountability is also one of the basic principles of a human rights approach to poverty reduction. But because of its special significance in the context of human rights and poverty reduction, it is singled out for discussion in a separate section.

In Section II of the Guidelines, the discussion of each right is structured around four parts. Part A outlines the relevance of the right in the context of poverty. Part B sketches the scope or content of the right as set out in international human rights instruments. For ease of reference, boxes reproduce some of the most relevant international human rights provisions; they also refer to recent world conferences, as well as the most relevant General Comments or Recommendations adopted by United Nations human rights Treaty-bodies. (General Comments and Recommendations offer guidance to State parties on the contours and content of human rights and the measures that might be taken to better secure their implementation.)

Part C identifies key targets in relation to each right and lists, for each target, some indicators that will help assess the extent to which these targets are being achieved over time. Part D sets out key features of a strategy for achieving the specified targets. Some brief comments are in order regarding the targets, indicators and strategies identified in these Guidelines.

For each right, the targets were derived from the scope of the right as set out in international human rights law (and discussed in Part B under each right). The choice of targets was guided by the following question: given the scope of the right, what are the major targets whose fulfilment would ensure realization of that particular right for the poor? Achieving these targets, for all the rights that are relevant to poverty, should be the ultimate goal of the human rights approach to poverty reduction. Many of the targets draw upon, and are similar to, those set out in the Millennium Development Goals (MDGs) adopted by the United Nations General Assembly in September 2000.

These targets may not all be achievable immediately – they may be subject to progressive realization. Nevertheless, a human rights approach to poverty reduction requires States to move as expeditiously as possible towards fulfilment of the targets. In the light of progressive realization, States should identify appropriate indicators, in relation to which they set ambitious but realistic benchmarks (i.e. intermediate targets) corresponding to each ultimate target, so that the rate of progress can be monitored and, if progress is slow, corrective action taken. Thus, indicators measure progress towards both intermediate and ultimate targets.

Several points relating to indicators are worth noting. First, the construction of human rights indicators is an ongoing enterprise and this document does not claim to have entirely resolved the matter. Nonetheless, an attempt has been made to derive from the existing literature, including that on Millennium Development Goals, a set of indicators that seem most appropriate for the targets in question, keeping in view the context of poverty. It is important to bear this poverty context in mind when inquiring why certain targets and indicators have been chosen, and not others.

Second, even in the context of poverty, the proposed list of indicators is by no means exhaustive. At the same time, it is not expected that all the indicators proposed here are applicable to all countries at all times. The list is intended for reference only. Each country must decide for itself which indicators are most appropriate for its specific circumstances.

Third, while using the indicators, it should be borne in mind that the objective is to indicate the conditions of the poor, and of specific disadvantaged groups among the poor, and not the average condition of the population as a whole. Some indicators are such that even if they refer to the overall population, any improvement or deterioration indicated by them will basically reflect changes in the condition of the poor – for example, the proportion of all children with access to primary education, or the proportion of homeless people in the country. Other indicators do not have this property – for example, the rate of specific crimes against women. These will have to be disaggregated to reflect the condition of the poor and of specially disadvantaged groups among them, e.g. poor women, minorities, indigenous peoples and so on.

Exactly what type of disaggregation is appropriate will depend on the nature of the target in question and the particular circumstances of the country.

Fourth, most of the indicators proposed in these Guidelines have a striking resemblance to the standard indicators of socio-economic progress. So this raises the question, in what sense can they be characterised as human rights indicators? In brief, a human rights indicator derives from, reflects and is designed to monitor realisation or otherwise of a specific human rights norm, usually with a view to holding a duty-bearer to account. Thus, because there is overlap between human rights targets and socio-economic progress, there is likely to be a resemblance between human rights indicators and the standard indicators of socio-economic progress-although it should be observed that some human rights indicators, especially those relating to civil and political rights, do not usually figure in measures of socio-economic progress. Essentially, what tends to distinguish a human rights indicator from a standard disaggregated indicator of socio-economic progress is less its substance than (i) its explicit derivation from a human rights norm and (ii) the purpose to which it is put viz human rights monitoring with a view to holding duty-bearers to account.

Some remarks should be made to clarify the strategies proposed in connection with each right. First, the intention is not to offer a complete strategy for implementing the right in question. A strategy is offered only to the extent that it is relevant to poverty reduction. Even in the context of poverty, the idea is not to formulate comprehensive and detailed prescriptions, but to identify some broad principles that follow from human rights concerns. The details are to be worked out by the people engaged in preparing poverty reduction strategies, and these details are bound to vary depending on the context.

Second, for each right the proposed strategy consists of two distinct types of recommendation. First, there are recommendations that follow directly and clearly from the explicit human rights laws and their elaboration by the UN human rights Treaty-bodies. Second, there are recommendations that may not be explicitly stated in any treaties or human rights jurisprudence, but are considered to be consistent with the spirit and intention of the law. In general, a prescriptive tone is adopted here for the first set of recommendations, while the second is presented rather as a set of suggestions. It should be understood, however, that when the prescriptive tone is used it is only because the recommendations are in the nature of legal obligations. Moreover, these obligations have not been imposed from outside; they have been voluntarily incurred by States with a view to upholding the dignity and freedom of their people. The prescriptive language is intended merely to remind States of what they have voluntarily undertaken to do.

Third, even taking the prescriptive and suggestive elements together, the proposed strategy for any particular right cannot be regarded as comprehensive in any sense. This is partly because of the interdependence of human rights discussed earlier. Thus, the strategy proposed for implementing the right to food will not succeed for everyone unless progress is made in realizing the right to work, because most people who are not directly involved in food production have to work to purchase food from the market. Furthermore, successful implementation of any right will depend on the institutions for participation, monitoring and accountability – issues that are common to all rights and have therefore been discussed in separate sections instead of being repeated for each right. Thus, the strategy proposed for each right has to be seen as part of a comprehensive approach rather than as being adequate in isolation.

Fourth, a comprehensive approach does not prevent a State from prioritizing among rights. It is not expected that any country will find it feasible to implement all the recommendations with respect to all the rights simultaneously and immediately. Each State is free to set its own priorities and take up some of the recommendations for immediate implementation, while deferring others, so long as it abides by the principles of progressive realization. In choosing priorities, however, each State should be alert to the interdependence of human rights so as to maximize the effectiveness of its policies.

2

Contributions of Human Rights and NGOs Management

The narrative of the human rights movement in India and its historical origins has always been contextualized in the post-colonial democratic era. The turning point with respect to human rights activism in India was undoubtedly the Emergency period during the reign of Indira Gandhi. The Emergency was a period characterized by the curtailment of civil liberties through amendments to the Constitution to clamp down on the right to enjoy the fundamental rights enshrined within it, the promulgation of ordinances that legitimized the government's actions, such as arresting people on the pretext of 'preventive detention' as well as the establishment of new intelligence outfits, such as the CBI and RAW, which assisted the government with its agenda.

As a result of the severe repression of civil liberties by the government, several individuals and organizations came to the forefront, as champions of basic human rights. The most prominent among these was Jayaprakash Narayan's 'People's Union for Civil Rights'. A similar organization that was established was the 'People's Union for Democratic Rights'. The importance of these organizations was that they were autonomous of the government and critical of its actions.

Since then, the human rights movement in India has progressed with the establishment of other human rights NGOs, fighting for a variety of causes: The Human Rights Organization of Manipur, Civil Liberties Committee of Andhra Pradesh, Naga People's Movement for Human Rights of Nagaland, etc. are NGOs dealing with the human rights of minority groups in India; The Other Media works with human rights in Kashmir, the National Centre for the Protection of Human Rights coordinates several human rights activities; NGOs such as the Indian Association of Lawyers, the Lawyers Collective, the

Human Rights Trust deal with human rights in their publications; the South Asian Human Rights Documentation Centre deals with documentation, research as well as implementation of human rights; the Punjab Human Rights Organization works with Amnesty International and the UN Human Rights Commission; the National Campaign on Dalit Human Rights works with Dalits, whose rights have been violated.

K. S. Krishnaswamy identifies six functions performed by human rights NGOs, namely:

- o Gathering, evaluating and disseminating human rights,
- o Advocating human rights,
- o Lobbying and mobilizing public opinion,
- o Providing legal aid,
- o Providing humanitarian relief,
- o Developing human rights norms.

It is submitted that in a developing country like India, it is important to equip citizens with the proper awareness about human rights, such that they do not remain distant concepts and the government does not take advantage of marginalized groups. However, in addition to creating awareness and aiding the formulation of public opinion, providing assistance in terms of physical resources may often be of tremendous importance.

The human rights movement has come a long way since the Emergency, with the proliferation of human rights NGOs ever since. Human rights violations in India have been manifested in different forms in India even after the Emergency, often with the state being a party to these violations or showing indifference to the plight of the victims. According to many writers, the human rights movement has expanded itself ever since its origin during the period of Emergency. It now focuses on a wider range of issues, with economic and social rights (in addition to civil and political rights), problems relating to inter-community tension, the struggle for natural resources and women's rights being some key illustrations.

These changes have been attributed to a variety of factors, such as the change in the way development is viewed, the nature of government programmes and the priorities of donor agencies.

Some examples of human rights violations in India may be enumerated here: the implementation of draconian legislation such as the Prevention of Terrorist Activities Act, human rights violations during communal riots in Gujarat, atrocities carried out by the Indian army in Kashmir, minorities such as transgendered individuals and Dalits being denied human rights, etc.

As is evident, human rights NGOs in India have constantly had to mould themselves according to the specific nature of human rights violations that they are dealing with. Aswini Ray points out that this is a challenge that the human rights movement has not been able to deal with sufficient ease: "They are periodically called upon to respond to them with indigenous theoretical and conceptual innovations in view of the paucity of comparable resources in the asymmetrical western liberal democratic experience.

This challenge still remains inadequately responded because of the limited empirical base of political theory within the western experience"

CONTRIBUTIONS OF HUMAN RIGHTS NGOS IN INDIA

Expansion of the Rights Discourse: Human rights NGOs have been instrumental in expanding the rights discourse to include certain rights, which were previously not part of the human rights discourse, due to the limited sense in which the state projected rights. As a natural consequence of this development, the state has been compelled to take steps for the implementation of human rights. These NGOs have created awareness about the state being a human rights violator, by carrying out atrocities in Gujarat and Kashmir, for example, and through the passage of draconian law. In order to formulate an effective defence against these accusations, the state has had to bring about reform in its policies and actions.

Recognition of the Rights of Marginalized Groups: Human Rights NGOs in India have played a significant role by taking steps to guarantee human rights to marginalized groups, such as women and members of oppressed classes. It is due to the efforts undertaken by these NGOs that the rights of these groups have been taken cognizance of, by the state, and have also been widely recognized in society.

CRITICISMS OF HUMAN RIGHTS NGOS IN INDIA

Lack of A Comprehensive Approach: One criticism levelled against human rights NGOs in India has been that their approach is not a comprehensive one due to the rather rigid manner in which they focus only on a single issue. For example, the NGOs dealing with providing human rights to women may not engage with the problems of the peasantry. This would lead to issues such as those of women's exploitation in the farmers' movement being neglected.

Neera Chandhoke points out the perils of such an approach: "if each discourse occupies its own space and fights its battles independently from other discourses of resistance, the fragmented arena resulting from these particularistic practices is peculiarly vulnerable to being occupied by the state and by the dominant classes".

It is submitted that the NGOs must pursue a more flexible approach, for concentrating on single issues without thinking about inter-related rights of other groups may prove to be myopic.

Isolation of Human Rights NGOs: It is the view of several experts that with human rights NGOs isolating itself from other actors in civil society and the masses, they are plagued by a fundamental structural problem and as a result, they are rendered ineffective.

Guha argues that due to their restricted social base, NGOs do not enjoy popular support, to the extent that their exclusivity lends them the character of powerful class-based movements, often the kind that they are opposed to.

Moreover, the media and the middle classes begin to view them as groups pursuing their vested interests and working as per the whims of their donors.

The Issue of Funding: Possibly the biggest criticism that human rights NGOs in India face is related to the issue of funding. It is alleged that many human rights NGOs formulate their programmes, such that the interests of their donors are given priority to. As a result, many of the areas of human rights that NGOs focus on, such as women's rights, are in fact, a product of the manipulation that their donor agencies exercise. As per one report, foreign donors donated to the tune of Rs. 4,871.9 crore to Indian NGOs in the year 2001-2002.

NGOs carrying out rehabilitative activities after the tsunami floods came under suspicion when it was reported that these NGOs were quite affluent and that there was no transparency or accountability as regards the manner in which they utilized the funds that were provided to them by their donors for the specific purpose of rehabilitating those affected by the tsunami floods. Little is known about where the funds are utilized by the NGOs and which groups have been provided shelter.

In another instance, a UK-based organization, Enable, accused an NGO in India, to which it had donated money, of misappropriating aid worth Rs. 6 crore in the course of five years.

In fact, many human rights NGOs are run, not by the councils that they claim to have, but by individuals, who are in control of the funds granted to the NGOs. The situation is such that there are no means of keeping a strict watch over the flow of foreign funds and ascertaining who their real beneficiaries are.

Strident critics of NGOs in India believe that when NGOs fail to be accountable to the citizens they claim to be working in the interest of, they have no right to try to hold the government accountable for its actions. Often, NGOs have been found to be funded to a large extent by the government. Hence, the concept of funding can shake the very foundations on which an NGO is based, that is, the idea of critically assessing the government. Some governments have made moves to pass legislation that would bind NGOs to comply with norms that would make sure that they worked in a manner that was transparent. NGOs have protested against such moves, on the ground that they should remain in a sphere free from the government.

One of the recommendations to improve the situation has been to structure the functioning of NGOs along the lines of the functioning of corporate bodies. Taking measures, such as establishing strict accounting standards, carrying out regular audits through the setting up of an Audit Committee, separation of the Chairman and the Chief Executive, restricting the service contracts of executive directors to three years, the pay of officers to be regulated by a remuneration committee, etc. would bring about some measure of transparency to the functioning of NGOs.

INGOS AND NGOS: A COMPARATIVE DISCUSSION

Global v. Local: Baxi opines that NGOs find security in creating "global spaces", as opposed to "local spaces", that is, there is a greater possibility of NGOs from different countries coming together to protest against a global cause, rather than a local cause.

It is submitted that this is a natural outcome of the fact that human rights NGOs in India are likely to pursue goals that may be unique to their home country, owing to the peculiar nature of the problems that they are protesting against. Several NGOs identify their goals in terms of protest against specific policies of the governments of their respective countries, which result in human rights violations of citizens of that country. It follows that it may often be difficult to generate global awareness or solidarity about causes that are specific to the countries of origin of many local NGOs, and hence the solidarity expressed at a global level pertains to global issues of human rights. Further, most of these NGOs may not even possess the resources to bring their local cause into the global space, given the limited space that they operate in.

Resources and Power: Another point of difference between INGOs and NGOs is the quantum of resources at their disposal, and as a result, the number of people they seek to target. It is noteworthy that INGOs, such as

Amnesty International, OXFAM and Greenpeace have more members than citizens in small countries, such as Fiji, Nauru and San Marino. Hence, it cannot be doubted that in the scope of their organization, and manner of operation, INGOs are far larger than NGOs. Often, NGOs in India may be small organizations, which take up a particular cause and deliberately aim at targeting a very small section of people. For example, an NGO in India may take up the issue of trying to guarantee tribals residing in a particular region their human rights. The localized presence of many human rights NGOs can be seen in contrast to the massive scale at which some INGOs operate. Moreover, the small-scale operation of an NGO may be due to a lack of greater resources, but it is also often a matter of choice, with domestic NGOs finding that effectiveness would be best guaranteed by local projects.

The Importance of Associationalism: Putnam, in his discussion on the fragility of civil society, records the observation that there is a considerable deal of anxiety revolving around the 'collapse' of civil society in the United States owing to a decline of associationalism. Hence, the view held in the west is that the scarce resource of "social capital" has been lost. It is of note that INGOs that operate in the world today are of western origin.

On the other hand, the idea of civil society in India seems to be flourishing, with the rapid expansion of the human rights discourse and the simultaneous increase in number of human rights NGOs. Contrary to the trend in the west, where INGOs could well be diminishing in number, the culture of associationalism is thriving in India, which is evident from the proliferation of human rights NGOs.

The human rights movement today would be incomplete without the contribution of civil society, particularly non-governmental organizations, which have been indispensable in the human rights movement, not merely for redressing the wrongs done to victims of human rights violators but also for successfully creating a comprehensive discourse on human rights.

Without NGOs contributing to the field of human rights at the international level and the domestic level in various countries, the state would exist without having any specific agencies to be accountable to, for the violation of specific human rights. Further, these organizations have helped in bringing instances of human rights violations to the notice of the state, so that they can take action in that regard. The protection of human rights has become an issue of prestige in the current day scenario, with no state being able to afford complacency on its part. NGOs have also been instrumental in equipping marginalized groups-women, children, indigenous peoples, to name a few-with the ability to demand their rights.

However, the functioning of these agencies has, by no means, been without its share of criticism. The issue of funding has come up time and again, in the international as well as Indian context. There is no doubt about the fact that NGOs need to bring about more transparency in the manner in which they conduct their work, for anything short of that would make their credibility in the human rights movement suspect. There is also a growing realization that the human rights discourse must be expanded-both at the international as well as Indian level. At the international level, INGOs must ensure that their definition of human rights does not reflect a bias towards the North. At the domestic level in India, NGOs would gain by developing an inter-related approach to human rights, one that would take into account the human rights of groups that may be related to the ones whose cause they are advocating. Creating such alliances may lead to better mobilization of the victims of human rights violations. It would also make the human rights movement more effective, since it would reduce the fragmentation that currently exists therein.

Another constructive suggestion that can be made at this juncture would be to encourage NGOs and states to enter into a relationship that could lead to better cooperation. Although the goal of NGOs to apply pressure upon the government should not be lost sight of at any cost, it may be more beneficial for the state and non-state actors to enter into a non-confrontational relationship, one that could lead to an improved implementation of human rights. Lastly, it must be said that the human rights movement is in a state of constant change, with new doctrines and ideas being added everyday to the human rights discourse. This will doubtless affect the working of the human rights NGOs. Whether it will assist them in developing a more comprehensive mandate or whether it would lead to constant disagreement between them resulting in a weakening of the human rights movement remains to be seen.

GUIDING PRINCIPLES ON NGOS

Recognizing that non-governmental organizations (NGOs)* are essential to the development and success of free societies and that they play a vital role in ensuring accountable, democratic government,

And recalling the right to freedom of expression, peaceful assembly and association enshrined in the UN Universal Declaration of Human Rights, the International Covenant on Civil and Political Rights and the UN Declaration on Human Rights Defenders,

We hereby pledge our commitment to the following principles and our determination to work for their full implementation throughout the world:

1. Individuals should be permitted to form, join and participate in NGOs of their choosing in the exercise of the rights to freedom of expression, peaceful assembly and association.
2. Any restrictions which may be placed on the exercise by members of NGOs of the rights to freedom of expression, peaceful assembly and association must be consistent with international legal obligations.
3. NGOs should be permitted to carry out their peaceful work in a hospitable environment free from fear of harassment, reprisal, intimidation and discrimination.
4. Acknowledging governments' authority to regulate entities within their territory to promote the public welfare, such laws and administrative measures should protect--not impede--the peaceful operation of NGOs and be enforced in an apolitical, fair, transparent and consistent manner.
5. Criminal and civil legal actions brought by governments against NGOs, like those brought against all individuals and organizations, should be based on tenets of due process and equality before the law.
6. NGOs should be permitted to seek, receive, manage and administer for their peaceful activities financial support from domestic, foreign and international entities.
7. NGOs should be free to seek, receive and impart information and ideas, including advocating their opinions to governments and the public within and outside the countries in which they are based.
8. Governments should not interfere with NGOs' access to domestic-and foreign-based media.
9. NGOs should be free to maintain contact and cooperate with their own members and other elements of civil society within and outside the countries in which they are based, as well as with governments and international bodies.
10. Whenever the aforementioned NGO principles are violated, it is imperative that democratic nations act in their defense.

THE GROWING INTEREST OF NGOS IN MANAGEMENT

The concept of 'participatory management' has become important to development organisations. Holcombe (1995), for example, points out that many NGOs now speak of an 'empowering' or 'participatory' style of management, in which staff are seen as a source of skills and capacities, and are encouraged to take the initiative in solving problems. Moreover, Chambers (1995: 197) argues that: The institutional challenge for all development agencies is... to flatten and soften hierarchy, to develop a culture of participatory management, to recruit a gender and disciplinary mix of staff committed to people, to adopt and promote procedures, norms and rewards which permit and encourage more participation at all levels. However, despite growing interest in the concept, 'participatory management' is a term which remains both complex and unclear (Anheier and Cunningham, 1994).

A degree of rhetoric surrounds the concept, in the same way that this is a problem for the concept of 'participation' in development (Clark, 1991). Moreover, despite the assumed tradition of participation in the management of NGOs, and the increasing popularity of 'participatory management' as a management style for NGOs, relatively little has been written on the subject.

The heightened interest in 'participatory management' must be seen, first of all, in the context of increasing importance attached to participatory development paradigms. People's participation, according to the Human Development Report (UNDP, 1993: 1), 'is becoming the central issue of our time'. Smillie (1995: 223) points out that: ... it is the NGO community through which most bilateral and multilateral agencies choose to apply participation, and from which most take their lessons.

NGOs are assumed to be participatory in approach, and this contributes to their perceived comparative advantage (Hudock, 1995). While NGOs have been examining ways to increase participation of beneficiaries in development initiatives, they have, at the same time, come under increasing pressure to 'professionalise' and, in particular, to address a widespread neglect of management (Korten, 1990; Smillie, 1995).3 In this regard, the growth of NGOs (James, 1994), and their increasing dependence on donors for their income, have been important factors. Organisational growth, and the demands of donors, however, are not the only reasons for the pressure on NGOs to professionalise. Whilst NGOs have traditionally not acknowledged the link between 'internal organisational capacities and their programme performance in the field' (Sahley, 1995: 46), there is a growing realisation among them that management is a key determinant of project success (Campbell, 1987). Moreover, the growth in interest in NGO management is due, in part, to increasing organisational problems, in particular problems related to organisational growth, changes in funding, and changes in organisational role. At the same time, managers of NGOs increasingly see development as a professional practice.

One result of such pressure has been the widespread use of instruments and techniques such as Logical Framework Analysis, Objective-Oriented Project Planning (or ZOPP), Participatory Rural Assessment and Rapid Rural

Assessment. It has also led to attempts to improve the administrative aspects of programme work, such as proposal writing, budgeting and reporting. Moreover, it has also resulted in a growing interest in management approaches, strategies and techniques prevalent in the business world (such as 'management by objectives', 'strategic planning', 'stakeholder-analysis', and 'mission-based management'), and a willingness to import them, often uncritically, to the world of NGOs (Smillie, 1995). The appropriateness of this latter trend, however, is questioned.

The 'NGO Management Debate'

Several researchers and consultants have applied themselves to the question of which theories and models NGO practitioners can use in the design and management of their agencies. Although it is 'still very much in its infancy', the tentative emergence of the study of NGO management has provided the focus for a wideranging debate about how NGOs can be more effectively organised. Indeed, there is, at present, no consensus regarding the nature of NGO management principles and practices, although the importance of management is generally accepted (Campbell, 1987).6 Four schools of thought have been outlined by Campbell (1987) and form what I will call the 'NGO management debate'.

Three of the four perspectives presented argue that NGOs require a distinctive management style. The first school of thought insists that the critical issue is that NGOs are voluntary organisations and should draw on voluntary sector principles. A second view is that NGO contexts are critical in determining the type of management they need, and that the principles of development management should therefore strongly influence NGO management. To these schools of thought can be added a cultural perspective which questions the applicability of western management models, discusses the need for 'indigenous' approaches, and argues that the cultural environment in which the NGO operates must determine the nature of NGO management.

The arguments for a distinctive approach to NGO management, however, are not unanimously accepted. Dichter (1989), for example, argues that the distinction between the management of non-profit and commercial organisations is largely irrelevant as management principles should apply to all organisations whatever their nature and function. The priority need for NGOs, he argues, is straightforward, basic, 'nuts and bolts' management to meet equally straightforward basic weaknesses in organisational management. He points out that 'people inventions, and argues that 'means' are confused with 'ends'.

In particular, the fact that the participation of people in their own growth is a valued goal does not necessarily imply that the western management models which stress this value will be useful or appropriate in the Third World context. Such a view is echoed by DeGraaf (1987) who, while arguing that the nature of the development task does shape NGO management, insists that to say NGOs should adopt a participatory style of management because participation is important in development is over-simplistic.

'Participatory Management' and the 'NGO Management Debate'

The debate about the nature of NGO management has become polarised. In particular, to argue for a distinctive approach to the management of NGOs does not mean to reject the need for basic organisational systems (Drucker, 1990). Moreover, there are many new theories and concepts in commercial management which are very relevant to NGOs including, for example, 'strategic management', 'In Search of Excellence' management, and not least, 'participatory management' (Campbell, 1987).

Secondly, the view that a participatory approach to the management of NGOs constitutes a distinctive approach is untenable, as there is a long history in the business world of employee involvement in organisational decision-making.

Indeed, since the turn of the century, and particularly since the early 1960s, interest in, and support for, employee participation has been rapidly increasing (Brannen, 1983). Generic management has clearly distinguished between a taskoriented authoritarian approach to management, on the one hand, and an employeecentred, democratic or participative style on the other.

'Empowerment' is now widely used in business and management as well as in development (Wright, 1994), and 'participative management', such as that proposed by Likert's (1961) 'System 4', is a recognised approach to management.

In particular, Japanese corporations such Hitachi, Nissan, Honda, Mitsubishi and Toyota are often cited as exemplars of employee-participatory practices. At the same time, forms of employee participation have flourished in the 1980s in the guise of managerial policy initiatives inspired by the new 'excellence' movement, and have been expounded as a key instrument in the creation of Human Resource Management (HRM) strategies. Finally, in recent years, inspired by Japanese management practice, various forms of team-working based around customer care and Total Quality Management (TQM) programmes have witnessed a considerable rise in popularity.

THE APPROPRIATENESS OF 'PARTICIPATORY MANAGEMENT' FOR NGOS

The NGO management debate has attempted to address the question: what style of management is appropriate for NGOs? In so doing, the debate is valuable. However, given that participation in decision-making is a feature of governmental and commercial organisations, the association of a participatory style of management with a distinctive approach to NGO management is unhelpful. It is more useful to examine the advantages of participation to organisations generally, and to NGOs in particular, and then identify those factors in the NGO context which make a participatory approach more appropriate for them.

There are a number of perspectives on the increasing interest in participation in the commercial sector. Guest and Knight (1979) argue that it represents part of the search for... a new means of overcoming industrial and economic problems, changing market conditions internationally, rising expectations of the workforce, and interest in the concept of industrial democracy. The emphasis on changing environmental conditions is taken up by Lawler (1986: 19) who insists that 'the societal, business, product, and work force changes that have occurred argue strongly for a change in management style', and who believes that 'in most situations some form of participative management is the best answer' (Lawler, 1986: 11). At the same time, Wall and Lischeron (1977: 1) point out that in contemporary society 'participation, in one form or another, is seen as one means of improving the quality of working life'.

However, the increased interest in participation cannot simply be seen as stemming from changed contextual factors and a desire for greater work humanisation. An instrumental view of participation-that greater participation will lead to greater efficiency, and consequently greater profits-is fundamental in the commercial sector (Beardwell and Holden, 1994), and is particularly reflected in the 'hard', rather than the 'soft' approach to Human Resource Management (Storey, 1987).8 That participation is linked to improved performance is evident from Ouchi (1981) who states:

Decision-making by consensus has been the subject of a great deal of research in Europe and the United States over the past twenty years, and the evidence strongly suggests that a consensus approach yields more creative decisions and more effective implementation than does individual decision-making. Moreover, the participation of staff is inextricably linked with the concept of 'learning organisations'. Senge (1990: 3), for example, argues that 'the organisations that will truly excel in the future will be the organisations that discover how to tap people's commitment and capacity to learn at all levels of an organisation'. 'Participatory management' and 'participatory development' As noted earlier, several authors argue that a participatory approach to management is particularly suitable for NGOs whose work involves the promotion of participation and the empowerment of beneficiaries. Chambers (1983: 210), for example, insists that such a management style is more in keeping with 'bottom-up development' or a participatory development approach. NGOs require a 'new professionalism' based on fundamental 'reversals' in the values, attitudes and behaviour of NGO staff, so that the people whom the NGO aims to support are truly empowered. Carroll's (1992: 205) study of NGOs in Latin America demonstrates that an open, collegial management style builds confidence and trust among beneficiaries and support organisations, and is, therefore, a key organisational quality for promoting popular participation. Similarly, the British Overseas Development Administration points out that 'culture, management structure, goals and sources of funding, all influence the manner and extent to which an aid agency can enhance the participation of other stakeholders' (Eyben, 1994: 4.3). Indeed, Roche (1992: 188) argues:

Experience suggests that a decentralised structure with semiautonomous, self-managed federated units, coupled with information and cooperative learning, is perhaps the most appropriate organisational design for supporting micro-development. A second theme that emerges in the literature is that NGOs need to develop decentralised and participatory decision-making structures, and adopt a problemsolving rather than a predictive blue-print approach to management, to ensure flexibility and maintain the ability to adapt to constantly changing realities.

In particular, participatory planning processes are important as it is the field staff who normally have closest contact with beneficiaries (Sahley, 1995). This 'effectiveness' argument is also taken up, for example, by Brodhead and Herbert-Copley (1988), who suggest that NGOs must adopt a participatory approach in order to have wider impact.

A third theme which emerges is the expectations of NGO staff. Clark (1991: 61), for example, states that: NGO staff are generally highly committed to their work because of widely shared values and a belief in the social change mission inherent in their work. This generates a sense of ownership which, when combined with the widespread expectation that organisations promoting democracy and participation should themselves be democratic (Billis and MacKeith: 1993), means that 'an autocratic style simply wouldn't work: the staff require participation' (Clark, 1991: 61).

Moreover, Hodson (1992: 135) argues that as NGOs grow 'decentralised and consensual forms of decision-making' are of particular importance 'if decisions are to be seen by staff as legitimate'. In addition, there is an assumption that respect for workers leads to improved organisational functioning. Clark, (1991: 62), for example, suggests: Naturally an organisation of principled and committed workers will function best if staff feel respected, and listened to. The 'NGO management debate' cannot be easily resolved. In particular, a number of questions about the appropriateness of a participatory style of management for NGOs remain unanswered. Moreover, the debate about the appropriateness of 'participatory management' is constrained by a degree of definitional ambiguity which needs to be addressed.

A Case Study of Concern Mozambique

The aim of the case study is to explore the reasons why CONCERN Mozambique is seeking to adopt a more participatory style of management and to outline the proposals which emerged about the direction such change might take. The process of change in CONCERN Mozambique is underpinned by a number of assumptions made by management staff about the importance of participation, and its role in the management of an organisation committed to promoting participatory development. These are as follows:

(a) A 'natural' approach for participatory development?

In the first place, the consensus among interviewees is that CONCERN's commitment to participatory development necessitates a participatory style of management. Such a management style is considered, for example, to be 'a natural approach', given that the organisation is committed to promoting participation in its development programmes. As one Programme Manager stated: You cannot do participatory development without participatory management. In particular, it was noted that an organisation must practise what it preaches, and that since CONCERN Worldwide is promoting participation of the beneficiaries, the participation of staff is therefore essential. As another Programme Manager remarked:

One can't expect staff to mobilise, animate and facilitate interest groups to analyse their own problems and set their own objectives if the organisation does not have a similar empowering approach with staff.

(b) Programme responsiveness

Secondly, there is among programme management a widespread belief that greater participation of staff, and particularly field-workers, in the management of the organisation will result in improved programme responsiveness. This view is reflected in the 'CONCERN Mozambique Policy Framework' (1995) which states: As an agency that targets the poorest we need a management style that is flexible and responsive to the needs of the poor. A participatory management style enables those staff who are closest to the poor, those at project operational level, to guide the organisation in its programme design and implementation to allow the needs of the poor to be identified and met.

Furthermore, the interviews with the Country Director reveal a fundamental belief that staff at project level are in the best position to make decisions for that project. This view is echoed by one interviewee who remarked: We get reality in decisions... if people further down the line are involved in the decision-making.

(c) Staff empowerment

At the same time, the general view is that 'participatory management' is not just about involving staff, but about 'empowering' them, and creating 'voice'. As the Country Director remarked: CONCERN is here to deliver a service. The most important people in that service delivery are the field workers (they are the most important people in the organisation in many ways). Space has to be made for those people to have a voice in the organisation.

While most programme management staff spoke about 'participatory management' resulting in improved decision-making and ownership of decisions, a number of Programme Managers also suggested that 'participatory management' is an appropriate management style given that CONCERN Mozambique is committed to building up local staff capacity, and in particular, to creating the conditions necessary for sustainable development.

(d) Better 'downward' accountability

'Participatory management' is also seen as enhancing 'downward accountability'. This is evident from the 'CONCERN Mozambique Policy Framework' (1995) which incorporates the idea, originally suggested by CONCERN Worldwide's Southern Africa Division (correspondence, September 1995), that teams and teamwork at management and project level will 'avoid the emergence of a tall hierarchical structure between the target group and field management' and, more especially, will 'ensure that field resources are not diverted away from the poorest'.

(e) Promoting democracy

Finally, while Programme Managers, in general, see 'participatory management' in terms of its having a crucial role in improving organisational effectiveness, the wider implications of adopting a participatory style of management were noted by one Programme Manager who commented on the importance, in a fledgling democracy, as Mozambique is, of promoting democracy within the workplace. In summary, the case study suggests that while a number of different reasons may be identified, they are all related to the ultimate aim of improved development practice, and in particular, are inspired by a fundamental commitment to participatory development.

IMPROVED DEVELOPMENT PRACTICE

Participatory management is seen therefore not as an end in itself, but as means of reaching organisational goals more effectively. As one senior staff member commented:

The only reason we have participatory management is to facilitate our development approach. It is not for its own sake. The study revealed the crucial role of leadership. It is clear that, on a practical level, CONCERN Mozambique has initiated this process of institutional change because the Country Director strongly believes in the importance of such an approach, and more significantly, has acted on that belief by taking advantage of a number of opportunities which have enabled the process to take place. The most important of these has been the support for the initiative from CONCERN Southern Africa Division, including its willingness to allow the budget flexibility necessary for the development of the new systems. At the same time, according to the Country Director, that this belief is shared by the Programme Managers and key national staff has also been crucial, as has their willingness to accept the new responsibilities that a participatory style of management involves.

The case study indicates, in the first place, that management staff in CONCERN Mozambique clearly see 'participatory management' not as a collection of tools and techniques, but as a fundamental approach to management. At the same time, it is understood as something which must be created, or allowed to evolve, over time: as one Programme Manager pointed out, it is essentially a process of 'introducing things bit by bit'.

Secondly, though the possibility of including other stakeholders had been briefly discussed, the general understanding among CONCERN programme management staff is that 'participatory management' is, for the time being at least, only about the greater involvement of staff members, and in particular field staff, in decision-making. It is therefore perceived as overlapping with, but distinct from, CONCERN Mozambique's commitment to 'participatory development', which pledges it to securing 'the participation of interested parties in all stages of the programming process-government, team, target groups, informal structures etc.' (Policy Framework for CONCERN Mozambique, 1995).

At the same time, 'participatory management' is not seen as representing in any way a rejection, or diminution, of standards of professionalism and accountability. There have been no changes to the financial or administrative systems, nor are any intended, and auditing and input control remain crucial. Indeed, at a meeting of senior programme staff with the Southern Africa Regional Director in March 1995 it was agreed that 'by ensuring that tasks are better defined, such control mechanisms can be enhanced by participatory objective-led planning'. These changes also require a firm hand. 'Participatory management' is not about the adoption of an unstructured, 'laissez-faire' style of management. On the contrary, it is seen (though not always positively) as quite procedural, and very structured. As the Country Director remarked:

Participatory management is not less structured; it is more structured if anything. It's quite prescribed, but people are involved in the prescription.

Finally, 'participatory management' is linked to a 'reversal' in the way in which the organisation is conceptualised and represented. In the first place, it is informed by an understanding of the organisation as directly related to, and in service of, the beneficiaries (who are conceived of as 'clients'). In addition, it is underpinned by a view of the NGO as a 'bottom-up' organisation in which the most important members are those closest to the clients. The present CONCERN Mozambique organogram, which is based on the concept of an 'inverted triangle', reflects these views.

The study also reveals that there is a crucial link between the adoption of a more participatory style of management and institutional change. Indeed, as one Programme Manager remarked:

A participatory approach to development requires changes at all levels of the organisation. The resulting programme proposals CONCERN Mozambique's commitment to such change is evident in the five programme proposals, each of which states: CONCERN Mozambique is going through a process of institutional change aimed at creating a management style that is conducive to the type of community development programme being proposed here. These changes commenced in 1994 and are still ongoing, are structural and cultural in nature, and have taken several forms.

(a) A 'flatter' Organisation

'Participatory management' is clearly identified with the creation of a 'flatter' or more 'horizontal' form of management, and the reduction in the layers of authority between senior management and field-workers. This facilitates speedier and more participatory decision-making, and is assumed to increase programme responsiveness. Additionally, it narrows the gap between the organisation's target group and senior management.

(b) Team Structures

Secondly, the study reveals that the adoption of a team approach, both at project and country levels, is central to the style of management adopted by CONCERN Mozambique. A project team (referred to as a 'General Assembly') has been formed in each of the five programme areas, and is the most important aspect of the new structure at project level. Comprising all staff directly involved in project activities, it meets every three months. Its responsibilities include the design of work plans using the ZOPP methodology, the evaluation and re-design of existing methodologies, and the evaluation of the management team. Furthermore, two new fora have been established at country level, and meet annually: a 'Wider Group', which is concerned with national policy and strategy, and a 'Steering Committee', which is responsible for ensuring that policy is implemented.

(c) Other Changes

The study also reveals that adoption of a more participatory style of management is not just about changing organisational structures. It is also clearly seen to involve the creation of an environment in which dialogue, communication, and particularly organisational learning, are facilitated and encouraged. The establishment of the staff magazine, in June 1995, is an important development in this regard. Furthermore, the conducting of an evaluation, by the staff in early 1996, of CONCERN Mozambique's strengths and weaknesses during the previous year, and the publication of the results in the staff magazine, reflect the link between 'participatory management' and a commitment to the development of a culture of openness.

Levels of Participation

The study confirms that, in CONCERN Mozambique, staff are now more involved in both project and country management (see Table 1). This parallels 'participative management' practices at 'shop-floor' and 'plant' levels (Guest and Knight, 1979). Moreover, the involvement of employees at country management level, in decisions that relate to the entire country programme rather than just projects, illustrates that the participation of staff in CONCERN Mozambique is, to use Strauss and Rosenstein's (1970) framework, both 'immediate' and 'distant'. At the same time, however, the adoption of a participatory style of management does not, for the time being at least, imply the participation of non-management staff in decision-making at levels higher than the Mozambique country programme.

Secondly, the study reveals that the participation of staff in the design of work is perceived by senior staff as central to 'participatory management'. In this regard, the ZOPP methodology, introduced in 1995, is crucial. As the Country Director remarked:

ZOPP is at the core of participatory management: it gives staff a language, puts people on an equal footing, and gives people the confidence and the skills to sit with their boss and argue.

At the same time, 'participatory management' is understood to involve more that just the design of work. Four of the eleven field-workers surveyed, for instance, mentioned their involvement in deciding the responsibilities, tasks and procedures of the project team as an example of the way in which they are now more involved in decisionmaking. Indeed, staff are increasingly invited to participate in decisions about work conditions (for example, staff salaries and benefits) as well as in decisions about administrative issues (such as staff appraisal, staff selection, and transport policy).

The study also reveals that there are different degrees or 'intensities' of participation within CONCERN Mozambique, and suggests that 'participatory management' is more than just improved information-sharing and greater consultation of staff. More authority has been delegated than previously, and indeed, there has been, and continues to be, a transfer of power. However, the degree to which this takes place varies according to situational factors, and more particularly, occurs within carefully defined parameters. The study also suggests that the intensity of participation depends not only on the level of the decision-making, but on the nature of the decision. The decision-making power of the Steering Committee is a good example: Moreover, when looking at areas of decision-making not related to the design of work, there has, to date, been more in terms of consultation than delegation. This is indicated by the results of the focus group discussion with the national staff of the Maputo office, during which staff were asked to identify recent decisions made and staff participation in them.

In summary, the case study has shown that CONCERN Mozambique has commenced a process of institutional change aimed at facilitating its development approach. This process is still emerging, and is inspired by a fundamental commitment to providing a better service to organisational beneficiaries. Important lessons can be learned from this experience, and these will be the subject of the next and final chapter.

EMERGING ISSUES

Important practical issues are raised by the case study of 'participatory management' in CONCERN Mozambique. In the first place, the case reveals that the initiative in CONCERN Mozambique is primarily an attempt to arrange internal structures and procedures in such a way as to most effectively and efficiently undertake the organisation's tasks and purposes. In this regard its objectives may be no different from the objectives of 'participative management' in the commercial sector. However, the aim of organisational efficiency in NGOs is not the making of profits, as it is in the commercial sector, but improved service to the NGOs' beneficiaries or clients.

At the same time, the case study also reveals the importance of a 'process orientation' in NGO management, and suggests that the nature of the task has an important, if not a crucial role, in determining organisational processes. It suggests that attention to 'process', or what Paton (1991) calls the 'expressive aspect of management', may be of greater significance for NGOs, particularly those involved in the promotion of participation. 'Participatory management' may therefore represent a conscious effort to exercise management authority and responsibility in ways which are consistent with the broader social values and purposes of the NGO. In particular, it may be seen as an attempt to address the management challenges that the task of promoting participation imposes on an organisation. As Batsleer (1995) points out, however, none of this is new among voluntary organisations.

The study also suggests that at the heart of the task dimension of 'participatory management' is the assumption that the participation of staff leads to improved decision-making and, therefore, greater effectiveness. This is not new, however, either in NGO management or management generally. In the NGO context, it has been explored by Carroll (1992) whose study of NGOs in Latin America concluded that effective NGOs use a participatory style which relies on local knowledge and dialogue with beneficiary groups, and have a less hierarchical and more collegial internal organisation than public or private organisations.

However, that greater staff participation will lead to improved decision-making, and that this in turn will result in more responsive programmes, are both assumptions which need to be tested. As a consequence, an important aspect of the relationship between 'participatory management' and improved development practice remains unproven. At the same time, the study highlights the close connection between 'participatory management' and organisational learning, which is increasingly promoted as crucial to organisational effectiveness.

The case study also suggests that 'participatory management' is not necessarily concerned with increasing staff motivation. However, the study also suggests that 'participatory management' may be a strategy which effectively capitalises on expectations among staff throughout the organisation who, according to Sahley (1995: 52), 'need to feel that they can contribute to the development of policy and strategy'.

At the same time, a participatory style of management may be bolstered by a ' view of staff relations-which assumes that management and employees are working to the same goal of the organisation's success (Fincham and Rhodes, 1992). Secondly, it is clear that management staff in CONCERN Mozambique see 'participatory management' largely, though not exclusively, in terms of its benefits to the organisation, rather than to staff.

While such an instrumental view is dominant in the generic management literature, the participation of staff may, nonetheless, be seen as an end in itself. As noted earlier, 'participative management' may have as its objective the improvement of the 'quality of working life', or the promotion of industrial democracy.

That these are not explicit concerns of the management in CONCERN Mozambique suggests, however, that 'participatory management' may be seen in the context of the 'hard' rather than the 'soft' side of Human Resource Management (Storey, 1987).

The study also indicates that different objectives may be attributed to 'participatory management' even within the same organisation. In addition, different aspects of the process of adopting a participatory style of management may be associated with different objectives.

One of the implications is that the perceived 'success' or 'failure' of 'participatory management' will depend on the aims attributed to the greater involvement of staff in decision-making. Consequently, the question: 'Is Participatory Management effective?' has no simple answer. At the same time, the study suggests that there is a danger that a participatory approach to management may be perceived by NGO staff as appropriate only to those NGOs involved in 'participatory development'. However, the generic management literature clearly suggests the advantages to organisations, generally, of increased employee participation.

Issues for Researchers

While the case study suggests that 'participatory management' may represent a distinctive approach for NGOs, it also reveals that such an approach to management is not fundamentally different from management approaches adopted by some organisations in other sectors.

Indeed, the adoption of participatory styles of management among NGOs may be seen as part of the tradition of importing management concepts, prevalent in the business world, to the NGO sector.

At the same time, the study demonstrates that NGOs may learn a great deal from for-profit organisations about the importance and nature of participation in management. The case study also confirms the view that 'participatory management' is more than a collection of participatory techniques and involves institutional change that is both structural and cultural in nature. It implies a pro-active 'formalisation', or 'institutionalisation' of participation, so that existing patterns of participation are transformed into structures of participation. Such structures are necessarily expressions of the organisation's fundamental and long-term commitment to a participatory process. 'Participatory management' can be seen, therefore, in the context of the challenge facing NGOs to lose their 'shyness' of management and take on a strategic management orientation rather than focusing on logistics or project management (Korten, 1987: 155). At the same time, the study shows that translating a policy commitment to participation on the part of the organisation into a meaningful set of strategic and operational choices may be problematic. In particular, there is an inherent irony in promoting participation from the top down.

The case study demonstrates that the concepts and categories used to describe participation in the generic literature are of considerable use in understanding the nature of participation in NGO management. In particular, it reveals that 'participatory management' in NGOs is a multi-dimensional and multi-faceted concept, and is no less complex than participation in commercial organisations. Participatory schemes may pervade many or all levels of the organisation, and may take different forms. Moreover, the study endorses the view, expressed by the British Overseas Development Administration, that 'from any stakeholder's perspective participation may be seen as a spectrum model with a range of possibilities from being manipulated to being in control' (Eyben, 1994: 2.1).

The participation of staff will, therefore, vary in intensity according, for example, to the nature of the work, the experience and capability of staff, and the stage of development of the organisation. In this respect, White's (1995) conceptual framework, which argues that participation may by 'nominal', 'instrumental', 'representative' or 'transformative' (with only the final category truly empowering), may usefully be applied to, and inform, our understanding of 'participatory management'.

While interest in participation in the management of commercial organisations is generally confined to the involvement of employees, the study reveals that participation in the management of development NGOs may refer to the involvement, not just of staff, but of other stakeholders, even the beneficiaries.

'Participatory management' may thus be seen in the context of an NGO's attempt to structurally and systematically engage its multiple stakeholders (Fowler, 1995). However, the study also suggests that, in practice, participation in the management of NGOs may be confined to the greater involvement of NGO staff. This is in accordance with the view that the involvement of beneficiaries in the management of the organisation may not be feasible. In this regard, 'participatory management' may differ little from employee participation in the commercial sector.

There is no trade-off between greater participation of staff in decision-making and maintaining high standards of professionalism.

It demonstrates that 'participatory management' does not mean being non-directive, and, somewhat paradoxically, requires strong leadership.

Indeed, it suggests the accuracy of Clark's (1991: 66) view that achieving the right balance between strong leadership, which ensures resolute pursuit of strong ideas, and openness of style, which ensures that all staff feel properly valued, is the greatest management challenge for NGOs, particularly as they grow in size.

'Participatory management' inevitably raises questions about the nature of the relationship between those who manage and those who are managed. Such debate has been vigorous in the commercial sector throughout this century (Beardwell and Holden, 1994: 6). In particular, 'participatory management' implies a conception of the organisation as an environment in which managerial discretion is permitted freer rein, and staff are given greater 'voice' (Hirschmann, 1970). As such, it is essentially no different from 'participative management' in the commercial sector in which employees are enabled, to varying degrees, to have a greater say in decision-making.

The case also demonstrates that 'participatory management' may represent a management style in which 'worker empowerment' in practice takes place very much within the boundaries set by management. In this regard, too, it is no different from employee involvement practice in the commercial sector (Beardwell and Holden, 1994: 584).

At the same time, there is likely to be a dilemma, within management, in terms of how much power to extend to the workforce. Management will want to harness the workers' creative energies, but at the same time not undermine managerial prerogatives, particularly accountability. 'Participatory management' may be seen, therefore, as an attempt to reconcile the tension between participatory ideology and the hierarchical requirements of institutional action.

The research also highlights the important link between a more participatory style of management and democracy within the organisation. It suggests the accuracy of Pateman's (1970) argument that it is possible for 'partial' participation at both immediate and distant levels to take place without a democratisation of authority structures, and that 'full' participation may be introduced at the lower level within the context of a non-democratic structure overall. However, while it may be possible for a more participatory approach to be introduced within an organisation which is not participatory in management style, the case suggests that official endorsement (at the organisational or 'company' level) is essential if such practices are to be legitimised, and therefore truly 'formalised' and 'institutionalised'.

The importance of a gender focus in 'participatory management' needs to be made explicit. In the first place, 'participatory management' requires an examination of popular assumptions about the position of women in organisations. Secondly, as Goetz (1995) points out, unless women and men are represented equally at all levels of an organisation, management can never be truly 'participatory'. Moreover, an organisation whose management is not gender equitable will ultimately fail to address the priorities of women, who, as Kabeer (1994) points out, have been and continue to be marginalised by deeply entrenched, and hence barely visible, biases in development theory and practice.

'Participatory management' must be informed by culture and, like any management approach, must 'spring from the cultural values which govern social interactions and dominate intra-and inter-organisational relations' (Bjur and Zomorrodian, 1986: 415). However, culture is an extremely complex phenomenon (Wright, 1994), and although writers such as Hofstede (1980) and Laurent (1983) have attempted to examine the influence of cultural factors on management generally, our understanding of such factors remains unclear.

The treatment of the relationship between participatory styles of management and culture, therefore, needs careful investigation. In particular, the idea that 'participatory management', as a people-centred approach, is a western construct (Dichter, 1989), and therefore foreign to Third World contexts, needs to be seriously challenged.

While 'participatory management' and 'participatory development' are sometimes used interchangeably, the study suggests that this is a terminological rather than a conceptual problem.

For senior management staff in CONCERN Mozambique the distinction is clearly unproblematic. 'Participatory development' is clearly about the involvement of beneficiaries in the planning, implementation and evaluation of external interventions. 'Participatory management', on the other hand, is about the participation of staff (and possibly other stakeholders) not only in the design of organisational activities, but in decisions about organisational policy, strategy and operations.

It is essential, therefore, to avoid confusing the terms, and in particular, to link the two more precisely. What emerges from the study, but is not discussed in the literature, is the degree to which 'participatory management' may be highly formal and procedural.

In particular, it requires the transformation of existing patterns of participation into formalised structures. Ironically, this may result in stronger managerial control. At the same time, the study suggests that the structured and controlled nature of 'participatory management' may strengthen rather than weaken accountability.

In particular, it may support programming, monitoring and evaluation systems which are important 'downward' accountability instruments (Wils, 1995). The case also suggests that 'participatory management' is an aspirational concept, and thus may be best described, in the Weberian sense, as an 'ideal type' (Fincham and Rhodes, 1992: 190).

It indicates that the degree to which any organisation may facilitate the greater involvement of non-managerial staff in decisionmaking is inevitably limited, and will be contingent on the complex interplay of a number of organisational variables. Moreover, like other management approaches such as Total Quality Management, 'participatory management' will remain open to a variety of definitions and interpretations. As a result, NGOs will need to create their own model of 'participatory management'. This, however, is not necessarily a constraint. Finally, the case study also suggests that 'participatory management' must be seen in the context of Campbell's (1987:

3) assertion that 'there is not, nor can there be, only one correct way of managing an organisation'.

This 'contingency approach', which is the dominant approach to the management of organisations generally (Child, 1988), must be the context within which 'participatory management' is discussed. In this way, 'participatory management' can be completely consistent with Dichter's (1989) view that what is needed is not a search for universal principles but a clearer focus on the actual field conditions, as it is these which must determine which management style is appropriate.

3

HIV/AIDS Transmission in India: Recent Trends

Although numbers of recorded cases of HTV and AIDS in India are still relatively low, the rapid increase in seropositivity rates amongst sentinel populations suggests that the scale and pace of HTV transmission in the country is already significant. By March 1995, 2 505 704 people in India had been screened for HIV infection. 18 222 were found to be seropositive using the Western Blot method and 1108 individuals have developed full blown AIDS (NACO 1995). Seventy-nine percent of recorded HTV positive cases are located in the four states of Maharashtra, Tamil Nadu (including Pondicherry), Manipur and Karnataka.

This partly reflects the more advanced medical and screening facilities in Bombay, Madras, Vellore and Bangalore. Thus, if the data are adjusted to take account of numbers screened, high prevalance rates are also found in the southern states of Goa, Kerala and Andhra Pradesh, together with Uttar Pradesh, Punjab/Chandigarh and Delhi in the north. Significantly, 24 of the states or union territories in the country have already reported HTV infection.

The dominant mode of HTV transmission in India is heterosexual intercourse. The strong double standard that expects women to preserve their premarital virginity and to remain exclusively faithful to their husbands, but which tacitly accepts that men may engage in premarital or extramarital intercourse, has resulted in a sizeable demand for female prostitution. At the same time, there are large numbers of impoverished women who find few opportunities for economic survival other than commercial sex. Up to one million women are estimated to work in the Indian commercial sex industry (ICMR 1992), 100 000 in Bombay alone. Low levels of condom use and high rates of client turnover have facilitated the transmission of sexually transmitted diseases, including HTV. Approximately 30% of prostitutes in Bombay are believed to be HIV positive (ICMR 1991) and in Madras, where the first case of HIV infection in the country was detected, seroprevalence levels amongst commercial sex workers had reached 15% by June 1993 (personal communication, Dr. Jayapaul).

Intravenous drug use has also emerged as an important risk factor of HIV transmission in India. The highest rates of HTV have been recorded in the north eastern state of Manipur where cheap and easily available good quality heroin is fuelling an HTV epidemic amongst intravenous drug users, or IDUs (Naik et al. 1991). By March 1995, 97 per 1000 people screened in the State were found to be HIV positive, yielding a seroprevalence rate of 171 per 100 000 population (NACO 1995). The neighbouring states of Mizoram and Nagaland are also recording steady increases in HTV. High rates of injecting drug use in this region have been associated with its proximity to the 'Golden Triangle' of Burma, Laos and Thailand where 20% of the world's heroin is estimated to be grown and processed. However, intravenous drug use is not confined to the north east.

Of the estimated 2 million drug users in India, 50 000 are believed to inject drugs (Jayaraman 1992). In Delhi the recorded seropositivity rate amongst IDUs rose from 43.5 per 1000 in 1993 to 333.3 in the first 6 months of 1994 {*Pioneer* 1994). Whilst trends in HIV prevalence amongst commercial sex workers (CSWs) and IDUs have commanded the most attention of both the Indian media and government officials, evidence suggests that HIV is firmly entrenched in the general population. The number of people who have been infected by blood and blood products is unknown, although this factor currently accounts for more full-blown AIDS cases in India than intravenous drug use. CSWs and their clients also provide a point of contact for HIV transmission between large numbers of otherwise disconnected people.

As a result, growing rates of seroprevalence are being observed in so-called lowrisk groups. Extrapolating data on HIV prevalence rates in pregnant women and blood donors, GOI and WHO suggest that the AIDS epidemic in India will exceed that of neighbouring Thailand. By the end of 1992 more than one million people in the country were estimated to be infected with the virus. This figure is expected to double or even triple by 1996 (NACO 1993).

THE EVOLUTION OF HIV/AIDS POLICY IN INDIA

During the early 1980s, the official response to AIDS in India was one of denial. AIDS was seen as a 'foreign' disease from which ordinary Indians would be spared. The detection, in 1986, of HIV antibodies in Indian CSWs did little to dispel this belief. Although women engaged in prostitution were vilified for 'importing' the disease by having sex with foreigners and were identified as a potential 'reservoir of infection' which threatened the general population, the stigmatization of CSWs served to distance them from an indifferent public and to reinforce the view that AIDS was restricted to specific, well-defined groups.

This view prevailed when cases of seropositivity were identified in 1987 amongst professional blood donors. Rather than using this sample (albeit biased towards impoverished men) to interpret possible trends in HIV infection in the genera] population, professional blood donors were branded a 'high risk group' and charged with sexual promiscuity and drug addiction.

The emphasis placed upon high-risk groups rather than high-risk behaviours both reflected and contributed to the first policies and laws relating to HIV/AIDS. In 1986 the Indian Council of Medical Research (ICMR) in collaboration with the Directorate General of Health Services (DGHS) and individual State Governments initiated a national programme of serological surveillance. This provided the springboard for (indeed, came to be synonymous with) the National AIDS Control Programme which was formally launched in 1987. Rather than developing a system of sentinel surveillance, efforts focused on the unsystematic collection of samples from 'high-risk' groups.

The latter were defined as sexually promiscuous men and women, homosexuals, IDUs and people who had received repeat blood transfusions. However, as little guidance was given with regard to the practical problem of identifying and testing such individuals, samples were taken from 'captive' populations (STD patients, women detained under the prostitution laws, blood donors and hospital patients). As access to the latter depended upon the extent to which individual Surveillance Centres could liaise with hospitals and social welfare or police departments in their states, there was a large variation between the centres in both the numbers of individuals and the proportions of specific groups tested.

By October 1989, for example, Tamil Nadu State alone accounted for 43% of all people screened in India. By contrast the State of Uttar Pradesh, which comprises 16% of the total Indian population, had tested less than 2% of all screenees.

As targeting procedures clearly differed from centre to centre and state to state, it became difficult to draw reliable conclusions about the prevalence of HIV in specific groups or regions, let alone piece together a national picture.

However, ICMR felt compelled to publish its findings. With insufficient information to assess the prevalence, distribution and likely spread of HIV in the population as a whole, the Council could do little more than draw the public's attention to its sero-surveillance data on high-risk categories. Such selective reporting inevitably reinforced the impression that AIDS was restricted to the most marginalised of groups and strengthened calls for discriminatory legislation.

During the 1980s, various legal measures were proposed to prevent the so-called importation and spread of HIV in India, from compulsory testing to the isolation of HTV positive individuals and AIDS patients. Despite popular support, most were rejected on the basis of human rights. The notorious AIDS Prevention Bill of 1989, for example, gave government and health authorities sweeping powers to infringe upon individual rights (de Souza 1990). The draft Bill included provisions to require medical practitioners to notify local health authorities about any drug addicts, HTV positive people and AIDS patients in their care; to empower health authorities to forcibly test and question individuals suspected to be at greater risk of infection and isolate HTV positive cases; and to introduce criminal penalties for the transmission of HTV by professional blood donors. Not surprisingly, the Bill received widespread criticism for victim blaming and denying human rights and, following a series of amendments, it was finally withdrawn in 1992.

The absence of legislation has not prevented the application of highly discriminatory measures in practice. Questions have been raised, for instance, about the methods used in surveillance activities. Although the collection of blood samples from high-risk groups is technically 'voluntary', it is doubtful whether the consent of screened individuals is always obtained and whether they have the knowledge and freedom to refuse testing. Other problems relate to the treatment of individuals found to be HTV positive. Information about people's HTV status is frequently leaked to the press who have not only named HTV positive individuals, but printed their photographs.

A number of states have illegally detained HIV and AIDS sufferers as well as people suspected to be at high risk of infection. In 1988, for example, HTV positive sex workers arrested under the Prevention of Immoral Traffic Act in Madras were kept under detention even after serving their official sentences. The case provoked a strong response from local activists and in 1990 the Madras High Court ordered the release of five prostitutes who had been detained at the Government viligance home (Nataraj 1990).

In the face of both international and national pressure, GOI began to revise its AIDS policies. In 1989 a medium-term plan for AIDS control was drawn up in collaboration with WHO. This focused on the need to establish an effective programme management structure with a view to coordinating multi-sectoral policies. In 1990 responsibility for surveillance activities was transferred from ICMR to the office of the National AIDS Control Programme in DGHS (NACO 1993). As the latter had already initiated blood safety and AIDS case management programmes (whereby existing medical colleges and institutes had been designated as regional centres for the clinical treatment of AIDS), this paved the way for the creation of an umbrella organization responsible for coordinating a broader range of AIDS-related policies.

In 1991, proposals for a new bureaucratic structure encompassing such an organization were developed in a 5-year Strategic Plan for the Prevention and Control of AIDS in India. The following year, the National AIDS Control Organization was officially established and the more comprehensive National AIDS Prevention and Control Programme was launched.

The creation of NACO represented a turning point in Indian AIDS policy. Although some emphasis is still placed on surveillance, NACP now acknowledges the need to focus more resources upon HTV prevention strategies as well as counselling and care. To this end, the Programme aims to encourage safer sex practices and condom use amongst the general public as well as vulnerable groups; to further develop STD (sexually transmitted disease) prevention and control activities; to ensure that HTV postive individuals and AIDS patients are provided with care, counselling and support in order to live their lives in dignity; and to integrate AIDS Information, Education and Communication (IEC) programmes with existing health programmes, including mother and child health and family planning, and with other sectoral programmes in education, youth affairs, women's issues, welfare, urban development and labour affairs. In order to implement this comprehensive approach, NACO explicitly calls for intersectoral and NGO (non-governmental organization) collaboration together with grassroots mobilization.

NACO suggests that grassroots approaches are particularly relevant to the development of targeted programmes for groups practising high-risk behaviours (sex workers, their clients and employers; IDUs; men who have sex with men; school leavers; migrant labourers and prison inmates) and identifies NGOs as major partners in such initiatives. It accepts that no standard formula can be applied to community based strategies and that programmes should be adapted to local level circumstances. In the absence of detailed knowledge about the socio-demographic characteristics and social structures of vulnerable groups such as CSWs and IDUs, the need for qualitative assessment of local needs and potential strategies is also acknowledged

(Government of India 1991). With its commitment to project integration, community participation and non-governmental involvement, GOI's response to AIDS has undoubtedly changed for the better. However, the 5-year Strategic Plan is ambitious and problems of translating policy into practice in the Indian context may have been underestimated. The following section examines NACP's specific components in more detail and considers factors that have enabled and constrained their implementation.

AIDS CARE AND HUMAN RIGHTS IN RURAL INDIA

The role medical ethics has gained more importance with the spread of the AIDS epidemic. A key element of this emphasis is on care givers such as doctors, nurses and counsellors to provide good quality care in a non-judgmental fashion. Although the principles of medical ethics hold true for all human beings, the socio-cultural context in which medical care is provided is not uniform. Further, the health care infrastructure in many societies does not permit universal access and availability of care. This is the case in rural India where HIV is spreading rapidly. Although the Indian government outlines a very sound AIDS policy, there are several gaps in the translation of this policy to action. These gaps are the result of various issues ranging from stigma in the community to lack of skills and resources among medical providers to effectively manage HIV infection. This paper analyses these gaps and recommends some strategies to enable upholding human rights of persons and families living with HIV/AIDS in rural India.

There are an estimated 3.5 million HIV infected persons in India. A review of documents from the National AIDS Control Organization (NACO) reveals a comprehensively written policy. NACO is the national body in India that provides leadership in AIDS prevention and control. The policy addresses key issues of prevention, care, and human rights protection. Additionally, the policy also recognizes several challenges to its implementation and emphasizes the need to address them.

These include the often slow response and action from the government sector, the recognition of violation of rights such as denial of care for PWHAs by medical practitioners, the need to enhance technical and managerial capabilities of program managers, to name a few. This recognition is a key first step to addressing the epidemic. The NACO AIDS Policy (NAP) also details specific policy initiatives. They are program management, advocacy and social mobilization, participation of non-governmental organizations (NGOs), surveillance and monitoring, policy on blood safety, HIV testing and counselling, initiatives for PWHAs, control of sexually transmitted diseases (STDs) and condom education. In maintaining a focus on AIDS Care services, this paper will discuss the last four initiatives.

AIDS Care services in general include prevention education, access to prevention technology, voluntary testing and counselling, and care for PWHAs. The NAP emphasizes the need for wider out reach in these services in rural areas. Although the level of awareness is as high as 70% in urban India, it is only around 30% in rural areas. Thus the mandate for intensification of prevention efforts in rural India is indeed important. In terms of HIV testing and counselling, the NAP stresses its stand against mandatory testing, and strongly advocates voluntary testing with pre-and post-test counselling. The policy additionally affirms the rights of PWHAs to education and employment. It also points out the need for protecting confidentiality, and proper counselling emphasizing the importance of access to medical care. Control of STDs and condom social marketing are highlighted as essential efforts that will facilitate prevention.

Despite public and private sector attempts, there are some gaps in the translation of NAP particularly in rural areas. The first gap is in the area of prevention education. Prevention education efforts may take the form of AIDS programs and lectures and may not always be evaluated for impact. It is not uncommon for AIDS awareness activities to take the form of a series of lectures delivered by prominent residents and politicians to a gathered crowd on occasions such as World AIDS Day or World Health Day. While such AIDS awareness campaigns have a higher out reach and increase knowledge and awareness about AIDS, they are rather limited in achieving behaviour change and change is risk perceptions. The need for focused approaches tailored to the needs of various segments of rural population-men, women, adolescents-is urgent.

The second gap is in the provision of counselling and testing services. HIV disease is typically detected at the primary care physician's office where the person goes to when s/he becomes sick usually with opportunistic infections. Thus, the primary care physician bears the onus of pre-test counselling and taking consent. In a private practice where a doctors may see an average of 40 patients a day, this is sometimes a difficult onus to bear. Many doctors in private practice cite reasons of staff fear, and resources to avail of universal precautions, as some reasons that limit their caring for HIV infected persons. Further, there is a debate of whether counselling is a service that a medical doctor is qualified to provide. In the final analysis, several PWAs are often referred to the government hospitals.

FROM POLICY TO PRACTICE

As a civil society committed to promoting health, it is important to provide access to information and prevention of AIDS to rural residents of India. Half-hearted education attempts, awareness programs that have no measurable benefit, lack of provision of care, absence of testing and counselling are more than violations of national mandates to control HIV-they ultimately are actions that further the conditions under which HIV may be transmitted. How can the implementation of national policy then be enhanced to preserve human rights and promote health? The following are some areas of action.

Sensitize Health Providers in the Private Sector. In the rural periphery, private doctors far exceed public sector doctors. Private doctors are in several instances, the first point of contact for several PWHAs in rural areas. Doctors in rural areas may not have upgraded their skills in several years. Besides qualifications of some may be moot and they may exploit the poor and illiterate. Several doctors in rural India also claim to have a cure for AIDS. The need to educate all rural doctors and empower them with skills is critical. This is the first step to ensure protection of human rights in AIDS Care.

Invest in networking of health care providers, and NGOs. Isolation of rural areas is not limited to geography. Intellectual isolation can indeed be rather pervasive. Networking among regional doctors is the first step to sensitization.

This will provide an opportunity to learn from best practices and encourage sensitive treatment of P.WAs. The vastness of rural areas in India calls for intensive localized efforts with people from the region who are prepared to address its needs. Here, NGOs can work with doctors offices in the periphery to provide counselling services. The out reach of some NGOs and people's groups extends to remote rural areas. This might encourage close monitoring of health care service delivery for violations of human rights. In strengthening the capacities of these groups lies the beginning of a concerted response to PWAs in rural areas of India.

Facilitate People's Movements for Strict Enforcement of Human Rights. The role of people and advocacy groups is key in enforcing human rights. A well informed public can take these issues seriously and serve as watchdogs to the government. The state then follows by implementing Acts that preserve rights. The organization of female sex workers in Calcutta to prevent oppression and taking steps to prevent HIV infection is one example Similar organizations of PWAs and persons interested in human rights can lead to action in rural areas.

Educate Enforcing Bodies. The link between laws and their implementation is only as strong and fair as their enforcers. There are several reports of police brutalities in India. The earlier mentioned detention of HIV positive sex workers is an example. There is a need to facilitate dialogue between police and the community.

The NAP should provide for tangible links between the law enforcers and the public in terms of AIDS control and prevention. Police and other enforcing bodies should also be equipped with technology to enforce law better. The village government or Gram panchayats are to be empowered under NACO plans to implement AIDS Projects. Gram panchayats consists of elected individuals who manage the implementation of development efforts at the village level. However, these bodies in some states are influenced by the higher castes where there is potential for power and politics to violate rights. The political will in AIDS Care and Human rights should be vocalized by politicians and other leaders, and committed bodies to handle rights violations should be supported.

Focus more efforts on men and laws favouring women's rights. The need to work with men has been stressed in the literature, in the context of women's health. There is evidence for the urgency of this need in light of AIDS. Male behaviour has been documented to facilitate HIV infection in monogamous women. The large number of liquor shops in Belgaum district facilitates consumption of alcohol. While alcoholism in both men and women can increase violence, studies in India have shown a link between excess male alcohol consumption and domestic violence. Despite these challenges to achieving women's health goals, laws can effect women's health and well being. In the state of Kerala for example, where women have women access to basic health care and favourable property and inheritance laws, we see high litearcy rates in women and small families. In addition to NACO mandate of working with women, more intensive efforts targeted at rural men, and elders is needed. This might begin to influence groups that directly impact women's health rights.

Recognize the interaction of human rights and rural context in planning AIDS Care services. Communities in rural India are complex entities. Health workers in rural India report on the importance of taking permission from village elders and leaders, in order to initiate any discussion with the village residents. These roles of family and community need to be considered in AIDS counselling. There are reports that caste, occupation, religion, and economic status already are grounds for discrimination in several poor districts of India. Thus, translation of NAP in rural villages requires addressing these dynamics.

There is also a need to appreciate the inter-state diversity in iliteracy, program planning, and governance. NAP also needs to lobby for implementation of several pending and unfinished projects to provide basic necessities to India's rural residents. Unless these needs are met, violations against PWHAs may simply be a part of the larger oppression that many in rural India face. These structural issues must be brought into the fore front of public debate by NACO, and other advocates of humanized AIDS Care.

Seriously enforce education of young people. In a review of textbooks used by grade 11 and 12 students, there was reference to HIV/AIDS and even STDs. However, although there was mention about the microbiology of the disease, the real issues of transmission and prevention were covered only cursorily. This quote is illustrative of young men's frustration with the sex education practived in schools in rural Karnataka: "The teachers skip the reproductive system altogether.. this is usually a choice between this and another system in biology exam.. so they think we can leave it in choice. While students are most eager to read about this.. the teachers are not. " Peer training and education is a viable strategy to empower young adults who will soon be sexually active. Sensitization of this population to these issues will also create community consciousness and go a great length in creating human rights awareness.,

AIDS has brought to light the issue of human rights. It is now important to take this opportunity to seriously consider enforcing these rights to all Indians in all sectors of societal function and governance. The strategies listed above may provide a beginning to address AIDS Care in rural India. But they do require larger reforms, political will and responsible spending of public funds. Successful initiatives such as Polio Plus campaigns in India bear evidence to committed implementation to address serious health issues. It is hoped that such commitment of resources will be replicated in addressing AIDS in rural India.

AIDS BASED NEW RURAL MARKETS

Every year, more than six million people die either of AIDS, tuberculosis and malaria alone. Today there is no effective vaccine for these and many such diseases and the low income countries have average health budget expenses of $17 to $ 36 per person and only afford to spend pennies per dose on vaccines. This has resulted in heavily coming down on the exchequers on the one hand and low morale of pharmaceutical and biotechnology companies on the other due to very thin margin on developing such life-saving vaccines.

In fact ten percent of the world's health research and development is devoted to diseases that affect ninety percent of the world's population.

While remarkable efforts to contain the spread of HIV have been made worldwide since the onset of the epidemic approximately 15 years ago, the number of people infected with HIV and with full-blown AIDS has continued to increase unabated. From the beginning of the epidemic in the early 1980s until mid-1996, an estimated 29.4 million people worldwide were infected with HIV. The largest number of persons infected with HIV, totalling 19 million, or 68 percent of the global total, live in sub-Saharan Africa. World Health Organization (WHO) projections for sub-Saharan Africa paint a gloomy picture for the future. In 1980, HIV infections for this region were estimated to number 620,000. This number increased to 2.5 million infections by 1985, 10 million by 1990, and was projected at 40 million by the year 2000. Between 1992 and 1995 alone, it was estimated that sub-Saharan Africa experienced a 47 percent increase in new infections, representing more than 3.6 million new cases of HIV. The position of Kenya is absolutely at stake.

"Although Kenya is in many ways ahead of other countries in understanding the epidemic, the country, however, lacked a cohesive program document before the launching of the book. It is hoped that new policies coupled with recommendations will be pursued in order to prevent the further spread of HIV and to mitigate its impact."

The face of HIV/AIDS has also changed during the 6 years of the AIDSCAP Project. In the early years of the epidemic, persons most often infected with HIV were adult males in their mid-to late-twenties and their partners, who were often commercial sex workers (CSWs). Recent statistical information reveals disturbing changes in this profile. More new infections seem to be occurring in young people aged 15 to 24, and many of them show risk factors that are less evident. Infection rates among women, particularly young girls, are increasing at a faster rate than among their male counterparts. This increase is due, in part, to young girls experiencing sexual activity at an earlier age, marrying older men (who are thus more likely to be infected), or exchanging sex for money. In Kenya, Rwanda, and Tanzania, more than 10 percent of the women surveyed in urban areas attending antenatal clinics are found to be HIV-positive, with rates exceeding 30 percent at some surveillance sites. Most of these women are housewives infected by their partners.

There are significant regional variations in levels of HIV infection among countries and between urban and rural areas within countries. Countries such as Malawi, Tanzania, and Rwanda have high prevalence rates ranging between

4 and 30 percent in sexually active urban populations; the rate is as high as 40 percent among groups who engage in sexual risk taking. Rates of HIV infection as high as 80 percent have been recorded among Commercial Sex Workers surveyed in Nairobi and Abidjan. In countries where the epidemic is at an earlier stage, such as Senegal and Nigeria, the estimated seroprevalence ranges from 2 to 12 percent among at-risk groups in urban areas. However, throughout Africa, differences between urban and rural infection rates are narrowing, sometimes rapidly

AIDS is a dreaded syndrome which kills not only people but also their morale when they are alive. There are instances of suicides attempted by the AIDS affected persons simply because of their low morale and poor economic conditions. This article attempts to develop enough scope for such of those patients who can serve as a role model in the National and local awareness drives besides engaging themselves as marketers of necessary preventive and consultative product/information agents for reasonable charges, by which they can create new markets, especially in rural areas, where the level of awareness is relatively low and mindset to help poor patients for something in the form of information or experience or tips or products of small value. Of course this effort could be a certified one by relevant Government agencies as part of rehabilitation process undertaken at national/regional levels.

CONDOM SOCIAL MARKETING

In 1992, lack of access to condoms was common in most of the countries of the LAC region. To address this constraint, AIDSCAP and its subcontractors initiated or strengthened condom social marketing programs in four of its major countries in the region.

These interventions sometimes had dramatic results, not only on sales of the socially marketed product but also on commercial sales and government policy.

For example, during a 4-year project in Brazil implemented by DKT do Brazil, an affiliate of Population Services International, sales of Prudence — the DKT condom — totaled more than 71.5 million. Of this number, approximately 45.8 million were sold in AIDSCAP target areas.

Prudence is the third largest brand in Brazil. Prior to this program, Brazil had one of the lowest rates of condom use in the world, with nationwide sales of approximately 50 million condoms in 1991. By the end of 1996, sales had more than tripled. A DKT position paper is also credited with the president's 1995 decision to decree a yearlong tax holiday on the 60-percent duty charged on imported condoms. This holiday expired after a year, but the duty was lowered to 10 percent.

On the same lines above, it is suggested to create AWARENESS MARKETS for and by those already infected and could run a business of their own in rural centres or village schools for spreading AIDS education at a reasonable fee [say 5 USDs per head]. Such a nominal fee may be collected from the students of the same school or the locality where the programme is implemented so as to meet the daily requirements of the infected persons. This would give self-employment to millions of affected people to engage themselves on turn-duty basis and to share the regular and considerable income from awareness drive which will have a positive effect on the society as a whole particularly on the young minds in schools to lead a safe life.

AIDS Prevention Markets

This is a kind of marketing in which the preventive aspects/products related to AIDS could be taken to people at grass root level and sold at reasonable prices. "In Haiti, there are many rural markets [commercial outlets] in which these products find a good offer from locals and it makes the sellers enjoy a sizeable margin for wholesales, distribution and retailing. Condom social marketing [CSM] is an area like treasure hunting which serves as preventing the incidence of AIDS in high-risk areas/situations". It cannot only improve the level of understanding of prevention but also serves those unaware of the facts and fallacies of AIDS. This kind of marketing is successful in Cameroon, South Africa, Ethiopia, Rwanda, Tanzania and Nepal. The role of NGOs is appreciable in this and their care for AIDS infected persons.

THE NATIONAL AIDS CONTROL PROGRAMME: SPECIFIC COMPONENTS

As outlined above, AIDS policy in India prior to 1992 focused almost exclusively on serosurveiliance. Between 1987 and 1991, 85% of the national AIDS budget was devoted to the screening of individuals, blood and blood products (NACO 1993). By contrast, in 1992 there were only five government centres for the care of AIDS patients in the whole of the country (Baweja and Katiyar 1992). Health education activities were also woefully inadequate and relied on the limited number of non-governmental organizations who were willing to work in AIDS prevention. Recognizing the need to focus resources more effectively on preventive activities, NACP incorporated an IEC component, STD control and condom promotion in addition to the existing surveillance and blood safety programmes. Strategies for reducing the impact of HIV and AIDS were also included in the new plan. In order to implement this more extensive range of activities, attention to and funds for programme management were substantially increased.

Strengthening Programme Management

As NACP objectives and activities, together with the budget available for HIV/AIDS policy, have expanded, the management demands of the Programme have become significantly more complex. On the one hand, a centralized management structure is required to provide overall policy directions, to coordinate multi-sectoral collaboration, to extend technical and operational support to staff and organizations implementing programme activities, and to approve budgets and disburse funds. At the same time, there is an increasing awareness of the role of regionally specific factors in the transmission of HTV and thus of the need for management to be decentralized so that appropriate action can be taken by state and district authorities and by local NGOs. Political pressures have also propelled the decentralization of AIDS programme management to the state level. Health is constitutionally a state responsibility in India and individual states have considerable power to either accept or reject centrally organized and centrally funded programmes. It is therefore both necessary and desirable for state governments to fully participate in the design, implementation and management of the country's AIDS programme.

The new National AIDS Control Programme has a hierarchical structure, each level of management corresponding with a level of bureaucracy in the state machinery. The National AIDS Control Organization (NACO) is accountable to and receives policy guidelines from multi-sectoral committees chaired by the Minister and Secretary of Health. Nevertheless, it holds sufficient administrative and financial powers to constitute a centralized body for the planning and management of policies relating to HIV and AIDS. It is at this level that specific programme components are designed, coordinated and monitored; that funds are allocated and disbursed; and that liaison takes place with associated ministries, state governments, multilateral and bilateral agencies and NGOs. All government ministries and departments, for example, have been invited to designate officers responsible for developing programmes in collaboration with the Organization. NACO is also supported in its functions by a National Technical Advisory Committee which endorses operational guidelines and which may advise on the need for training and educational materials.

In order to decentralize the planning, implementation and management of AIDS prevention programmes to a more appropriate level, the basic organizational structure of NACP has been replicated at the state level. State AIDS Control Programmes are managed by State AIDS Cells (the counterparts of NACO), which are supported by State Technical Advisory Committees and overseen by Empowered Committees. Like their national level counterparts, the latter are expected to have multi-sectoral representation so that partners from various government sectors, industry, women's groups, NGOs, trade unions and so on can contribute to the development of strategic plans. Arguing that the factors associated with HIV transmission vary regionally, NACP envisages that each state will develop its own approach to AIDS prevention and control. To this end, the involvement of NGOs is strongly encouraged as such organizations tend to have the freedom and flexibility to respond to local needs.

The new organizational structure of NACP demonstrates a commitment by the Government of India to mount a serious response to the growing challenge of AIDS by fostering collaboration between central and state governments, different ministries and departments, and between governmental and non-governmental organizations. In practice, however, this has proved hard to achieve. The most serious setbacks to the Programme have occurred at the state level, due to the failure of state governments to observe NACO directives and to promote the participation of the NGO sector. Between 1992 and 1993, 22 states and union territories used less than 10% of the funds allocated to them for AIDS prevention and control. Several state governments failed to create AIDS Cells and in some cases money was diverted to other programmes. Even where AIDS Cells have been established there have been problems with staff recruitment and programme implementation.

Staff are normally transferred to the Cells from health and other government departments. However, because AIDS Cell posts are perceived to have a limited life-span (they are supported from a five-year World Bank loan) and because of the stigma attached to AIDS-related work, these appointments are treated like 'punishment postings' (*Pioneer* 1993). By July 1993, only three of the 11 vacancies in the Delhi Cell had been filled, and in the Punjab officers were reshuffled every three months. Such procedures are unlikely to result in an efficient and dedicated staff. Problems have also emerged in programme implementation, most particularly in attracting NGO involvement in the design and implementation of HIV prevention activities. Contrary to national guidelines, very few state governments (Tamil Nadu being a notable exception) have created Empowered Committees with multi-sectoral representation.

The absence of NGO participation in management has done little to counter bureaucratic conservatism in policy development and resource allocation. For example, rather than placing funds directly at the disposal of the new State AIDS Cells, Finance Departments have typically released the money to Health Departments. The latter have proved reluctant to support programmes of a more innovative nature and to support the non-governmental sector. In response to demands from NACO and the Ministry of Health, state governments have begun to review their funding procedures. In metropolitan cities, for example, efforts are being made to set up separate administrative departments within municipal corporations (NACO 1994). These umbrella organizations would plan and coordinate the implementation of AIDS prevention and control activities by different agencies and sectors.

The creation of umbrella organizations at the city and state levels would be a positive development for NACO's aim of promoting integrated HIV/ AIDS policies. The Organization recognizes that this disease cannot be addressed by the health sector alone. However, although it has had some success in establishing intersectoral collaboration at the national level, this has not brought about the desired shift towards a more comprehensive approach to HIV and AIDS. Good examples of collaborative ventures include the incorporation of HTV/AIDS awareness activities into the 'Universities Talk AIDS' programme (implemented by the National Service Scheme of the Department of Youth Affairs and Sports of the Ministry of Human Resource Development (HRD), and developed with close collaboration between NACO, the Ministry of HRD and WHO) and the allocation of free prime time on national television for HTV/AIDS awareness campaigns.

These and other planned collaborative efforts are very positive developments, given the need for integrated approaches to HTV/AIDS prevention. However, they are also highly selective in orientation, reflecting the continued tendency to conceptualize HTV transmission in terms of individual behaviour rather than social change. In order to be effective, HTV intervention strategies must focus upon the social, cultural and economic factors that give rise to risk behaviours in the first place and that constrain less risky activity. To date, however, little progress has been made in incorporating HTV/AIDS prevention efforts in India into broader development and empowerment strategies.

HTV/AIDS SURVEILLANCE

Some of the problems of the surveillance programme have been discussed above. These include the lack of a systematic sampling strategy, wide regional variations in numbers and proportions of different categories screened, inconsistencies in the reporting and processing of data, and the lack of attention paid to ethical issues such as consent and confidentiality. ICMR began to acknowledge the limitations of its data in 1990 (ICMR 1990). However, responsibility for surveillance activities has filtered down to the state level and, due to bureaucratic inertia, the structure and mechanisms of the programme have remained largely unchanged.

The vast majority of samples continue to be drawn from so-called 'high-risk' groups with sample collection depending upon individual centres' targeting procedures and access to captive populations. As a result, screening efficiency and intensity vary widely. In Delhi, for example, the percentage of positive samples collected by 8 centres which had screened more than 10 000 individuals by June 1994 ranged from 0.0003 to 0.05. The pattern of surveillance is also highly uneven at the state level, rates of screening by March 1995 ranging from 6868 per 100 000 population in Pondicherry to 10 per 100 000 in Bihar.

In addition to yielding data of doubtful reliability, the surveillance programme has come under attack for infringing human rights. India is a signatory of the World Health Assembly resolution which calls upon governments to protect from discrimination persons or groups known or suspected to be HIV positive. To this end, NACO has requested that states organize a sound and rational testing policy which includes unlinked anonymous testing for surveillance and screening of blood; linked testing for those with acute symptoms of AIDS where counselling is available; and voluntary testing facilities only in the presence of sound counselling and support services.

In practice, many samples collected for surveillance are linked (indeed, names continue to be leaked to the press) and although testing is technically voluntary, many of those screened have neither the knowledge to give informed consent or the freedom to refuse to be tested. Counselling of HTV positive individuals is inadequate, amounting to little more than post-test advice on how to avoid infecting other people and little is available in the way of social, psychological and medical support.

Acknowledging the failings of the surveillance system, NACO has decided to adopt a sentinel surveillance system whereby in a limited number of selected sentinel sites, selected populations will be screened for HTV prevalence at certain intervals to monitor the progression of the epidemic and to identify trends. A standardized protocol for sentinel studies has been developed and introduced. Efforts are also under way to improve the quality of counselling offered to people with HIV and STDs. To this end, a grassroots counselling training module has been developed and a counselling training programme established with appropriate modules and manuals.

Behavioural Change through Information, Education and Communication

Because the dominant mode of HIV transmission in India is heterosexual intercourse, strategies to modify sexual behaviour are a key component of HTV prevention. Nearly a decade after HTV infection was first detected in an Indian national, there is little evidence to suggest that such behavioural change has been achieved. Levels of knowledge and awareness about HTV and AIDS are very low in both the general population and vulnerable groups; condoms have a negative image and are almost exclusively associated with family planning; and, as sexual relations are inherently unequal, few women have the power to protect themselves against HTV.

During the earlier phase of the National AIDS Control Programme, cultural taboos about openly discussing sex fostered a reluctance to initiate AIDS awareness campaigns. Official apathy and indifference were also linked to the belief that AIDS would be confined to highly marginalised groups. Notwithstanding such cultural sensitivities, NACO now recognizes that there is a pressing need for activities designed to generate awareness about HTV and AIDS and to bring about changes in risk behaviours. To this end, the Organization is disseminating information about AIDS through the television, radio, press and other channels of communication. The 'Universities Talk AIDS' programme currently reaches approximately 10 million students in 6500 colleges and universities in India. Efforts are also under way to devise educational materials for members of the services, railway workers, industrial workers and prisoners (Dasgupta 1994).

Until recently, attempts to introduce AIDS education to schoolchildren proved unacceptable to educationalists who believed that sex and AIDS education would encourage early sexual experimentation (Muley 1994). However, an extra-curricular package on HTV/AIDS and STDs has now been developed by the National Centre for Education Research and Training (NCERT) in collaboration with NACO, UNICEF, UNESCO and WHO. This package has been discussed by various groups, including teachers and parent-teacher associations, and forms the basis for proposals from 15 states for school-based AIDS awareness programmes.

In addition to general awareness campaigns, NACO is promoting the development of HTV prevention programmes to bring about behavioural change in highly vulnerable groups such as CSWs and their clients. Targeted interventions are a recent development in Indian AIDS policy. Nevertheless, a number of ambitious pilot projects have been intitiated with technical assistance from WHO. In Madras, for example, a pilot scheme was established in 1992 for the design and implementation of IEC strategies amongst members of the commercial sex industry (Asthana and Oostvogels, forthcoming). Due to the isolation and powerlessness of sex workers themselves, the recruitment of peer educators proved problematic. The project therefore tested strategies which involved close affiliates of the target groups.

These included madams, pimps and brothel keepers. It also recognized that it was important to include clients in out reach efforts since their cooperation in using condoms is essential. Brokers (who procure clients for CSWs) were identified as a potential conduit for the dissemination of AIDS information and condoms amongst this target group. Finally, the cooperation of a wide range of players with more peripheral links with the sex industry was enlisted. These included local police; general practitioners who provide STD services; the employees of cinemas, wine shops and bars; political and religious leaders; and the local media.

By endorsing community-based strategies of this type, NACO is in tune with international AIDS policy. Nevertheless, there remain powerful obstacles to promoting behavioural change amongst targeted groups. Official attitudes to CSWs, for example, are still highly contradictory. The Suppression of Immoral Traffic Act of 1956 (SITA), amended in 1986 (PITA), did not originally seek to abolish prostitution, but to abolish the practice of exploitation of women by others. However, the client is not an offender under the Act and sex workers can be penalized under Sections 7 and 8 for soliciting (Singh 1991).

In practice, moreover, it is prostitution rather than exploitation that is targeted for legal action with over 90% of the 15 000 or so cases that are registered annually under SIT A/PITA being taken against sex workers rather than pimps and procurers (personal communication, Dr. R Oostvogels).

Vulnerable to stigmatization and criminal prosecution, it is hardly surprising that CSWs remain suspicious of official involvement. Confidence has been expressed in the ability of NGOs to gain access to marginalised groups. However, care should be taken in assuming that the non-governmental sector is, by definition, more virtuous than its governmental counterpart. Evidence suggests that a growing number of Indian NGOs which have jumped on the AIDS bandwagon are motivated by self-promotion rather than altruism. Many organizations would appear to be more interested in attracting international funds and attending international conferences than working in the communities they claim to serve. Finally, NGO projects that have been initiated with outside assistance may not prove sustainable once that assistance has been withdrawn.

Other obstacles to the promotion of behavioural change stem from the nature and organization of the commercial sex industry itself. Whilst street workers are fairly visible because of where they work, other CSWs are engaged in disguised prostitution and are thus difficult to identify. Women who continue to live in regular households but who sell sex without the knowledge of their families and neighbours maintain a close secrecy about their working lives. It can also be difficult to gain access to brothel-based women. In Madras, for example, the premises in which brothels are housed regularly shift in response to police raids or complaints from neighbours. Information about the location of brothels is thus restricted to regular clients and brokers (Asthana and Oostvogels, forthcoming).

Finally, HTV prevention strategies are undermined by the powerlessness of commercial sex workers. Improved access to condoms has a limited impact on sexual practices if targeted individuals cannot insist upon their use. Yet, evidence suggests that it is the client rather than the sex worker who determines condom use and the few client surveys that have been undertaken in India reveal very little enthusiasm for safe sex. Brothel owners can play a key role in defining the sexual practices of the women they control and may be persuaded that there are business advantages to being able to advertise safe sex. In practice, however, many brothel owners will put the immediate needs of their clients before those of CSWs, and if condom promotion is perceived to threaten client interest and satisfaction, they will not insist upon condom use.

Control of Sexually Transmitted Diseases

The prevention and control of sexually transmitted diseases (STDs) is recognized as one of the major strategies of HTV prevention as genital ulcer diseases and STDs characterized by discharge facilitate both the acquisition and transmission of the HIV virus. Official data on STD prevalence rates in India are limited as they are based on cases reported to public hospitals and STD clinics. Evidence suggests that only a very small percentage of STD sufferers attend public facilities, the majority seeking clinical care from private doctors, going directly to drug sellers (where both diagnosis and case management tend to be inadequate) or resorting to self-medication. Women are particularly likely to go without treatment; first because women with STD are frequently asymptomatic, second because they may not be aware of the significance of genital tract symptoms, and third because of the fear and stigma attached to seeking care for an STD. Those in rural areas are further disadvantaged due to the lack of female doctors and problems of physical access to health facilities. Recent evidence also suggests that because women who do seek treatment are often too inhibited to be physically examined, health workers are forced to rely on verbal accounts (Ramasubban 1990). This clearly increases the risk of misdiagnosis.

As a first step towards developing STD prevention and control activities, NACO has commissioned a number of baseline surveys to evaluate the extent of the problem. In Tamil Nadu, samples were collected from selected populations in 1992. Rates were highest amongst female remand prisoners (a group likely to comprise a high proportion of CSWs), 36% of whom were infected. However, 10% of antenatal clinic attenders were found to suffer from a sexually transmitted disease and 2% from syphilis. STDs were also found to be a significant problem in rural areas, with 6% and 4% of men and women being affected. Four percent of rural men were found to suffer from syphilis (NACO 1993). These figures suggest that STDs constitute a major health problem in India and that large numbers of people in the country are potentially at risk of contracting HTV.

Recognizing the severity of the problem, NACO has proposed that, in addition to offering technical assistance to individual states and union territories, central funds are to be channelled into STD prevention and control efforts. A national STD programme has been in existence since 1946. However, during the first two decades of the programme, health officials were more preoccupied with combating major epidemic diseases such as smallpox and malaria. Because STDs were regarded as less life threatening, they commanded a lower medical and administrative priority (Arnold 1993). In the 1960s and 1970s STD clinics began to be established at both state and district levels. However, rather than developing community approaches to STD prevention, emphasis was placed on diagnosis and treatment. NACO has proposed that policies need to be aimed at both preventing STD infection and providing better diagnosis and case management of these diseases.

To this end, it is developing EC strategies which promote safer sex and condom use. Prevailing attitudes to STDs need to be challenged as high-risk groups are more likely to rely on antibiotics to cure venereal disease than methods to prevent it in the first place. Many brothel owners, for instance, arrange for their girls to have weekly injections of antibiotics from AIDS policy in India private doctors. This may promote complacency amongst sex workers who come to believe that HIV, like other STDs is curable. Even when efforts are made by sex workers and their clients to prevent STD transmission, evidence suggests that they place their faith in folk remedies and myths rather than condoms. Qualitative research undertaken by a WHO-funded team in Madras found that many sex workers believed that washing one's genitals after intercourse in urine, soda water or lime juice would prevent STDs.

Another idea was that whilst intercourse by a roadside or railway track encourages the spread of disease, sex in a confined room does not (Asthana and Oostvogels, forthcoming). Such ideas act as barriers against the use of condoms and suggest the health education regarding STDs and AIDS is a priority.

In addition to raising knowledge and awareness, NACO aims to improve access to health care for sexually transmitted diseases by strengthening existing facilities and by extending STD services to nonspecialist centres (such as MCH/Family Planning and antenatal clinics). Staff at the existing 372 STD clinics in medical colleges and hospitals are to receive laboratory equipment and training in diagnosis, case management, surveillance, education and counselling. Under the new policy, however, the emphasis has shifted away from these higher order centres and from the laboratory diagnosis of STDs, to first level health workers and the use of the syndromic approach to the management of people with STDs and their partners.

Thus, although STD clinics will play a role in training paramedical personnel and will act as referral centres for the diagnosis and management of difficult cases, the STD programme will be decentralized to the primary level. Efforts are also under way to provide orientation and training for private health care providers. This is one of the most difficult aspects of the component, first because of the size of the private sector and second because the STD training modules are likely to attract doctors who already have some interest, knowledge and awareness about STD case management. The participation of medical staff who are providing poor quality STD services will be more difficult to achieve.

Condom Programming

High rates of STDs amongst the general population and amongst sex workers in particular reflect very low levels of condom usage by sexually active individuals in India. Factors that have contributed to the generally negative image that people hold about condoms include the tendency to associate STD control with cure rather than prevention, the poor quality of condoms sold on the Indian market, and medical attitudes and practices regarding family planning. Condoms are associated with contraception rather than disease prevention and are presumed to negatively affect sexual pleasure.

As a result, they are rarely used in encounters between CSWs and their clients. Indeed, sex workers may be abused for insisting upon their use. For many clients, particularly those who hire the services of a prostitute with a group of friends, it is simply not macho to use a condom. Sex workers also hold negative beliefs about condoms, such as the fear that they might get lost in the vagina or that they will prolong the sexual encounter. Health education is needed to counter such beliefs. Thus, targeted IEC strategies incorporate condom promotion as a central component. Negative attitudes amongst potential users also stem from the belief that condoms are not particularly effective. Experiences of breakage are not uncommon and are usually due to poor condom quality. NACO has therefore undertaken to improve the quality and image of condoms available on the Indian market (including the Government's own brand, 'Nirodh').

A major legislative achievement has been to revise Schedule 'R' of the Drugs and Cosmetics Act which stipulates the statutory minimum quality standards for condoms manufactured in the country. Manufacturers are also required to improve their methods of quality assurance. Thus, the production and distribution of unlubricated condoms has been phased out (lubricants reduce friction and thus the likelihood of breakages) and better quality testing (e.g. for strength, ageing and holes) introduced. Methods of social marketing to increase demand amongst target populations are also being investigated. These include using packaging and advertising to make condoms more exciting and distributing condoms through vending machines to reduce the embarrassment of purchasing them. More emphasis is also being placed on improving the commercial distribution of affordable condoms, first because freely distributed condoms are associated with the Government's family planning campaign and second because the sale of condoms tends to raise their value in consumers' minds.

In spite of the association that is commonly made between condoms and family planning, it is estimated that only 5% of eligible couples actually use this method of contraception. At present the most popular forms of contraception advocated by family planning agencies are sterilization and intra-uterine devices (IUDs), followed by oral contraceptives and finally condoms. The emphasis on permanent or long-term methods of family planning stems from the lack of follow-up given to women, especially those who gain access to these services through large rural family planning camps. There is also a tendency amongst health professionals to assume that barrier methods are too unreliable to be widely promoted amongst low-income and illiterate groups. As a result, there is little demand for condoms in the general population.

The growing incidence of HIV in the country means that more emphasis needs to be placed on methods that achieve the dual purpose of family planning and disease prevention. Moreover, as IUDs are contra-indicated for women who are at risk of contracting STDs, including HTV, the active promotion of this form of contraception is not desirable. In an important example of inter-sectoral collaboration, NACO has coordinated with the Department of Family Welfare and the condom is now promoted as a 'dual benefit product', protecting against both conception and disease. Nevertheless, there remain important obstacles to improving the uptake of this method. Many women are not in a position to negotiate safe sex, either because they are under pressure to conceive or because it is culturally unacceptable for them to suggest the use of condoms, even to husbands with other sexual contacts. Couples wishing to practice birth control may also find condoms impractical if they lack privacy or if they cannot dispose of them easily.

Blood Safety Programme

Blood transfusion is the most efficient and also, at least in theory, the most easily preventable mode of HIV transmission. However, infected blood and blood products account for the second largest number of recorded AIDS cases in India (12%), preceded only by multiple partner sex (75%). HTV was first detected in a professional blood donor in 1987, after which surveillance centres were instructed to intensify screening of blood donors. The seropositivity rate in this group rose sharply from 0.3 per 1000 in April 1988 to 1.5 per 1000 six months later and in 1989 the screening of all donated blood and blood products became mandatory. Since 1990, 180 zonal blood testing centres have been established in 112 cities.

The high risk status of professional blood donors is uncertain on the basis of risk *behaviour.* It is likely that samples have been double counted due to the tendency of professional blood donors to sell blood to different blood banks under different names (ICMR 1989). Commercial blood banks may also take several units from a single donor but use different names in order to evade regulations which state that individuals should donate no more than one unit every 12 weeks (Girimaji 1992). Both practices would be expected to inflate the seropositivity rate of paid donors. Nevertheless, sentinel studies have consistently recorded higher rates of HTV infection in professional than in voluntary and replacement donors. As most professionals are destitute, without kin and travel from city to city, it is sometimes suggested that they are more prone to visit prostitutes (Ramasubban 1990). Another possible explanation is that the process of plasmaphersis (whereby red blood cells are re-injected after separating and retaining liquid plasma) exposed professional blood donors to the HTV virus due to the inadequate sterilization of equipment (Girimaji 1992).

Although testing of all donated blood has been mandatory since 1989, three years later an estimated 85% of the nation's blood supply was not being screened for HTV (*India Today* 1992). Blood banks in smaller towns and cities lacked access to screening centres and few had the skills or equipment to undertake testing themselves. Whilst linkages had been established between zonal blood testing centres and government blood banks in metropolitan cities and large urban centres, many private blood banks were not sending their samples to be screened. The private sector includes commercial blood banks which in 1989 supplied 24% of the nation's blood supply and which are estimated to rely on professional blood donors for 94% of blood collected (NACO 1993). It is therefore likely that a significant proportion of infected blood has been missed by the screening AIDS policy in India 195 programme.

There is also evidence to suggest that professional blood donors responded to the tightening up of screening procedures in metropolitan areas by migrating to smaller towns and cities. Problems of blood safety are not confined to blood donated by professionals. Because demand for blood outstrips the public supply, relatives of patients requiring operations are encouraged to donate their own blood (replacement donations). HIV prevalence is also increasing in this group. In 1992 HTV prevalance rates of 6.7 and 8.2 per 1000 were recorded in voluntary and replacement donors in Maharashtra State, compared to 16.8 per 1000 in paid donors (Bharucha 1992). The rate in the replacement group may result from the practice of professionals posing as relatives if the latter are unwilling to donate blood. Nevertheless, it suggests that improvements in both the supply and the screening of blood must be made if HIV transmission is to be avoided during emergency surgery.

Recognizing the urgency of improving blood safety in India, NACO has undertaken to improve testing of blood and blood products, strengthen existing government facilities and external quality control, promote voluntary blood donation, develop and improve facilities for plasma fractionation, and to improve the management, monitoring and evaluation of blood transfusion services. Central funds will continue to support zonal blood testing centres, and district level blood banks which handle small quantities of blood are being provided with rapid HTV test kits. NACO is providing central assistance to states to upgrade blood banks in the public sector and the Drugs and Cosmetic Act has been amended to ensure that the Government has better control over the licencing and inspection of private blood banks.

Before blood banks are to be granted a licence, they must be approved by the Drug Controller of India. Legal requirements introduced in the Act include qualification and experience requirements for blood bank personnel, mandatory testing of all blood and blood products, maintenance of complete and accurate records, and quality control. Blood Transfusion Officers have been appointed to coordinate the Programme's management at the State level and provision has been made for two drug inspectors in the major states and one in the smaller states to regulate the practices of blood banks. Voluntary blood donation is also being promoted through IEC strategies involving the mass media, government institutions and NGOs, and attempts are being made to educate health professionals programme. There is also evidence to suggest that professional blood donors responded to the tightening up of screening procedures in metropolitan areas by migrating to smaller towns and cities.

Problems of blood safety are not confined to blood donated by professionals. Because demand for blood outstrips the public supply, relatives of patients requiring operations are encouraged to donate their own blood (replacement donations). HIV prevalence is also increasing in this group. In 1992 HTV prevalance rates of 6.7 and 8.2 per 1000 were recorded in voluntary and replacement donors in Maharashtra State, compared to 16.8 per 1000 in paid donors (Bharucha 1992). The rate in the replacement group may result from the practice of professionals posing as relatives if the latter are unwilling to donate blood. Nevertheless, it suggests that improvements in both the supply and the screening of blood must be made if HIV transmission is to be avoided during emergency surgery.

Recognizing the urgency of improving blood safety in India, NACO has undertaken to improve testing of blood and blood products, strengthen existing government facilities and external quality control, promote voluntary blood donation, develop and improve facilities for plasma fractionation, and to improve the management, monitoring and evaluation of blood transfusion services. Central funds will continue to support zonal blood testing centres, and district level blood banks which handle small quantities of blood are being provided with rapid HTV test kits. NACO is providing central assistance to states to upgrade blood banks in the public sector and the Drugs and

Cosmetic Act has been amended to ensure that the Government has better control over the licencing and inspection of private blood banks.

Before blood banks are to be granted a licence, they must be approved by the Drug Controller of India. Legal requirements introduced in the Act include qualification and experience requirements for blood bank personnel, mandatory testing of all blood and blood products, maintenance of complete and accurate records, and quality control. Blood Transfusion Officers have been appointed to coordinate the Programme's management at the State level and provision has been made for two drug inspectors in the major states and one in the smaller states to regulate the practices of blood banks. Voluntary blood donation is also being promoted through IEC strategies involving the mass media, government institutions and NGOs, and attempts are being made to educate health professionals to use blood and blood products more rationally.

Improved surveillance of donated blood has already had an impact on HIV transmission through blood transfusions, at least in the metropolitan areas. According to the head of the Delhi AIDS Cell, the rate of infection in blood recipients had fallen from 20 per 1000 in 1993 to 10.5 per 1000 in 1994 (*Pioneer* 1994). However, there are formidable obstacles to ensuring that all donated blood is screened. Bottlenecks have occurred in the implementation of the Blood Safety Programme at the State level due to the failure of State Finance Departments to release centrally allocated funds and, as there remain acute shortages in the nation's blood supply, unregistered blood banks continue to operate. There is little comfort, too, for the thousands of people suspected to have been infected with HTV by blood or blood products. In 1994 a woman who received HIV infected blood at a charitable hospital in Bombay lost her claim for damages on the basis that she had been treated free of charge (*Times of India* 1994). It is likely that this court decision will set a precedent regarding compensation for people with HIV and AIDs.

REDUCTION OF IMPACT

Whilst efforts to prevent the continued spread of HIV have been stepped up since 1992, there are already sufficient numbers of infected people to have profound social, economic, medical and psychological impacts on affected individuals, their families and communities. Although NACO has said little about the social and welfare costs of a disease that predominately affects people in their prime productive and reproductive years, it has started to plan for the impact of AIDS in the health sector. Health costs of HIV/AIDS include increased demands on hospitals, medical staff and health budgets, together with new demands for counselling and psychological support.

Recognizing that the current health care delivery system will have difficulty coping with the projected numbers of people with AIDS, NACO has proposed the development of community and home-based care programmes in which family members are trained in basic nursing skills and hygiene, and are supported by community level workers and local health facilities. An adequate referral system will need to be in place to ensure that hospital treatment is readily accessible for severely ill people with AIDS. In order to ensure that hospitalized AIDS patients are not stigmatized, NACO has requested that they are no longer isolated, but treated in general wards. Training programmes for health personnel have also been proposed to encourage less discriminatory practices.

Whether in the community or in a clinical setting, the new emphasis is on the need to protect the rights of those affected by HTV and AIDS and to support rather than marginalize them. To this end, efforts are being made to develop HIV/AIDS counselling activities. To date, counselling has involved little more than a discussion of the medical implications of HTV/AIDS and of methods of preventing HIV transmission. The new strategy introduces the concept of psychosocial support and emphasizes the need for dialogue rather than instruction.

Since the creation of the National AIDS Control Organization in 1992, there have been many positive developments in policy and legislation relating to HTV and AIDS in India. NACO has reacted positively and quickly to new approaches in international AIDS policy, most particularly those advocated by the World Health Organization's Global Programme on AIDS. Thus, the earlier official response, which was characterized by conservatism and discrimination, has been replaced by an approach which emphasizes the rights and dignity of people with HIV, which seeks to communicate with those who are vulnerable to the disease rather than instruct them, and to support rather than punish them. Considerable progress has been made in establishing the structure and mechanisms of a coherent National AIDS prevention and control programme and in directing resources towards interventions to prevent the transmission of HTV. To this end, NACO officials have confronted highly sensitive issues and have demonstrated a willingness to challenge cultural taboos surrounding sexual behaviour in India.

The progressive approach of national-level policy makers has been countered, however, by conservative forces at the state and local levels. With important exceptions, state governments have shown a reluctance to launch health education campaigns that talk openly about sex and condom use. Bottlenecks have occurred in the distribution of funds for AIDS projects and in the recruitment of personnel. Due to the stigma attached to working with high-risk groups, especially in the context of AIDS, many government officials are happy to pass the responsibility for HTV prevention activities to the non-governmental sector. Whilst this has paved the way for projects of a more innovative and challenging nature, it has permitted the growth of NGOs which seek little more than funds and prestige. Problems of implementation have also stemmed from conflicts of interest between different State sectors. On the one hand, health departments are expected to take an inclusionary approach to groups such as CSWs and IDUs. On the other, State bodies in charge of public order and law enforcement are expected to arrest them.

Whilst such constraints are of a short-term nature, a more fundamental problem with NACP is that it continues to emphasize medical aspects of AIDS at the expense of social and economic dimensions. As a result, it takes insufficient account of the wider social context that puts targeted individuals at risk in the first place. Individual vulnerability to HIV is generally increased by poverty, lack of education, poor self-esteem, poor health and nutrition (associated with increased need for blood transfusions or injections), low social status and lack of sexual autonomy. These factors cannot be addressed by 'selective' programmes that focus exclusively on HTV/AIDS prevention but demand an integrated and comprehensive approach that concentrates on broader development issues.

In the Indian context this means challenging double standards which result in the strict control of women's sexuality, sexual freedom for men, and commercial sex for large numbers of impoverished women; abolishing the social inequalities that sanction the rape and sexual exploitation of lower caste women by upper caste men; and addressing the economic inequalities which deprive large numbers of people of access to adequate health and education facilities, which promote long-term migration and the breakdown of normal family life, and which result in the entry of impoverished men and women into the commercial blood and sex industries. Such goals may be outside the sphere of influence of India's health planners, but if the AIDS epidemic in India is to be effectively challenged, they must be on the policy agenda.

CAN MASS MEDIA PREVENT AIDS

Mass media are generally defined as those channels of communication which are capable of reaching heterogeneous audiences simultaneously with uniform messages. These include radio, television, the press and cinema. Despite the overwhelming evidence of mass media effectiveness in raising awareness, increasing knowledge and changing attitudes and behaviour, doubts still remain among non-specialists and some media critics. These may be due to a failure to realize that there are two distinctive ways of media utilization, the first being the usual media coverage of news events, regular programmes and entertainment material, and the second is the use of the media in the context of a planned and systematic process for the clear purpose of influencing attitudes and behaviour.

REGULAR ENTERTAINMENT AND MEDIA COVERAGE

Mass media regularly cover all sorts of issues, such as health, arts, crime, sports and political events. In countries which have a "free" press, the guiding principle is more or less to sell more newspapers, reach a larger audience, or sell advertising space. The objective in other countries may be to act as government or political propaganda tools. In all cases, however, the media do not even claim to play a role in health education in their regular treatment of health-related issues. The fact that acquired immunodeficiency syndrome (AIDS), for example, has received more "regular" media coverage in some countries than any other health issue in the history of humanity could very well be due to the fact that AIDS is a disease that involves sex and death, thus providing journalists with all the ingredients for sensationalist copy.

Not only is this coverage not motivated by the desire to provide health education, but it may often be a negative force in this regard. For example, journalists often report AIDS in a manner which reflects their own prejudices. In fact, the media coverage of AIDS has been described as having been slow, erratic, distorted and bizarre. Journalists have consistently emphasized rare or bizarre ways in which human immunodeficiency virus (HIV) can be spread, rather than concentrating on the common modes of transmission.

While it may seem that news organizations are doing a public service by communicating important health information to their audiences, they do so not because of an altruistic desire to better the human condition, but to sell more newspaper space or charge higher rates for commercial time. A leader in the news media puts it even more bluntly, asserting that the media "will not and cannot serve as direct relays for campaigns to reduce smoking, to use safety belts or condoms, or to submit to frequent breast examinations". He claims that it is unrealistic to expect that the media will "systematically pass on repetitive messages from the medical community or anyone else".

Usual media programming may even run in the opposite direction. For example, it has been reported that Russian television has aired regular shows hosted by psychotherapists who claim to cure the audience's mental and physical illnesses from a distance. Millions of people watched those shows where the audience was instructed to put bottles of water in front of their television screens; the bottles were "energized" by the hosts of the show, and as a result, became a kind of "medicine". Among other examples of such media coverage were the distinctions repeatedly drawn by the media between "innocent victims" of HIV, such as children, and those "other" patients who are perceived as guilty of causing their own affliction.

Regular entertainment material also has the potential both to misinform and mislead the public. There is sufficient evidence that soap operas, music videos and movies are among the most popular television material, especially for women viewers and young adults. There is also sufficient evidence as to the impact of this entertainment material on the audience. Striking examples of the possible negative impact are the documented reports that violent fictional television stories trigger imitative deaths and near-fatal accidents.

Data provided by the United States National Centre for Health Statistics for 1979 show that the incidence of suicides, motor vehicle deaths and accidents rose immediately following soap opera suicide stories. With respect to AIDS, one would be concerned with how sex is presented and if safe practices are emphasized, considering that sex is a major theme in entertainment. An investigation of the content of two soap operas shown in the United States of America (USA) throughout 1980 (*All my children* and *General hospital*) revealed that the most common themes presented were deceit, murder and pre-and extra-marital sex.

Content analysis of a random sample of one week of network television soap operas shown during the summer of 1987 in the USA showed that the ratio of unmarried to married sexual behaviour in soap operas was 23.7 to 1. Even more important, there was no reference—verbal, implied or physical—to pregnancy prevention or sexually-transmitted diseases, including HIV/AIDS. In addition, a study of the 1986 USA prime time television season documented that soap operas contained: touching behaviour (24.5 times per hour); suggestions and insinuation (16.5 times per hour); sexual intercourse (implied 25 times per hour); and socially taboo sexual behaviours, such as sadomasochism and masturbation (implied 6.2 times per hour). In contrast, education was only touched upon 1.6 times per hour.

This has led communication researchers and analysts to conclude that Hollywood does not yet acknowledge safe sex, as condoms are non-existent in the movies or soap operas despite all of this sex. It has been argued that it would be very difficult for Hollywood to promote condoms, because Hollywood tends to cater to our fantasies and condoms, no matter how life-saving, will never figure in our fantasies. This is indeed a challenge, because it was not until Hollywood had the hero fasten his seat belt that it became more socially acceptable. Even when AIDS is a theme in television material, it is often not addressed in the most responsible way, because television is a business, and "customers" must not be offended. For example, it was found that, of the AIDS cases portrayed on television, 37% were caused by blood transfusion, while the actual figure does not exceed 3%.

All of this leads to the conclusion that unplanned, regular media and entertainment material will never, on its own, provide health education which would in any significant way influence HIV/AIDS-related behaviour. Yet media and entertainment are more like nuclear power: they are neither good nor bad in themselves; it all depends on how they are used and for what purposes. The following section, therefore, reviews a different side of mass media and entertainment: professionally planned efforts to harness the powers of the mass media and entertainment for the well-being of audiences.

Planned Media and Entertainment Material

Communication experts and planners have realized the need for, and importance of, professional media planning. Manufacturers of commercial products, in realization of this fact, have devoted a sufficient amount of their budget to the use of communication services, marketing and advertising professionals to plan campaigns to influence the buying behaviour of potential customers. Efforts to curb the HIV/AIDS epidemic cannot rely on news media to do it on their own. Communication experts have called for the mass education of the general public, and argued that this large-scale education has the potential for not only correcting misinformation, but also for creating and maintaining a more favourable environment for AIDS prevention. In addition, it is generally accepted among communication specialists that public education can change and maintain social norms and render the new attitudes more acceptable, more openly expressed and more likely to be acted upon. It is also believed that mass media publicity about AIDS influences people to take actions they might otherwise not. An expert group concluded at their meeting at the World Health Organization (1993) that mass media campaigns "have promoted widespread AIDS awareness, safer sex and condom use". In fact, an analysis of 10 major social marketing programmes concludes that mass media advertising has contributed more to increased condom sales than any other factor, including price, cultural attitudes towards family planning and the level of national socioeconomic development.

Evaluation studies show that there have been positive changes in condom use following AIDS prevention campaigns in the Netherlands, Switzerland, the United Kingdom and the USA. For example, the Swiss campaign resulted in an over 50% increase in the use of condoms, with over 70% among those between 17-20 years of age. This has led to the conclusion that large-scale education appears to have the capability of increasing the social acceptance of condoms and their use among persons more at risk. Radio spots used as part of a campaign to increase condom use among Kenyan commercial sex workers have led to a significant increase in condom use. Following mass media publicity, which included specific telephone numbers, calls to AIDS hotlines in the USA almost doubled from May 1990 to July 1991. In Mexico City, calls increased more than ten-fold, and in Israel, attendance at a major AIDS testing site increased 431% after the first major television programme on AIDS.

Planned entertainment material has achieved impressive results as well. In the Philippines, a popular music video, intended to encourage young people to postpone sex and avoid unwanted pregnancy, resulted in enhancing young people's communication with their parents. It also motivated over 150 000 Filipino youths to call a sexual responsibility hotline, as promoted in the television video featuring musical stars, and 25% of young people sought contraception information as a result of the song. As many as 240 000 women in Turkey are estimated to have adopted modern family planning methods as a result of television dramas and humourous spots. In Mexico, which has been a pioneer in the deliberate use of soap operas for educational purposes, soap operas were the primary cause of a 63% increase in attendance at adult literacy centres in one year, and a rise of 560 000 in those adopting family planning methods. A Ugandan film, *It's not easy,* was so effective that those who had seen it were more than twice as likely to have used condoms in the two months prior to the interview, as were those who had not seen it.

Entertainment material was the primary vehicle for spreading messages to curb alcohol-related traffic fatalities, a leading cause of death among young adults aged 15-24 years in the USA, through the popularization of the "designated driver" concept. This concept means that someone is "designated" or selected by another person or group to abstain from drinking, for a certain period of time or on a certain occasion, in order to be responsible for driving others home, so that they do not drive themselves after they have been drinking. The main vehicle used by the project, in addition to television spots, was to work with the communications industry to insert drunk driving prevention messages, including references to designated drivers, into scripts of top-rated television programmes such as *Cheers, L.A. law* and *The Cosby show.*

The approach was based on the conclusion that entertainment not only mirrors social reality, but also helps shape it by depicting what constitutes popular opinion, by influencing people's perception of the roles and behaviours that are appropriate to members of a culture, and by modelling specific behaviour. The strength of this approach is that short messages, embedded within dialogue, are casually presented by characters who serve as role models within a dramatic context, thereby facilitating social learning. Collaboration with the television industry in this project has yielded remarkable results. Among Americans under the age of thirty, 52% have actually been a designated driver. Among all alcohol drinkers, 28% have been driven home by a designated driver, and 43% of frequent drinkers have been driven home by a designated driver.

Does this suggest that all planned mass media and entertainment efforts succeed in achieving their objectives? Not by any means. In the United Kingdom, for example, injecting drug users, the intended target of a campaign using posters and television spots, did not even perceive that the messages were aimed at them. The slogan "zero grazing", which was used in the Ugandan campaign to mean "stay with one partner", was not even understood by the target audience, and another frequently repeated spot, using drum beats to spread a sense of fear, did not appeal to young people who interpreted the drums as an appeal for abstinence. Just as sensational news coverage can set back AIDS prevention efforts, poorly planned mass media efforts can do the same. In Nigeria, for example, frightening and confusing mass media material has resulted in negative attitudes towards people with AIDS and unfounded fears about the risk of infection. The level of fear aroused by the Australian campaign, which used death visuals, was apparently so great that those at highest risk practised denial and did not respond.

What is needed, therefore, is not just planned campaigns, as opposed to regular media programming, but *well planned* campaigns which utilize the full potential of mass media and entertainment. The "technology" and methodology for planning and implementing such campaigns do exist. Research has established that mass media are most likely to change behaviour when the information is targeted at specific audiences, comes from a credible source, and provides a personally relevant and engaging message. Effective use of mass media requires careful planning, audience research, message development, pre-testing, dissemination strategy, evaluation, coordination with existing services, and linking mass media with interpersonal communication. This methodology has been detailed elsewhere.

Measures for Prevention of AIDS through the Mass Media

The potential for what the mass media can do in the prevention of AIDS is influenced by how, and how well, the media are used. For example, the media may be used to achieve one or more of the following:

- general advocacy
- endorsement of society's leaders
- community endorsement/support
- community involvement
- specific programme support
- religious leaders' participation
- general public information and education.

To be effective, the media, in particular, and communication programmes in general, have to achieve specific "hierarchical" objectives. The effectiveness and success of media interventions should be evaluated in terms of the extent to which each one of the following ten objectives or outputs has been accomplished:

- exposing audience to the message;
- attracting attention to the message;
- creating interest in and liking of the message;
- audience comprehending the message—becoming aware of what the problem is;
- audience being taught those skills related to solving the problem;
- audience understanding of the message—understanding why they should behave in the prescribed manner;
- yielding—audience changing pre-existing unfavourable beliefs and attitudes;
- audience retaining new information;
- audience deciding to comply with the message and adopt changes;
- audience behaviour changing in accordance with message.

Finally, a legitimate question which can be raised at this point is this: if we have the methodology and the evidence, why have not all countries implemented well planned mass media and entertainment campaigns for AIDS prevention?

OBSTACLES AND CHALLENGES TO MEDIA

Political commitment to AIDS prevention is the most important first step. Policy-makers have generally been reluctant to air prevention messages on the mass media, which constitutes a major obstacle. Carefully designed materials have not been released because of opposition from politicians, broadcasters, or other gatekeepers afraid of arousing religious or other resistance. An evaluation of 21 public service announcements about AIDS from public health departments in Canada, Denmark, Norway, Sweden, the United Kingdom and the USA, revealed that three of the five spots considered most effective by 56 knowledgeable reviewers had been rejected for general broadcast. The announcements judged least effective, on the other hand, were broadcast much more frequently.

Communication planners and others have tried to overcome this hurdle for many years. For example, a workshop intended to increase awareness of the social and economic impact of AIDS persuaded policy-makers in Papua New Guinea to promote and support mass media AIDS educational efforts; and pre-test and impact evaluation reports, as well as audience research results showing the desire of the public to receive clear information, have persuaded policy-makers in Peru and Colombia to do the same. Non-governmental organizations and other AIDS advocacy groups can bring pressure to bear on government officials to counteract anticipated pressures from other sources.

The role of international health and development organizations in promoting, supporting and advocating the use of well planned mass media campaigns can also make a significant difference.

High Start-up Costs

When given the choice, many policy-makers tend to hesitate in choosing well planned media campaigns because of their initial high start-up costs, despite the fact that mass media may be the cheapest approach to use, on the basis of per capita cost.

However, using mass media effectively requires more investment at the beginning than other approaches, which may discourage many countries from effective use of mass media opportunities available to them. Even though the available data on mass media costs are less than would be desired, some good examples are already available.

In Turkey, a multi-media campaign cost about US$0.04 to reach one woman of reproductive age and about US$0.67 to gain one user of a modern contraceptive method. It is also reported that in Zimbabwe, a radio soap opera for men cost about US$0.16 for each man reached and US$2.41 for each new contraceptive user. Mass media effort is therefore more cost-effective than other approaches, such as group talks or printed materials.

A meeting in WHO on effective approaches to AIDS prevention concluded that "although mass media education is often expensive, it may be cost-effective in terms of costs per person reached". It also recommended certain measures to reduce mass media costs, such as the provision of free air time on radio and television for AIDS prevention campaigns.

Lack of Sufficient Technical Expertise

An in-depth analysis of the mass communication component of medium-term plans (MTPs) of national AIDS programmes of a sample of seven countries revealed that the plans lacked definitions of appropriate "media-mix" or audience segmentation.

They did not seem to be based on good knowledge of media habits and preferences of the various segments of the target audience in different regions of the countries, and among different socioeconomic groups and different age groups, as well as between males and females.

These are only a few of the basic components of a good AIDS prevention communication plan which are often neglected, despite their extreme importance. For example, the media-mix selected for a specific campaign should be closely linked to specific audience segments which may require tailored messages, such as women, unmarried youth and people who practise high-risk behaviour or are likely to be in more high-risk situations.

Each one of those segments may have different preferences and media habits and thus requires a different approach. Furthermore, when the audience is segmented, it becomes possible both to involve each segment in the design of messages which are intended for it, and engage them in the pre-test of those messages in order to ensure better impact.

In addition, AIDS prevention materials have to compete with commercial advertising for air time and audience attention, which requires that AIDS messages be more professionally and creatively packaged. The high quality of the Ugandan AIDS film *It's not easy* has enabled this film not only to reach 90% of the Ugandan work force, but to also reach beyond Africa to Asia, Latin America and the USA. The film is considered an unusual case of a developing country's product being used to change attitudes and behaviour in an industrialized country.

LOCAL SITE DEMONSTRATION PROJECT

Welcome to the CDC PMI Local Site Demonstration Project Web site! ; the information itself is quiet interesting and accepting in nature. This site has been designed primarily for HIV prevention community planning groups and program planners in state and local health departments, community-based organizations, and other agencies. It provides information about an approach that was successful in motivating reductions in HIV risk behaviour in adolescents. Also it would yield income to meet the costs and rehabilitation of the infected persons utilized in the organization or their kith and kin.

The PMI Local Site Demonstration Project was a five-year effort (1993-1998) to reduce sexual HIV risk behaviour among young people under age 25. CDC and its national prevention partners supported five local sites (Nashville, TN; Newark, NJ, Northern VA, Phoenix, AZ; and Sacramento, CA) in planning and implementing Prevention Marketing programs. In each site, coalitions of community volunteers representing AIDS service organizations, youth-serving agencies, other sectors of the adult community, and youth from the target audience learned about social marketing and behavioural science and applied the information in planning sets of prevention activities.

The first of the steps in the Prevention Marketing process was organizing volunteer coalitions at the local level. Then the coalitions were given training and technical assistance that enabled them to conduct audience research and to plan interventions based on the research findings. The planning goal was to "fill in the blanks" in the coalitions' pictures of their target audiences, the behavioral objectives of the programs, the behavioral determinants that programs would have to impact in order to motivate risk behaviour change, and the kinds of interventions that would be most likely to impact those determinants. Site programs all included skills-building workshops that provided intensive, face-to-face exposure to prevention messages. In addition, sites planned to employ some combination of:

- mass media (e.g., billboards and radio and cable television spots),
- small print media (e.g., brochures),
- promotional materials (e.g., T-shirts and temporary tattoos),
- peer out reach, and
- Special events.

The sets of interventions were referred to as a "marketing mix," a multi-pronged, integrated strategy for getting prevention messages out to broad segments of the target audiences.

IMPROVED POLICIES AND CHANGED SOCIAL NORMS

Another result of the efforts of the AIDSCAP/LAC regional office has been an improved political and social environment for HIV/AIDS prevention. Governments' recognition of the costs of the HIV/AIDS epidemic and their commitment to providing resources to fund programs have increased, partly because of the socioeconomic impact studies sponsored by AIDSCAP. As mentioned earlier, model interventions with documented impact have been scaled up and supported by government resources. Important policy changes have improved the efficiency of HIV/AIDS prevention projects as well as the human rights environment for individuals at risk of, or already infected with, HIV.

Examples of the improved policies include the lowering of duties on condom imports in Brazil, passage of AIDS laws in the Dominican Republic and Nicaragua, adoption of national STI guidelines in Honduras and Haiti, and development of a national HIV/AIDS 5-year plan (1995) in Haiti.

Many countries in the LAC region also have seen widespread changes in social norms. For example, the Catholic Church in Haiti has reached out to HIV/AIDS prevention organizations and has taken an active role in providing care and support for HIV-positive individuals. Today, individuals who die from AIDS may be buried in Catholic Church cemeteries; 5 years ago they were not allowed.

While these results in building capacity, reducing risk, and improving policies and changing social norms validate AIDSCAP approach and attest to its persistent efforts, they do not provide justification for complacency.

Many of these results represent only the initial steps toward completely sustainable organizations, fully protective behaviors, effective policies, and supportive social, economic, and political settings. There is amputee number of SOS Children's villages in States south of Sahara, at present getting extended to Kenya, Malawi, South Africa, Zambia and Zimbabwe where in the AIDS Orphans are rehabilitated.

Out of 13 million AIDS affected children around the globe, ninety percent lives in African states and 2.4 million children are below 15 years of age. They pose a relatively bigger challenge to those countries they belong to, socially, economically, psychologically and otherwise.

They need better counselling rather than medical care on priority basis as they undergo a trauma of experiencing loss of parents when they are below teens and could not be consoled by grand parents. Again, it is suggested that concrete markets for consultation could be brought in these places by such of those infected persons who want to get employed and serve their young counter parts by which they can make money for their own well-being. Prevention Marketing is CDC's "brand" of social marketing. Prevention Marketing adds important qualities to social marketing an emphasis on behavioral science and the full participation of community members who have made a long-term commitment to a strategic planning process. Social marketers have always relied on target audience input to select and refine program materials. They usually obtain this input through focus groups, surveys and other means of data collection. In contrast, community members (including members of the target audience) participate in all steps in the prevention marketing process.

Prevention Marketing has as its foundation the belief that, working with specialists in the sciences of behaviour and communications, community members themselves are best able to develop their own HIV prevention programs and to manage issues that could hamper program effect.

4

Role of NGOs in HIV/AIDS Prevention and Care

Widespread pressure for popular participation and a declining faith in the capacities of governments to solve the interrelated problems of social welfare, development, and the environment, lead to the global upsurge of organised private activity through a new non-profit sector. The non-profit sector has grown increasingly important in its efforts to provide alleviation of societal problems and injustices and the promotion of democratic values throughout the world in recent years. This sector has also become a major economic force with sizeable expenditures and multiple levels of paid and volunteer employment. Non-governmental organisations make up the subset of the non-profit sector involved in development work (Salamon 1997).

According to Brodhead and O'Malley, the term 'non-governmental organisations' applies to diverse organisations that "work together outside of government to address a need, advance a cause or defend an interest" (Brodhead and O'Malley 1989). However, the World Bank defines NGOs as "private organisations that pursue activities to relieve suffering, promote the interests of the poor, protect the environment or undertake community development". Brown and Korten further differentiate non-governmental groups into the commercial and voluntary sectors. According to them, "the voluntary sector is seen as a distinct class of organisations that are held together by common beliefs and shared values, rather than by political imperatives (government) or economic incentives (the commercial sector)". They include locally-based groups as well as international organisations having local offices in project countries. Many are single-focus, narrowly targeted organisations while others attempt to meet broader needs in mainstream communities. All are characterised by their dedication to a set of shared social values that guides their organisational mission.

NGOs have in increasing numbers voiced their concerns in international discourse about numerous problems of international scope. Human rights activists, gender activists, development agencies, groups of indigenous peoples and representatives of other defined interests have become active in the international community. Since their inception, the United Nations and its various organisations have felt the direct and indirect impact of NGOs. NGOs are omnipresent in many aspects of international relations, and have become critical to the UN's future. NGOs have assumed a central role in activities involving human rights, complex humanitarian emergencies, the United Nations relationship, the global environment, the international women's movement, operational coalitions and state relations, and AIDS. They also bring local experience to bear on international decision making.

The NGO expansion, dubbed the "barefoot revolution", can be attributed to several external and internal factors to produce what has become a significant event in international policy making and execution. Three of the more important factors include: the end of the cold war, technological developments, and growing resources. The end of the Cold War was the first, and perhaps most important influence on NGO expansion. The demise of the Cold War brought with it the end of ideological and social orthodoxy. UN practitioners and diplomats became less reluctant to interact with non-governmental staff, opening up new avenues of communication and cooperation within the decision making process. The UN became a forum for discussions between governments and NGOs. When politics and security, especially over nuclear proliferation, dominated the international agenda, NGOs were at a comparative disadvantage. They had no weapons, and only limited access to people wielding decision-making power. Since the end of the Cold War, NGOs have had the capacity for direct action. They also contribute advanced knowledge on issues such as gender, environment, AIDS, relief assistance, human rights, and community development.

The development of new technology is widely considered a second factor in influencing the prominence of NGOs in UN activity. Governments hostile to NGOs often fail in their efforts to prevent information flow, interaction and networking through the Internet and telecommunications. Electronic media have made it possible to ignore national borders, and create communities based on common values and objectives that were once the exclusive privilege of nationalism.

A third factor is the growing resources and professionalism of NGOs. Indigenous and trans-national NGOs have attracted additional resources from individual donors, governments and the UN. Western governments, for example, have increasingly turned towards NGO projects on the basis of reputation and cost-effectiveness. This trend matches the progressively declining funding for foreign assistance and with domestic pressures in donor countries to cut back on overseas commitments. New communications technologies are also helping foster the kinds of interaction and relationships that were once possible only through air travel. Scaling up certain kinds of trans-national efforts from neighbourhoods and regions to the global level, and scaling down to involve local grassroots organisations are no longer logistically impossible.

NGOs facilitate the formation of international institutions and reinforce the standards promoted by these institutions through public education, organised attempts to hold states accountable to these, and enhance institutional effectiveness by reducing the implementation costs associated with international institutions. Increased networking capabilities also allows for improved capacity to monitor states' compliance with international agreements, promote institutional adaptation and innovation, and challenge failed institutions or projects. NGOs employ a variety of inter-organisational devices ranging from formal structures, to informal interpersonal ties to increase their persuasiveness and efficiency. Four types of inter-organisational devices can be identified: formal bridging groups, federations, UN coordinating bureaus, and connections to governments. Based on a close scrutiny of goals, relationships among various organisations, and operational methods, it was deduced that NGOs play two broad roles in society: (1) operational roles, and (2) educational and advocacy roles. Operational NGOs are more central to international responses in the post-Cold War world. They have the responsibility of fund-raising. The rendering of services is central to most NGO budgets, and the source for support from donors. Services rendered could include technical advice, tangible resources for disaster relief, development, etc. (Gordenker and Weiss 1996).

While the target of organisational NGOs is beneficiaries (or victims in case of emergencies), educational and advocacy NGOs seek to influence citizens, and through public opinion, bear fruit in the form of additional resources for their activities, as well as new policies, better decisions and enhanced international regimes. These NGOs help to reinforce various norms promoted through public education campaigns. This heightened awareness among public audiences in turn helps hold the state accountable for their international commitments (Gordenker and Weiss 1996).

Categorising NGOs, their trans-national relationships, and their impact on the community marks an initial step toward understanding non-governmental organisations. NGO interactions with the UN system and the global community forms part of a larger set of challenges as the international community copes with changing political trends towards decentralisation and democratisation of global governance. NGOs have played a key role in this global progression.

The role of NGOs in society cannot be ignored. This is true also in the field of prevention and treatment of HIV/AIDS. In areas of the industrialised world hardest-hit by AIDS, NGOs helped set trends that have now been institutionalised within AIDS prevention:

1. Advocacy for persons living with HIV/AIDS,
2. Targeting educational materials to specific groups,
3. Improved access to experimental drug trials and health care, and
4. Peer education.

In the developing world, the NGO response to AIDS emerged somewhat more slowly, reflecting both a lack of resources and experience, and a widespread reluctance to recognise publicly or acknowledge the threat. As the epidemic has progressed however, both well-established and newly organised NGOs have been among the first to respond, promoting the need for persons with AIDS and HIV to have access to counselling, support and health care. They have mobilised impressive efforts for training, education, and other supportive services while official declarations denied the existence of the problem.

The importance of NGOs in the national AIDS control programmes of developing countries has also evolved over time. When the World Health Organisation's Global Programme on AIDS (GPA) first began to assist countries to draw up national plans for AIDS control, NGOs were not regularly consulted during planning, nor represented on national AIDS committees.

Over time, GPA developed extensive links with a wide range of NGOs, and now supports their efforts to combat AIDS at global, national and local levels (Grose 1989).

A 1989 resolution from the World Health Assembly supported the importance of NGOs in the global strategy for the prevention and control of AIDS, acknowledging that "their commitment and versatility, and their knowledge and experience... can make a special impact on individuals and society regarding AIDS and the needs of HIV-infected people and those with AIDS".

down 200,000 from 1999. At the same time, 2.4 million people died in Africa of AIDS this year, up from 2.2 million in 1999, according to the report.

The report says the fall or stabilization of new infections may be due to effective prevention programs in countries such as Uganda and relatively fewer people likely to become infected, especially in countries where one out of four people have the HIV virus. World AIDS Day this year focuses on the role men play in the spread — and control — of the disease. "As fathers, grandfathers, brothers, sons, friends, husbands, and partners, men determine the shape of the epidemic," Dr. Gro Harlem Brundtland, director-general of the World Health Organization, said in a prepared statement. "The campaign recognizes that men could have the greatest impact on the speed with which the epidemic subsides. Men are also well positioned to address the consequences of HIV infection and to ensure adequate care for those who are affected."

Sometimes members of the faith community are oblivious to problems unless they are affected directly, and some blame the victims, Dr. Allan Handy sides, health director for the Adventist World Church, told Newsroom. "So the first thing we feel in the health ministries in the church is to bring an awareness to church members that this is not just a problem far away, it could be affecting somebody in the next pew to them," he said.

In October, the Seventh-day Adventist Church's General Conference created an AIDS study committee to track the impact of HIV/AIDS on society and the church and recommend more effective ways for the Adventist Church to respond to the worldwide epidemic. The 31-member committee includes Adventist health professionals and church leaders from Australia, Africa, Asia, Europe, and the Americas.

"I think that within the faith community there needs to be a change in attitude — that it is a sort of self-inflicted problem, that they caused it upon themselves — to one of more supportive, nurturing, and caring," Handy sides said. "And through education (we need) to try to rid some of the ignorance about HIV and AIDS. AIDS has a great deal to do with people's lifestyles and choices, but sometimes within faith communities there is a tendency to think they live on a higher plane and that is a mentality of being so heavenly they are no earthly good, or their heads are in the clouds."

People of faith can especially influence the behaviour of young people, who are especially at risk of contracting HIV/AIDS, he insisted. "We know that behaviour is often a reflection of attitudes in their subculture or local group, and we feel that the faith community ought to be emphasizing connections, positive relationships, that we ought to be building relationships

THE IMPACT OF RELIGIOUS ORGANIZATIONS IN PROMOTING HIV/AIDS PREVENTION

"Behaviour change" is a term much-used in AIDS prevention circles. It is often used narrowly to mean adopting condoms. But one could argue that the condom option is really a "harm reduction" solution for people who *don't* change their risky behaviour.

This paper is concerned with what might be called primary behaviour change. Examples of this are fidelity to a single partner, sexual abstinence, or young people "delaying" the age at which they begin to have sexual intercourse. It is useful to distinguish these behavioral changes from condom use or treatment of sexually transmitted diseases (STDs), both of which are "harm reduction" approaches. The latter are more passive than the former, and arguably involve less of a personal commitment to fundamental change of behaviors.

If we consider the simple ABC approach to AIDS prevention to which lip service has long paid (Abstain, Be faithful, use Condoms if A&B fail), it is clear that the vast majority of prevention resources have gone to condom promotion, and more recently, to the treatment of the treatable STDs.

Few in public health circles really believed—or even believe nowadays—that programs promoting abstinence, fidelity or monogamy, or even reduction in number of sexual partners, pay off in significant behavioral change. My own view on this changed when I evaluated HIV prevention programs in Uganda and Jamaica, and conduced a national survey of behavioral change in the Dominican Republic.

Findings are now presented from three countries that seem to best illustrate the positive impact of faith-based organizations (FBOs), Uganda, Senegal and Jamaica. We will see a pattern of behavioral changes compatible with the prevention strategies favoured by FBOs, as well as data showing stabilization and reduction in national HIV infection rates.

Uganda

Uganda is the country that has had the most dramatic decline in HIV infection rates. HIV prevalence declined from 21.1% to 6.1% among pregnant women between 1991 and 2000. In 1987, the major religious organizations in Uganda (Catholic, Anglican, Muslim) became significantly involved in AIDS prevention, with WHO/GPA funding, through the Ministry of Health. By 1992, HIV infections rates were still so high that USAID also decided to allocate some of its funds for FBOs to work in prevention, but on the FBO's own terms. The FBOs said that they wished to promote "fidelity" and "abstinence" rather than condoms. At the time, many working in HIV/AIDS prevention thought that fidelity and abstinence promotion would have few if any measurable results. However, this approach was and is strongly favoured by President Museveni, who is credited with being the most activist African head of state in addressing the AIDS crisis. Museveni stated his views in a speech to the First AIDS Congress in East and Central Africa (Kampala, 11/20/91):

Sex is not a manifestation of a biological drive; it is socially directed...I have been emphasizing a return to our time-tested cultural practices that emphasized fidelity and condemned premarital and extramarital sex. I believe that the best response to the threat of AIDS and other STDs is to reaffirm publicly and forthrightly the respect and responsibility every person owes to his or her neighbor.

As for condoms, Museveni said in the same speech: Just as we were offered the "magic bullet" in the early 1940s, we are now being offered the condom for "safe sex."... I feel that condoms have a role to play as a means of protection, especially in couples who are HIV-positive, but they cannot become the main means of stemming the tide of AIDS. Beginning in 1991, we see a downward trend in both STI and HIV infection rates in Uganda. We also have numerous studies after 1993 documenting behavioral change. Most studies show that reduction in the number of sexual partners (which may be causally related to the "fidelity" message), and delay of sexual debut among youth (which seems to be related to the abstinence message), are the major forms of behavioral change that have occurred in Uganda, more than increased condom use. Condom ever-use is at about 20% nationally. The proportion of Ugandans who report one or more non-regular sexual partners is between 6-8.7%. And about 20-25% of those surveyed age 15-49 report complete abstinence in the past year, most of this attributed to youth delaying first sexual experience (Uganda MoH 2000, 2001 in preparation). If sizable numbers of men and women reduce their number of sexual partners, can this have significant impact on HIV infection rates? Recent studies by N.J. Robinson and others that have modelled the impact of different interventions on HIV infection rates in east Africa suggest that reduction in number of partners can have great impact on averting HIV infections, in fact greater than either condom use or treatment of STDs.

Decline in infection rates is greatest among the 15-19 age group, and a UNAIDS analysis shows that this was mostly due to the rise in the median age of first intercourse by 2 years, increasing from age 15 to 17. Rise in age of sexual debut among females is particularly important because of the increased biological vulnerability of young females to HIV infection. It is noteworthy that male condom user levels were only 3-5% in Uganda before 1992. And this refers to the proportion of men who reported "ever" using a condom, not those who claimed regular use. It therefore seems unlikely that condom use contributed to the onset of decline in STI and HIV infection rates, even if increased condom use in subsequent years helped this process. Condoms were not widely available in Uganda until after 1993, and then mostly in urban areas. By 1998, 20% of Ugandans reported *ever* having used a condom (average national male rate, rural and urban). Some reports continue to claim that the world's great success story in AIDS prevention, Uganda, owes its achievement to condoms, but this is not true. It is also worth noting that apart from delay of sexual debut, about 7% of women and 10% of men aged 15-50 reported that they have adopted complete and sustained abstinence for HIV protection in the previous year by the mid-1990s. This rose to over 20% in 2000.

Has involvement of faith-based organizations impacted behaviour in Uganda? There is some evidence from impact studies, such as a UNAIDS "Best Practices" study of the Islamic Medical Association of Uganda (IMAU) which shows that AIDS prevention activities carried out through religious leaders has had significant direct impact on particular populations targeted. The Anglican Church of Uganda has also implemented special prevention programs aimed at youth, carried out in Sunday schools and primary schools. Moreover, religious organizations put emphasis (sometimes sole emphasis) on primary behavioral change, on what they called abstinence (or "delay") and fidelity, and these are the very changes that resulted, or were most likely to be found in surveys and studies. True, FBOs were not the only groups promoting primary behavioral change, but this was their intervention of choice and they probably helped promote this approach with other groups.

Finally, as behaviour has continued to change and HIV infection has continued to decline, the number of religious leaders and groups involved in AIDS prevention has expanded under district Ministry of Health AIDS prevention activities (funded by the World Bank's STI Project). As a result, there is now a high level of involvement on the part of religious organizations and leaders. How high? By 1995, only two years into the first FBO project, over 2,745 trainers and peer educators as well as 5,629 community volunteers in the Muslim IMAU project had reached 193,955 households and had counselled or sensitized 1,059,439 sexually active people, according to the external evaluation of the USAID-funded project that supported the first FBOs. In the Anglican CHUSA project, the project trained 96 diocesan trainers and 5,702 community health educators and had sensitized 736,218 members of the community, also by 1995. There was also a Catholic-run project.

In 1998, I evaluated HIV decline and behavioral change evidence in Uganda for the World Bank. I reviewed district workplans between 1995-98 and conducted interviews with relevant informants. I estimate that an average of 150 religious leaders (ministers, imams, deacons, elders, etc.) were being trained in each of Uganda's 45 districts *per year*, resulting in some 6,750 religious leaders trained in HIV/AIDS per year. Even if there may have been over-reporting of training numbers, we can reduce figures by a third and there would still be 4,500 trained per year since 1995. "Training" here refers to religious leaders being educated about AIDS and what they could do to help prevent it, usually in brief workshops. Those trained in this way then function as peer educators and group discussants or leaders, talking to others in their religious group or broader community about AIDS and how to prevent it.

Taken altogether, the foregoing amounts to at least suggestive evidence that religious organizations and other more conservative opinion leaders in Uganda (e.g., school authorities, traditional healers, and local political leaders such as chiefs) that have advocated abstinence and fidelity have had a significant impact on overall infection rate decline.

Senegal

Senegal is another country widely recognized as an AIDS success story. Like Uganda, it was one of the first countries in Africa to acknowledge AIDS and to begin implementing significant AIDS prevention and control programs. According to UNAIDS, Senegal currently has one of the lowest HIV seroprevalence rates in sub-Saharan Africa.

Data from antenatal clinics complied by UNAIDS show that HIV infection rates were 1.1% in 1990, and only 0.4% by 1997. A UNAIDS document reports, "In Dakar, the major urban area in Senegal, HIV-1 prevalence among antenatal clinic women has been 1% or less for all years up to 1998." Prevalence rates range from zero to 0.8% outside Dakar.

As in Uganda, we find evidence of primary behavioral change in Senegal, that is, partner reduction and rise in age of sexual debut. For example, researchers, compared two cross-sectional surveys using standardized questionnaires conducted in 1990-1992 and again in 1994. Even by 1994, "The proportion of men who declared casual sex partners in the past 12 months decreased from 39% to 21% (P = 0.01). Condom use ("ever used) was 3.6%

in 1993, almost the same low level as Uganda at that time. In a 1997 UNAIDS survey of women in Dakar, where condom use might be expected to be the highest, 23% of women age 16-50 reported *ever* using a condom.

According to Demographic and Health surveys, the median age of sexual debut has risen in Senegal, from 16.4 in 1993 to 17.5 in 1997. For age-specific comparisons, median age of debut for females 20-24 rose from 17.5 in 1993 to 18 by 1997. For females age 45-49, debut rose from 15.8 in 1993 to 17 by 1997. DHS data seems lacking for males before 1997, but by 1997 age of debut ranged between 18 and 20, depending on the age group. Many or most countries in east and southern Africa seem to have sexual debut median ages of 15 or less.

As in Uganda, FBOs became involved in HIV/AIDS prevention from early in the epidemic in Senegal. A conservative Muslim organization, Jamra, approached the national AIDS program in 1989 to discuss prevention strategies. Also as in Uganda, there was initial disagreement about the role of FBOs in condom promotion. The government conducted a survey of Muslim and Christian leaders to better define a role for them in AIDS mitigation. The survey found that religious leaders needed and wanted more information about HIV/AIDS, so that they in turn could educate those in the respective religious communities.

According to UNAIDS

In response, educational materials were designed to meet the needs of religious leaders. They focused in part on testimonials from people living with AIDS—the human face of the epidemic, often hidden where prevalence remains low. Training sessions about HIV were organized for Imams and teachers of Arabic, and brochures were produced to help them disseminate information. AIDS became a regular topic in Friday sermons in mosques throughout Senegal, and senior religious figures addressed the issue on television and radio.

A Catholic NGO, SIDA, also became involved in prevention as well as counselling and psychosocial support. In 1996, A meeting on AIDS prevention was held for Christian leaders; every bishop in Senegal attended and consensus was reached that AIDS prevention was an important national priority. The following year, Senegal hosted the First International Colloquium on AIDS and Religion, held in Dakar in late 1997, was attended by some 250 persons from 33 countries, including Muslim, Christian, and Buddhist religious leaders and the ministers of health of five African countries. The impact on Senegalese religious leaders of all faiths seems to have been to empower them "to act freely in the promotion of prevention strategies" Yet there was much to overcome before this was possible. A local researcher notes:

During the first stages of the AIDS epidemic the majority of religious (leaders) condemned those infected with the virus, calling the illness a divine curse. This attitude made AIDS shameful and a positive diagnosis difficult. Religion systematically condemned certain modes of prevention as well as certain individual and group behaviour

A recent LA Times article describes the role of FBOs and religious leaders today: While the religious leaders insist that they encourage abstinence over the use of condoms, they acknowledge the importance of dispelling myths about the disease, such as the common theory that AIDS is a curse or a punishment by God.

It may be argued that sexual behaviour in Senegal is conservative by general sub-Saharan African standards, therefore perhaps it is pre-existing norms and values rather than the impact of any interventions that have kept infection rates low. Furthermore, widespread male circumcision among Senegalese men certainly helps prevent heterosexual transmission of HIV. It may even be that the presence of HIV-2 limits the spread of HIV-1. But these considerations fail to explain why HIV-1 infection rates have risen in countries neighboring Senegal, countries comparable with regard to the factors just mentioned, including religious profiles. They do not explain why Senegal is unique in West Africa.

It should be noted that both Senegal and Uganda stand out in Africa as countries where governments supported AIDS prevention efforts boldly and strongly, at a relatively early stage. There is agreement in both countries that this support has made a major difference and has allowed prevention programs to have maximum impact. It is probable that one of the factors inhibiting a strong government response to AIDS elsewhere in Africa and beyond is fear of negative reaction from religious authorities. This only strengthens the argument for involving religious leaders and FBOs as early as possible.

At least the argument cannot be made in Senegal that behavioral change, followed by serprevalence stability or decline, was caused by fear, by simply seeing so much death—the argument often made to explain what happened in Uganda—since IV infection rates never exceeded about 1%, one of the lowest in sub-Saharan Africa

Jamaica

Risk factors are found in Jamaica that would predict relatively high HIV infection rates: an early age of sexual debut (median age of 14 for boys and girls), multiple sexual partners, a robust sex industry linked with tourism, lack of male circumcision, presence of chancroid, age disparity between partners (a pattern of older men having transactional or coerced sex with younger girls), relatively high levels of alcohol and drug use, and related factors such as poverty, labour emigration and male absenteeism, violence, homophobia, and major stigma associated with AIDS. Yet Jamaica has low HIV infection levels by regional standards: 1.6% or lower among the general population in 2000, down from 2% in 1996. This seems to be because of programs of STD case finding and syndromic management (resulting in declining infection rates of virtually all STDs); and behavioral change programs that have resulted in substantial reduction in number of sexual partners, a slight rise in the median age of sexual debut, and—unlike Uganda— high rates of condom use.

Jamaica is another country where there has been emphasis on promotion of "fidelity" and "abstinence," as well as condoms and treatment of STDs. This has come from the national HIV/AIDS Control program, through its BCC (behaviour change and communication) program. Notable among the vehicles for BCC have been schools and FBOs. As in Uganda, Jamaica's BCC program has emphasized face-to-face approaches and the use of peer educators.

SEXUAL BEHAVIOUR CHANGE IN JAMAICA

Has promotion of "fidelity" and "abstinence" resulted in behavioral change? The causal variables have yet to be sorted out, but a recent national population-based KAP survey of Jamaicans age 15-49 shows that the proportion of both males and females who reported 2 or more partners for the previous 3 month period declined sharply in 2000, compared to 1996. There was significant decrease among all age groups with the exception of females aged 15-19 (4.5% vs. 3.8% existing at time of a 1996 survey). Furthermore, the median and mean age of sexual debut rose from 13 to 14 for males between 1996 and 2000; it remained 14 for females. Earlier population-based, quantitative evidence showed that 50% of females aged 15-19 had sexual experience, down from 59% in 1993. Therefore, the age of sexual debut seems to be rising overall since 1993, albeit slightly.

There is also evidence from a recent qualitative study that some young people believed that 15 or 16 is the earliest that Jamaicans should begin to have intercourse. A focus group of "suburban" boys (those from higher-income neighbourhoods) believed that age 18-25 is "ideal" for first sexual experience. Yet sexual debut is at an earlier age. This means that there is a gap between beliefs, values and behaviour, a gap that FBOs can do even more to focus on in BCC interventions. The same study showed that boys who delayed first intercourse tended to be "raised in a Christian home" suggesting the influence of religion in delay of sexual debut.

Community Peer Educators interviewed by a recent USAID evaluation team reported that "mainstream" Jamaican churches have been particularly cooperative in their AIDS education efforts. With some churches, there was resistance at first. But it took only pointing out that members of a particular church were becoming infected with HIV to change these attitudes. The result is that Jamaica has had good, supportive relations between FBOs and national AIDS efforts in both the public or private sector, for many years.

The USAID evaluation team was unable to find direct evidence of any clergy or religious organizations opposing the work of the National AIDS program. There were occasional allegations that fundamentalist or Pentecostal churches criticized the promotion of condoms, but no real evidence of this emerged anywhere. On the contrary, individual clergy and faith-based organizations were cited virtually everywhere as helpful not only in the care, support and counselling of people living with HIV/or AIDS, but also in AIDS prevention efforts.

It is important to mention that FBOs in Jamaica have been relatively open about condom education and promotion. The government's condom social marketing program was even able to promote condoms among church groups on several occasions, and it encountered no church opposition to such efforts. Condom user rates in Jamaica are high by any country's standards. Over 90% of sex workers regularly use condoms with clients, and some 77% of men, and between 57-79% of women (depending on age group) reported using a condom during their last sexual encounter with a non-regular partner. Even condom use among *regular* partners is high by international standards, increasing from 47% in 1996 to 52% in 2000, using the same measure: whether or not a condom was used in the last sexual encounter.

In sum, Jamaican FBOs have been active in AIDS prevention (as well as in care and support of those already infected), just as we see in Uganda and Senegal, two other countries that have experienced stabilization and even decline of HIV infection levels at the national level. In view of these findings, as well as the modelling studies cited, it would seem that there ought to be greater equity in resource allocation between HIV/AIDS prevention programs promoting primary behavioral change —such as delay of sexual debut and reduction of number of sex partners—and the far more familiar programs that promote and provide condoms. There should also be more involvement on the part of faith-based organizations, and more AIDS prevention resources allocated to them—not because this is part of any political agenda, but because it works.

Of course, it is very difficult to attribute behavioral change in Uganda, Jamaica or anywhere to any one, or combination of, specific interventions. It is very hard to control for confounding variables. And few studies have looked specifically at the impact of FBOs. Indeed, very few countries have even supported major, national-level faith-based initiatives in AIDS prevention. The contribution of faith-based organizations has therefore not been recognized by national and international HIV/AIDS donor organizations, at least outside the countries discussed here. Yet there is now enough suggestive evidence to encourage FBOs to play greater roles in HIV/AIDS prevention, and for donor organizations such as USAID, the World Bank and UNAIDS to support more faith-based initiatives.

In conclusion, the following propositions are submitted for consideration and indeed for far more extensive empirical testing:

1. FBOs are best positioned of any group to promote fidelity and abstinence; this is their "*comparative advantage*." The behavioral change results of such efforts are measured as partner reduction and delay of first sexual experience, to use the language of public health.
2. These behavioral changes tend to be overlooked, yet we have highly suggestive evidence from a least three the few countries that have experienced national-level success in reducing HIV infection rates that they do occur when promoted, and that—according to recent modelling studies—such behavioral changes can have major impact on HIV risk reduction.
3. Religious orga This rose to over 20% in 2000. nizations ought to be given more support in doing what they do best, namely promoting fidelity and abstinence. If FBOs also want to promote condom use, so much the better.
4. It is reasonably well-established that consistent condom use protects against HIV transmission, therefore condom use should be promoted. Yet FBOs should not be forced to emphasize or even necessarily include condom promotion in their HIV/AIDS programs. There are enough other organizations in international AIDS prevention already doing this, and there are insufficient programs directed at partner reduction and delay of sexual debut among youth.
5. Until recently, little international funding has gone to FBOs. There have been few evaluations of FBO AIDS prevention programs; existing

evaluations results have not been much discussed or well disseminated; and religious organizations tend to be involved in care and support programs more than in HIV/AIDS prevention. Thus FBOs remain a great untapped potential in the global fight against AIDS. As new FBO programs are initiated, these should be carefully monitored and evaluated for lessons learned.

ROLE OF CHURCHES GROWS IN GLOBAL BATTLE AGAINST HIV/AIDS

Amid reports of continuing catastrophe, churches and faith-based groups are recognizing the importance of their role in the global fight against HIV/AIDS. "We have a mandate to care for those who are ill, to care for our brothers and sisters whoever or wherever they might be," said Betty Gittens, executive secretary for health and welfare ministries of the United Methodist Church in the United States. "The church has the ability, especially in Africa, to reach an awful lot of people, and the reason is that the church is one of the few groups that folks trust in society right now."

Religious groups are among those who can be especially effective in battling HIV/AIDS because of their ability to influence changes in behaviour, Mark Malloch Brown, administrator of the United Nations Development Program, said in a statement observing World AIDS Day on December 1.

"AIDS is such a formidable challenge in large part because of the difficulty of transforming societal, cultural, and gender norms and creating open dialogue about sex, empowerment of women, and the recognition of the role of men in responding to the epidemic," Brown said. "No government decree or planning document can do this. It requires a broad-based national effort involving communities, churches, women's groups, trade unions, and all types of organizations on the front line of AIDS prevention."

An estimated 5.3 million people worldwide were newly infected with HIV this year, according to "AIDS Epidemic Update: December 2000," released on Tuesday by the Joint United Nations Program on HIV/AIDS (UNAIDS) and the World Health Organization (WHO). That brings the estimated number of people living with HIV or AIDS to 36.1 million, up from 34.3 million last year.

Approximately 21.8 million people have died from AIDS since the epidemic started. The numbers are worst in sub-Saharan Africa, where an estimated 3.8 million people became infected with HIV this year, bringing the total number of people living with HIV or AIDS in the region to 25.3 million, up nearly 1 million from last year's figure. However, the number of new infections was

between young and old people," he said. "Because adverse behaviour increases dramatically in situations where there are not those positive relationships."

Gittens said the United Methodist Church is developing focus papers related to HIV/AIDS for the African American, Native American, and Latino communities in the United States. The church also has done extensive work in Zimbabwe conducting educational and prevention awareness programs, and is looking to expand its efforts with French-speaking and Portuguese-speaking partners elsewhere in Africa.

Dr. Harvey Elder, a specialist in infectious diseases and a member of the Adventist committee, said Christians have a responsibility to help AIDS sufferers. "No church that claims Christ can fail to respond to the AIDS crisis," he said. "We are called, as a church, to be a city of refuge, yet on the whole we are not. We need to develop a willingness to hold and to love, to be open to people, and to let the Gospel and the Holy Spirit work on their hearts."

Following are Examples of what Churches and Faith-based Relief Agencies are Doing to Combat HIV/AIDS:

- Adventist Development and Relief Agency (ADRA): Operates AIDS awareness and education programs in numerous countries in Asia and Africa. In Malawi, for example, ADRA trains volunteers for drama and music presentations that communicate strategies to avoid the disease.
- American Jewish World Service: Supports community based organizations in Ghana, Zimbabwe, and Malawi that are engaged in HIV/AIDS prevention, home-based care, care of AIDS orphans, and income-generating activities.
- Catholic Relief Services: Supports a variety of programs in 40 countries ranging from volunteer training for community educators and counsellors to medical care and programs for orphans and child-headed households.
- Christian Children's Fund: Supports AIDS orphans in Africa and Asia with food, health, education, counselling, and income-generating activities. CCF also conducts HIV/AIDS awareness programs in Africa, Asia, Latin America, and the Caribbean. Through CCF, donors can sponsor an AIDS orphan.
- Christian Reformed World Relief Committee: Works in AIDS prevention in Senegal with the Evangelical Lutheran Church, training church leaders and members to be prevention counsellors in their communities.
- Church World Service: Provides assistance to partners in Africa, Asia, the Caribbean, and Latin America for programs that include health

education and prevention; primary health care and treatment; sanitation and water development; and training for clergy, hospital chaplains, counsellors, and Christian health professionals on dealing with HIV infections.

- Heifer Project International: Works with a prostitutes rehabilitation program in Zimbabwe, with an AIDS orphanage in Kenya, and supplies a dairy cow to families who have adopted AIDS orphans.
- Islamic American Relief Agency: In Kenya, supports an AIDS awareness program, health care, and programs for AIDS orphans.
- Lutheran World Relief: Operates AIDS awareness and prevention programs, plus care and training for AIDS orphans and minors in East and West Africa and Southern Asia. In Kenya, AIDS education and community-based treatment is built into local health care and community empowerment programs. In Uganda, LWR helps a church centre provide long-term care and vocational training for AIDS orphans and minors. In India, 73 villages receive education and are creating a plan to combat HIV/AIDS.
- MAP International: Works to prevent the spread of HIV/AIDS in Africa and Latin America by actively engaging neighborhood churches and schools in culturally appropriate and locally sustainable HIV/AIDS education, prevention, and family support programs in these communities. MAP also provides medications for infections associated with AIDS.
- Salvation Army: Operates a variety of programs in more than 30 countries around the world. Many programs support people with HIV/AIDS and their families, including income-generation projects.
- World Relief: Helps churches in Rwanda, Malawi, and Mozambique conduct programs to prevent the spread of the disease and to care for the sick, the dying, and the orphaned. World Relief is developing biblically based AIDS prevention curriculum and pastoral counselling curriculum, and training church leaders and volunteers.
- World Vision: Conducts education and prevention projects and helps people living with AIDS, as well as AIDS orphans and their foster families in 10 countries. Among the agency's projects are assistance to AIDS orphans in Uganda, AIDS education for prostitutes and their truck-driver clients in Zambia, a Kids Club for children with HIV/AIDS in Romania, and a support group for people living with AIDS in Cambodia.

ACTIONS OF FAITH-BASED ORGANIZATIONS AND THEIR INFLUENCE ON HIV/AIDS-RELATED STIGMA

Our study aimed to explore perceptions of Uganda-based key decision-makers about the past, present and optimal future roles of FBOs in HIV/AIDS work, including actions to promote or dissuade stigma and discrimination.

Methods

We analysed FBO contributions in relation to priorities established in *the Global Strategy Framework on HIV/AIDS,* a consensus-based strategy developed by United Nations Member States. Thirty expert key informants from 11 different sectors including faith-based organizations participated in a structured interview on their perceptions of the role that FBOs have played and could most usefully play in HIV/AIDS prevention, care and support.

Results

Early on, FBOs were perceived by key informants to foster HIV/AIDS-related stigma and discrimination. Respondents attributed this to inadequate knowledge, moralistic perspectives, and fear relating to the sensitive issues surrounding sexuality and death. More recent FBO efforts are perceived to dissuade HIV/AIDS-related stigma and discrimination through increased openness about HIV status among both clergy and congregation members, and the leadership of persons living with HIV/AIDS.

Uganda's program continues to face challenges, including perceptions among the general population that HIV/AIDS is a cause for secrecy. By virtue of their networks and influence, respondents believe that FBOs are well-positioned to contribute to breaking the silence about HIV/AIDS which undermines prevention, care and treatment efforts.

Stigma is a persistent influence on HIV/AIDS, inflicting substantial personal, social and economic costs on individuals, friends and families, communities and nations. Fueled by deeply-felt responses including fear of infection, moral outrage, and shame, those living with HIV/AIDS may be shunned, denied care and support, or avoid life-saving medical care out of fear of rejection. Moreover, HIV/AIDS-related stigma and resulting discriminatory acts create circumstances that fuel the spread of HIV. It has been observed that religious doctrines and moral positions by religious leadership have helped create and support perceptions that those infected have sinned and deserve their punishment, thus increasing the stigma associated with HIV/AIDS. Yet, religious leaders have also been lauded for using their influential voices to mitigate stigma and discrimination against those infected and affected by the virus that causes AIDS.

Uganda, an early epicenter of the disease, is now frequently cited as sub-Saharan Africa's HIV/AIDS "success story" in response to its dramatic reduction in HIV/AIDS prevalence. HIV prevalence among pregnant women in Kampala fell from 31% to 6.2% between 1990 and 2003, while among army recruits aged 18 to 21 years, prevalence rates decreased by 12% over 5 years. Among a number of theories about Uganda's success are high level of political commitment to openness about the epidemic, involvement of all segments of society, and the "ABC" strategy – Abstain, Be faithful or use Condoms.

Regardless of strategy or vehicle responsible for Uganda's achievement, religious organizations are recognized for playing an important role in preventing new infections in Uganda. Uganda adopted a multi-sectoral approach in the fight against HIV/AIDS with an active participation among faith-based organizations as early as 1992. Nearly all of its major religious institutions, both Islamic and Christian, have been actively engaged in the country's struggle with HIV/AIDS. While there is general agreement supporting the critical role of the faith community in the dramatic reductions in Uganda's HIV prevalence, a better understanding of what faith communities are doing with regard to addressing the epidemic is critical.

Our study aimed to explore perceptions of Uganda-based key decision-makers about the past, present and optimal future roles of FBOs in HIV/AIDS work, including actions to promote or dissuade stigma and discrimination. We analysed FBO performance and contributions in relation to priorities established in *the Global Strategy Framework on HIV/AIDS*, an internationally-recognized, consensus-based strategy developed by United Nations Member States. This strategy encourages simultaneous efforts to reduce risk of HIV transmission, lessen vulnerability to HIV/AIDS, especially among women and other high risk groups, and mitigate the impact of the disease by providing care, treatment and support to those affected.

A key component of the overall strategy is to combat AIDS-related stigma that undermines the success of all three approaches. It is hoped that findings from this study will help FBOs to better understand how they are perceived, and how people in a variety of sectors think that FBOs can most usefully collaborate. Armed with this information, both faith and secular groups can capitalize on perceived strengths and address perceived weaknesses of FBOs to improve the collective response to reducing stigma and improving the lives of those living with the virus.

INTERVIEW FRAMEWORK AND PROCEDURES

By basing the interview questions on *The Global Strategy Framework on HIV/AIDS,* we sought to highlight and explore the "guiding principles and leadership commitments that together form the basis for a successful response to the epidemic," as they relate to faith-based organizations. We defined "faith-based organization" broadly to include the range from places of worship to development organizations with a mission of faith. This decision was taken for practical reasons in that the activities of the diverse faith-based actors in the country would be difficult to separate. Semi-structured, face-to-face interviews were conducted from September to December 2003. Lasting on average 60 minutes, interviews examined key informants' perceptions of the extent of FBO leadership, collaboration and contribution to strategies to reduce risk, decrease vulnerability, and mitigate the impact of HIV/AIDS. Interviews were conducted in the preferred language of the interviewee and were audio taped after permission was obtained. Tapes were transcribed verbatim and translated, if necessary, into English. Permission to carry out the study was obtained from the Uganda National Council of Science and Technology (NCST). Informed consent was obtained from all respondents.

Data Analysis

We aimed to reduce bias when analysing transcripts by "blinding" ourselves to the identity of the informant through the assignment of a number to each informant. Using qualitative analysis software, *Atlas. ti,* we coded all electronic transcripts with predetermined categories that referred to the general topic(s) that informants discussed. We then divided transcripts into sub-groups according to the sector ('FBO' and 'Non-FBO'). Data-derived codes based on themes emerging from data were identified from the typed text data.

For the purpose of this paper, we used a combination of codes to compile quotations that addressed the question, "What actions have FBO taken that promote or dissuade stigma and discrimination?" We studied our informants' responses in terms of FBO contributions, the conditions that define their participation, and the consequences of their involvement. Themes that resonated among a critical mass were further systematically analysed for communities, variations and disagreements. Lastly, we contrasted and compared these themes across sectors to synthesize our findings. The analysis is limited to what our key informants perceive and does not aim to validate the objectivity of these perceptions.

The findings are presented in two sections; the first relating to FBO actions perceived as promoting stigma, the second focusing on actions taken by FBOs to challenge stigmatizing behaviour. Emerging themes for the former include the use of stigmatizing language and messages; deeply-entrenched societal attitudes and norms; and limited involvement of persons living with HIV/AIDS (PLWHAs).

The latter section highlights themes focusing on the mitigation of stigma including increased knowledge; improved collaboration, inclusion and mobilization; and institutional capacity. All themes reflect an over arching consensus among both non-FBO and FBO respondents.FBO actions facilitating stigma

Stigmatizing Language and Messages

There was agreement among key informants that the language historically used by FBO leadership had often supported and propagated discriminatory views towards PLWHAs within their religious community.

You know for a long time we have lived with stigma in this country. When people have HIV they are stigmatized, they are looked at as cursed. There was a time when even some religious leaders could say, 'you have been cursed by God, you are a sinner, you have been misbehaving,' which I think does not go well as far as people coming out [disclosing their HIV status] is concerned. (FBO Key Informant)

In the beginning it was rather not very kind because whoever was found HIV-positive was looked at as a sinner and I think faith-based organizations have played a big role in enhancing stigma which was unfortunately very bad.

FBOs were also identified as sending out mixed messages in line with the Christian concept of 'hate the sin, love the sinner.' Respondents noted that while FBOs were largely unaware of the ill-effects of such language, these messages were as stigmatizing as more deliberate condemnation.

But when the church at the same place turns around and says, 'You know my son, you know my daughter, I will be there for you. I know you have sinned but I will be there for you,' again there is a mixed message there.

Some religious leaders say things they don't realize that they are stigmatizing, for example that this disease is a punishment from God. Deuteronomy says, 'If you obey, you will lead a healthy life, if you disobey, I curse you with boils, I will curse you with plagues, you will die an early death,' you see. How do you expect a person living with HIV/AIDS to come out and say, 'Here I am, I am positive' after realizing that God is punishing him, singling him out of the many who are disobeying and don't have AIDS? (FBO Key Informant)

Deeply-Entrenched Attitudes and Norms

Informants cited the use of religious teachings to ascribe blame without regard to deeply entrenched societal vulnerabilities. According to respondents, many of the traditional religious solutions offered by FBOs did not address the significant HIV acquisition risks faced by vulnerable groups, including women.

Many women who get infected in Africa have never had sex with more than one man. They are faithful but infected. So to say, 'be faithful therefore you don't get AIDS' is not a very good message. So to say, 'come to marriage'— you know that is the message sometimes the church leaders give. 'If you want to escape AIDS please come to Jesus and get married in church and things will be fine,' and you shake your head. How will Jesus save you from infection? Actually, getting married increases the risk. (FBO Key Informant)

Moralistic attitudes among various FBOs were also seen to foster both self-stigma among PLWHAs, as well as anger and withdrawal from religious activities.

What I have noticed in my church is that people who are HIV positive do not want to openly come out because of stigma. You know the church has that feeling that if you are a good Christian you should not get engaged in acts of sin…and to them, getting HIV, they take it that you got it through sin. And not only that, but even the person himself who is HIV-positive feels the self-stigma: 'How will they see me that now I have got HIV? They will take it that I'm a sinner.'

The Reverend said that people with AIDS eat from dirty plates — we call them 'myopalmus'. I said to myself, 'I have never eaten from the dirty plate. Get out of here! This is not a right place for you.' I do not give them my money when I go there.

FBOs were cited for equating positive behaviour change to being a 'good Christian', sending erroneous signals to its members. Religious organizations were also noted for embracing select elements of behaviour change, eschewing other more sensitive elements.

Up to now there are still problems of faith-based organizations accepting some of the elements of behaviour change. I know many people tend to think that behaviour change is being Christian but it is far from that. I think behaviour change means changing from past ways of life into a new way of life. And they did not support that in the beginning. We were not really found forth-coming because of the negative approach our religious institutions had as far as HIV/AIDS is concerned.

Limited Involvement of PLWHAs

According to most key informants, there has been limited involvement of PLWHAs in FBO activities. This lack of participation, often attributed to the fear of "breaking the silence," was cited by respondents as further fostering stigma and discrimination within both the organization and greater community.

It has been realized that we are not doing enough in involving persons living with HIV/AIDS in our churches, mosques, temples and so forth. And even many of our religious leaders living with HIV are living with it very silently. It would be nice to...I mean, we wish to do a lot more to see to it that we involve them more and more, whether they are lay people or they are ordained ministers.

Involvement of persons with HIV on the whole is inadequate because of the stigma. People are not very willing to come out, and if they come out there are still a lot of negative feelings. If a religious leader comes out, if he is positive, there is a lot of suspicion and so on. So, yes they have tried, but it is not yet adequate. Maybe it can be improved upon.

Increased Knowledge

As the epidemic has evolved in Uganda, respondents noted the changing attitudes of FBOs towards those with HIV/AIDS. Informants applauded FBOs for accepting HIV/AIDS as a problem without "borders" and for sharing this message throughout their respective organizations. Basically, FBOs are saying, 'HIV/AIDS can get me but it can also get you.' So when you have someone with HIV/AIDS in the community, you should support him, you should help him, because he may not be necessarily a sinner. Through participation in HIV/AIDS trainings, informants stated that FBOs have been armed with better information to fight discrimination and stigma within their institutions and congregations.

I should say where there has been training of the FBOs' leadership, where they have participated in seminars, they have had an impact on stigma and discrimination, because they have come to realize that there are many modes of HIV transmission and it is not just sex. And then they have come to know that even with HIV/AIDS you can still be productive. So to me, where they are trained they are effective in reducing stigma."...the planners, both national and for us the implementers in designing a communication strategy that would be able to reach out many people, we opted for using FBOs or approaches, that is using religious leaders of all faiths...because these are the normal communicators in the community.

Train them in HIV/AIDS issues including stigma and discrimination and ask them to pass the messages through sermons, group talks, home visits, and lectures and so on. So, we gave them more capacity to communicate on these issues. They have done it quite well, in fact very well in some instances. It is one thing establishing services and it is another connecting the services to the community, and that is where the faith-based groups did a good job...we are all satisfied with them.

Improved Collaboration, Inclusion and Mobilization

FBOs were reported as increasingly involving PLWHAs in their activities as well as being supportive to those that declare their HIV status. FBOs were applauded for their more recent support of PLWHA networks. All key informants interviewed cited improved FBO networking and collaboration with community-based organizations founded or led by people living with HIV/AIDS.

Given the fact that we set up a unit like this purely for HIV-positive patients means that we are fighting stigma. We are saying, 'you are welcome here, even if somebody else is not willing,' and I am sure [this is] the whole aim of whatever other FBOs are doing. Setting up a program for these patients means they are helping them, they are recognizing that there is a problem and they are willing to help.

Seeing FBOs launch a network of religious people who are HIV-positive and those who are directly affected by HIV in the recently-held conference in Uganda made a difference. I am sure it is going to make a difference as long as the question of stigma within faith-based organization goes away; we are blessed in changing the course of HIV/AIDS.

Most key informants were optimistic about these developments, particularly the involvement of religious persons who are positive.... I mean a person like me — I am a religious leader. I am positive and my church and fellow church leaders have really supported me to do what I have been able to do. And I am aware of other religious leaders who have become open and they have not been harassed. Even other members of the church who have taken the courage to share are really supported and involved in message delivery, program development. I know, for example, one faith group that involved one of their leaders who is HIV positive to do advocacy work. Sometimes they have used them to do advocacy to contribute to policy development.

Key informants also acknowledged that community mobilization efforts of FBOs have led to increased uptake of prevention services such as voluntary counselling and testing. Through these efforts, as well as educational and out reach programs, FBOs were observed to contribute to reducing stigma and discrimination in the community.

FBOs have continued to educate people about the disease and the more you educate people the more you change their mind about the disease. So maybe that is where I can say they have been contributing to the reduction of stigma by educating people more about it, by telling people about it, by getting involved into the programs. By allowing persons with HIV/AIDS to go for care and support in the missionary hospitals, that is bringing down stigma.

Well, the first thing really is to restore hope among these people, among the infected and the affected to help them rediscover their self-esteem, rebuild their self-confidence and promote positive living...

Institutional Capacity

FBOs were noted as possessing a comparative advantage in their ability to address stigma through their existing social mobilization channels. As trusted entities within the communities, FBOs were cited for their significant ability to influence the cultural norms of their congregations. I think around the issues of stigma, FBOs have a huge role to play. So many people go to Church on Sundays here or Mosque on Fridays. It has always been a powerful tool for social mobilization and developing and sustaining or changing social norms. Always, more powerful probably than political systems because on one level it seems people, although they listen to politicians, they do not really trust them.

FBOs were also cited as addressing HIV/AIDS-related stigma and discrimination through their institutions that provide care and support to PLWHAs. FBOs' post-test clubs, home care and income generating activities and support to orphans and widows were referenced as important programs in the fight against stigma and discrimination.

The primary focus is care, it is only care. We have several activities in care; we do medical and nursing care, we do home visiting then we do all types of counselling and we have some support for the orphans and preventive care also focusing on the youth.

I will pick out some few FBOs, which I know. For example, Nsambya Home Care has a department that is specifically dealing with HIV/AIDS. So what they are doing is one, they are looking at affected families, they are offering services to the orphans in terms of school fees and scholastic materials, In addition to that they offer voluntary counselling and testing services. But they do not end there. They go ahead to give support in relation to the needs of the persons living with HIV/AIDS, for example treatment that I think is free. And to me that is very important because we also have those who can't afford treatment.

THE AIDS SUPPORT ORGANISATION (TASO)-UGANDA

TASO was organised in response to the urgent need in Uganda for medical, emotional and practical support for people with HIV/AIDS and their immediate families.

Bombay Dost – India: In response to violence against the gay community and a lack of information about AIDS and other STDs, the newsletter Bombay Dost was started to reach out to people with alternate sexuality in the city of Bombay.

Rio de Janeiro Prostitutes Association (APRJ) – Brazil:

APRJ has worked out agreements with the local medical establishment for regular medical check-ups, and with BEMFAM, Brazil's largest private family planning agency to provide condoms.

Project Hope/Family Life Association (FLAS) – Swaziland: FLAS, a local NGO is collaborating with Project HOPE, an international NGO for an AIDS awareness and prevention programme. FLAS staff develop training programmes and educational materials for non-literate adults, out-of-school youth, staff of FLAS family planning clinics, and traditional healers, train 60 HIV/AIDS counsellors in Swaziland, and organise nationwide networks of regional counselling support groups.

Education Means Protection Of Women Engaged in Recreation (EMPOWER) – Thailand: EMPOWER offers support, assistance and access to education for women workers in Patpong, the entertainment district of Bangkok, Thailand. EMPOWER also provides referrals and health counselling on sexually transmitted diseases, nutrition, exercise, safe drug use and family planning.

Copperbelt Health Education Project (CHEP)-Zambia: CHEP offers street children a five-day survival skills course directly responding to immediate needs and long-term concerns including job training, small business management, staying within the law, avoiding drug and alcohol abuse, and preventing STD and AIDS. CHEP also runs training workshops for health workers and community leaders.

NGO Consortium – Kenya: NGOs formed a national consortium of organisations concerned with improving HIV/AIDS prevention and care, ensuring regular dialogue between NGOs and the AIDS Programme Secretariat, a government supported national AIDS committee. The sharing of information skills between NGOs leads to recognition for the role of NGOs played in the AIDS programme.

To identify the most effective roles for NGOs in HIV/AIDS prevention and care, it is imperative to recognise the strengths and weaknesses of NGOs. While not all NGOs share the same strong points, some strengths are common to most. For example, NGOs, being smaller and having more flexible administrative systems, and less cumbersome bureaucracies than governmental organisation, can devise and implement programmes faster. This allows NGOs to deal more openly with sensitive issues like sexuality and condom use. NGOs are often created and staffed by community members. This gives them credibility with and understanding of the communities they serve. Thus, NGOs are more likely to attract community participation for HIV/AIDS prevention and care efforts. They are also more likely to recognise what will be appropriate and effective for their constituencies, and in so doing, increase the potential for transforming community attitudes, beliefs and behaviours from within the community. This is a much-needed and valuable approach to HIV/AIDS prevention. Also, volunteers provide the energy and resources to staff many NGOs, and even paid staff often work at lower salaries because of personal commitment to the goals of the organisation.

NGOs are also willing to involve in their programmes those individuals who are poor and marginalised, and thereby, they succeed in reaching groups such as prostitutes or intravenous drug users, who are outside the mainstream society, and may be suspicious of public institutions. However, NGOs also have certain constraints and limitations that must also be considered in identifying their most effective roles in HIV/AIDS prevention and care.

Newer, smaller NGOs with small administrative staffs are not properly designed for large-scale budgeting or technical reporting. This leaves some organisations at a disadvantage when competing for AIDS-related funding from large international donors. Also, smaller NGOs are limited by their in-house technical capacity for complex projects. This prevents such organisations from meeting the requirements of outside funders for monetary and curriculum reporting, including evaluation of project efforts.

Since NGOs often operate with volunteer or modestly paid staff, they risk the likelihood of erosion due to burn-out. They need to maintain a balance between paid and volunteer staff in order to maintain project continuity, while preventing attrition which is especially common in the emotionally demanding field of combating HIV and AIDS. Also, it has often been the case that NGOs work in isolation, reluctant to collabourate with each other or with the government. This leads to limited sustainability, which does not focus on developing local capacities to carry on without NGO or other external support. This problem obscures NGO projects which are highly successful on a small scale. Early successes of a project are often found to be related to unique characteristics within the community or the NGO and may not be replicable on a large scale.

There is enormous potential for NGOs to play a major role in the effort to combat HIV and AIDS. In order for NGOs to perform at their full potential, Merceretal suggested several approaches supporting the role of NGOs in their response to the challenges of HIV/AIDS.

NGOs must be included in the design, implementation, and review of national AIDS programme plans. Also, the efforts of AIDS-related NGOs to form national and regional consortia, in order to strengthen their abilities to collabourate with each other and with their respective national AIDS control programmes, must be supported and strengthened.

Mercer et al. called for seed money and technical assistance to be provided to strengthen the administrative and organisational capacities of AIDS-related NGOs, especially in areas of great need. They argued the need for research about the best ways that this can be accomplished, even if it requires more funding for longer periods of time (1991). Collaboration has also been recommended, between larger, more established NGOs and their newer counterparts in a mentorship programme designed to strengthen capacity of small, indigenous NGOs. This would enable the newer organisations gain organisational skills more rapidly. International and indigenous NGOs need to collabourate on projects, and the success of such collaborations carefully evaluated.

NGOs should be funded based on their strengths. They should be encouraged to build on their strengths. In the area of HIV and AIDS, this requires recognition of NGOs' desire to provide support and care to persons with AIDS, as an integral part of their prevention activities.

By developing links with local universities, NGOs can substantially increase their technical capacities. Technical assistance in the field in key aspects of NGO programme interventions, provided by consultants or staff who have experience in working successfully with NGOs is a great asset, often preventing needless expenditure of misguided energy, and will assist NGO projects meet the needs of the people they serve. NGOs also need to analyse the roles played by television, radio and the press. These media act as agents of information, education or sensationalism. Their influence in creating public opinion can be monumental with regard to educational activities. Despite current literature concerning the work of NGOs, more research analysing ways to improve their efficacy is necessary.

Developing and evaluating the effectiveness of an interactive Internet programme or HIV prevention intervention models from the research arena to non-governmental organisations in developing countries with high HIV incidence will highlight areas of improvement (Kelly 2000). The study will incorporate Internet-based dissemination methods to establish a technology transfer approach that is rapid, widely applicable and cost-effective for national and international public health organisations including networks of NGOs. According to Kelly, previous research, found that technology transfer methods that provide intervention manuals, face-to-face staff training, and individualised consultation for implementing research-based HIV prevention interventions facilitate their adoption by service providers. This framework is now being expanded to test the use of Internet technologies to transfer an HIV prevention approach to NGOs in developing countries.

Each NGO will be assessed to determine its organisational characteristics, and the full repertoire of HIV prevention services it had offered. The assessment of the efficacy of the NGOs will determine maintenance of intervention use, tailoring or adaptations made to it, staff attitudes and satisfaction with the intervention, and implementation costs. According to Kelly, this study "will add to our scientific knowledge concerning approaches for transferring effective research-based HIV prevention approaches to community-based service providers; will test and develop a prototype model for using advanced Internet-based approaches for technology transfer; and will allow HIV prevention research advances to better benefit the global fight against HIV/AIDS" (Kelly 2000).

While NGOs and international agencies have set up specific programmes to stem the spread of HIV/AIDS, some of the consequences of wider development policies, such as increased mobility or migration or increased income to spend on recreation, can counteract these programmes and contribute to the spread of the virus. Unless HIV/AIDS prevention programmes adopt an integrated gender perspective addressing power relations within relevant social and economic context they are likely to fail. Many HIV/AIDS prevention programmes for youth in school fail because HIV/AIDS education is seen as irrelevant to their social and cultural circumstances. Youth education must therefore begin with an analysis of the needs and roles of young people in their particular community in order to respond appropriately to their needs.

After over a decade of research, it is recognised by NGOs and many governments that long-term solutions are needed to address the power imbalances. To date, solutions have been incomplete or inadequate and future strategies need to concentrate on power relations. There need to be changes in these relations and appropriate programme responses must be developed on this basis. Long-term solutions are needed so that women and young girls have equal access to employment, education and income generating opportunities.

International agencies and local NGOs need to recognise the link between development, gender relations and roles and the spread of HIV/AIDS and to promote awareness in a broad context with staff and within projects. Existing programmes should be modified to ensure they are gender sensitive.

Information and services must be provided to support people who are affected or infected with HIV/AIDS or other sexually transmitted diseases and infections (STDs and STIs). For example, confidential counselling and testing, information about safer sex and different control methods. The wider community must also be encouraged to use information services and consequently NGOs should produce accessible material and widely publicise these different services. NGOs are in a strong position to support advocacy and campaigns that can battle the spread of HIV/AIDS.

Mercer et al. (1991) suggested that "the need to adopt multiple approaches and involve diverse organisations in bringing about attitudinal and behavioural change at the community level," will prevent further destruction by HIV/AIDS. This review demonstrates how NGOs have embodied diverse objectives while maintaining effective local, national and international campaigns to combat the HIV/AIDS epidemic. Further development of NGO-governmental ties and research defining efficient strategies to affect social change at the individual level will determine the course of HIV/AIDS. Clearly, NGOs will play a role as the epidemic progresses

PARADIGM SHIFT AND CONTROVERSY IN AIDS PREVENTION

There is accumulating evidence that the prevailing model of AIDS prevention, designed by experts from America and Europe in response to an epidemic initially concentrated in high-risk groups, has been largely ineffective in sub-Saharan Africa, which has a different epidemic pattern. The model is based on risk-reduction interventions. For sexually transmitted HIV infections–

the major mode of transmission worldwide – this refers primarily to promotion and supply of male and female condoms. To a lesser extent it includes treating other sexually transmissible infections, the presence of which facilitates HIV transmission, with drugs. However, three out of four randomized clinical trials (RCTs) in Africa have suggested that mass treatment of STIs does not impact HIV infection rates significantly.

There have been no such RCTs to establish the effectiveness of condom use; indeed "for ethical reasons individuals cannot be randomized to a group that is not to use condoms." It is not possible to demonstrate a correlation between great condom availability or usage, and lower HIV infection rates, at the population level, in Africa.

Risk reduction can be contrasted with risk avoidance, which in this context refers to mutual monogamy or even polygamy (with an uninfected partner or partners), sexual abstinence or delay of age of first sex. Reduction in number of sexual partners, which can be an outcome of a Be Faithful message, would have to be classified as risk reduction, not risk avoidance. The remedies – based Western prevention model does not actively promote partner reduction, nor even address multi-partner sex. When HIV/AIDS first appeared in Africa, most governments preferred not to deal with the issue.

There was indignation that the West seemed to be blaming Africans for the origin of a deadly pandemic that was discovered among homosexuals in American and therefore, from the African viewpoint, was likely to be an American disease. There was also fear that evidence of AIDS would ruin tourism and foreign business investment. Yet Uganda's response to AIDS was rapid, and it became the first African country and one of the first in the world to experience HIV incidence and prevalence decline. Senegal seemed to soon follow the same pattern, although national HIV prevalence there barely exceeded 1%. These two countries are now recognized as the first two AIDS success stories in Africa. And it is important to look carefully at the type of programs both developed, largely on their own, and before Western AIDS organizations had geared up to assist Africa in the fight against AIDS.

The term primary behaviour change has been suggested to denote fundamental changes in sexual behaviour, such as partner reduction, mutual fidelity, or abstinence. Uganda developed AIDS prevention programs that emphasized primary behaviour change, along with risk reduction interventions. Put another way, it dealt with AIDS primarily as a behavioral issue requiring behavioral solutions, rather than merely as a medical problem requiring medical solutions. Since no other country can match Uganda's 66% decline in HIV prevalence, it becomes essential to understand what was different about its approach to AIDS prevention.

Risk-Reduction and its Limits

The AIDS prevention paradigm that was exported to Africa in the latter 1980s was developed for high-risk groups such as men who have sex with men in US cities like San Francisco. Part of the risk reduction model was to *not* address sexual behaviour. It was argued that this would amount to making value judgments, which is unscientific and would only drive away those who needed to be reached. AIDS experts settled for risk or harm reduction approaches, which assume that behaviour is difficult or impossible to change, although efforts can and ought to be made to mitigate the consequences of risky behaviour. Thus condoms and clean needles (if legal) were provided to reduce risk of sexually transmitted and blood-to-blood HIV infection respectively. There was and is virtually no discouragement of any form of sexual behaviour, or injecting drug use. AIDS experts applauded themselves for their open-mindedness and realism. This approach might have been suitable for San Francisco, or even Sao Paulo or Bangkok. But when this was exported to Africa, there was little attempt to adapt the model to other cultural settings or epidemic patterns, despite claims to the contrary. In the US, Europe and most of Asia, HIV infections are concentrated in a few fairly well-defined high risk groups. In (sub-Saharan) Africa, most infections are found in the general population. Actually, many are opposed to this distinction, arguing, "Let's not single out particular risk groups. That will stigmatize them—blame the victims—and make the general public feel that they are not at risk. So our message should be, "We are *all* at risk of AIDS." This has a nice, egalitarian ring, suggesting that we are all in this pandemic together. Nevertheless, differences in epidemiological patterns and cultural settings are real, calling for—among other things—different approaches to prevention.

David Wilson of the World Bank provides definitions of concentrated and generalized epidemics that point to appropriate interventions. "Epidemics are concentrated if transmission occurs mostly among vulnerable groups and if protecting vulnerable groups would protect wider society. Conversely, "epidemics are generalized if transmission occurs mainly outside vulnerable groups and would continue despite effective vulnerable group interventions." By definition, one cannot impact HIV prevalence in generalized epidemics by promoting riskreduction measures to high-risk groups, however successful those interventions might be. What does Wilson mean by vulnerable groups? "Universal vulnerable groups" are "injecting drug users (IDU), sex workers (SW) and men having sex with men (MSM).

They are universally vulnerable because of behavioral and biological factors. "In addition, their immediate sexual partners have elevated vulnerability, including clients of SW. They also include what may be termed situation-specific vulnerable groups, who may include prisoners and migrants to or from highly affected countries." Thus, different interventions are required for concentrated and generalized epidemics, and for different populations (high risk or general population in either type of epidemic. In this way, interventions can be targeted in ways that make sense and are likely to have some impact. For example, abstinence is not the primary behaviour promoted to prostitutes, just as condoms and syringes are not the primary behaviors and "technology" promoted to children in primary school.

The lack of fit between interventions and either type of epidemic or target population can be seen for example in responses found over at least 15 years to a related pair of questions about if the respondent had changed behaviour due to AIDS, and if so, in what way. When whole (general, national) populations were asked these questions, the answers consistently pointed to fidelity or remaining with one sexual partner, followed by abstaining or delaying sexual debut, usually among youth. Perhaps it would have taken an outsider to notice (and mention) that the protective behaviors most often cited were not the ones promoted. There clearly was a misfit between inputs and outputs. In 2000, the DHS discontinued asking this pair of questions.

There still seems to be little or no recognition among Western AIDS experts that general and high-risk populations require different interventions. An exception can be found in a consensus statement about HIV prevention in generalized epidemics, published in *The Lancet* and endorsed by over 160 global AIDS professionals as well as President Museveni of Uganda. It calls for the targeting of ABC messages on the basis of age and circumstances: primarily A (Abstain) for youth, primarily B (Be faithful or reduce partners) for sexually active adults and primarily C (use Condoms) for high risk individuals. And primarily does not mean exclusively; each primary or first-choice intervention is backed up by secondary interventions.

ABC model adopted by the United States

The ABC approach to HIV prevention has gained prominence and garnered controversy in recent years, as it has become the policy of the largest AIDS relief plan in the history of the pandemic. In December 2002, the United States Agency for International Development (USAID) adopted the Uganda ABC approach as the model of prevention for generalized HIV/AIDS epidemics. In 2003, the President's Emergency Plan for AIDS Relief (PEPFAR) was announced, and the ABC approach was adopted for all PEPFAR countries. The first PEPFAR strategy document to be released called risk "elimination" (or avoidance) a "cornerstone" of PEPFAR. The Office of the Global AIDS Coordinator (OGAC) later released further guidance on the ABC approach.

While this guidance has clarified the prevention approach to be followed by programs, considerable confusion and controversy remain. The evidence for and appropriate application of the ABC approach to HIV prevention remain widely misinterpreted and misunderstood.

And there remains great opposition to the AB components of ABC, a state of affairs that often mystifies laypersons, people not involved in AIDS issues. Surely people differ and therefore there must be a range of interventions to chose from? Surely there must be more to prevention than condoms, drugs, and testing? We attempt to answer some of the common criticisms about the primary behaviour change components of the ABC model that the US government has adopted.

What Evidence is there for the ABC Approach?

The sexual transmission of HIV can be directly prevented in three basic ways: by avoiding the exposure to risk through sexual abstinence; by reducing the risk of exposure through partner faithfulness and reduction in partners; or by blocking the efficiency of transmission through a barrier like a condom. In other words, by practicing A, B or C. The ABC approach therefore addresses the only three basic ways in which HIV can be sexually transmitted. Because Uganda provides the clearest case study of a successful ABC approach, this document makes frequent reference to Uganda. In Uganda, HIV prevalence decreased from 15 percent to 5 percent between 1991 and 2001.

During the same period, the following changes in ABC behaviors occurred:

- The proportion of young males age 15-24 reporting premarital sex decreased from 60 percent in 1989 to 23 percent in 1995. For females, the decline was from 53 percent to 16 percent.
- For all age groups, 41 percent of males had more than one sex partner in 1989. This declined to 21 percent by 1995. For females, the decline was from 23 percent to 9 percent. The proportion of males reporting three or more sex partners fell from 15 percent to 3 percent between 1989 and 1995.
- In 1995, about 6 percent of sexually active Ugandans used a condom with some regularity. By 2000, this rose to 11 percent of sexually active Ugandans, or 8 percent of all Ugandans.

There is increasing consensus that the main behaviour change that occurred in Uganda was a decrease in casual sex, as measured the proportion of men and women who report more than one sex partner in the past year. This has been a rather painful conclusion for major AIDS-related agencies and organizations, since, as noted, they did not fund significant programs to discourage casual sex—to "be faithful to one partner" or even to decrease the number of sexual partners. There has been a great deal of confusion between "abstinence" (especially "abstinence only") programs and those discouraging casual sex, such as Uganda's Love Faithfully or Zero Grazing campaigns. Most Ugandans ages 15 to 49 (the age group in which surveys such as DHS measure both behaviour and HIV status) are sexually active, not abstinent.

Yet partisans on both the liberal and conservative sides of the AIDS debate, and the specific "What Happened in Uganda?" This debate continues to refer to Uganda's early program (or, in a twist of irony, its most recent program) as an abstinence program. Data show that compared to other countries in Africa, it was with regard to B behaviors that Uganda was different condom use was not higher in Uganda than in other countries. Rather it is differences in "Be faithful" behaviors that Uganda stands out.

We wish to go beyond the basic evidence from Uganda, which we have only been able to summarize broadly, and devote the rest of this review to answering critical questions that have been posed about the ABC approach, which in effect means about the AB components added by changes in recent US AIDS policy.

Should condoms be promoted only to high-risk populations such as sex workers and truck drivers? Doesn't everyone need condoms? Condoms can be promoted to anyone and everyone, yet many years of experience provides persuasive evidence that only those in high-risk groups are likely to use them consistently, especially in rural areas of developing countries where a steady supply of condoms is problematic. *Consistent* condom use in Africa is rare, probably never exceeding 5 percent in any country. And most condom use outside of a very few high risk groups is *inconsistent*, in spite of major efforts that have gone into condom promotion and distribution, both for family planning and disease protection. Mounting evidence also suggests that inconsistent condom use does not protect people, at least at the population level in generalized epidemics.

In fact, now that DHS surveys are including a (population-based) sero-survey component, it is possible to compare the HIV status of condom users and non-users. In the first countries for which DHS data is available (Tanzania,

Kenya, Ghana) it has been found that condom users are more likely to be infected than non-users, whether the measure is condoms at last sex or last high-risk or last sex with prostitutes. These data are being called anomalous, yet they could be explained by factoring in inconsistency of use and the possible disinhibiting effect of condom promotion. So, to answer the question, condoms can be promoted to whole or general populations, i.e. to everyone, and there seems to be nothing in PEPFAR guidance documents that discourages or restricts such promotion.

The guidance does suggest that condom promotion be emphasized or targeted to high-risk groups, following the Uganda (earlier period) approach. This is for the simple fact that such groups are likely to use condoms, thus it is (or should be) a matter of practicality, of putting funds where they have a good chance of having some impact. Thailand is considered the world's great condom success story, with rates of condom use reaching 90 percent or above in Bangkok by 1996. But even in Bangkok, condom use reported by women in the general population (i.e., women not involved in commercial sex but possibly being in another risk category) was only 18.9 percent in 1966. Indeed, only 28.5 percent of Bangkok prostitutes reported using condoms with nonpaying sex partners, such as boyfriends. All these data are from a survey conducted by Family Health International in which condom use is defined as use during last sexual intercourse. If this is the best intense condom promotion can achieve in a condom-friendly city like Bangkok, hopes for rural Africa must be scaled downward. If we put aside models of Thailand that might seem appealing and focus on Africa, it appears that the actual market for condoms is quite small low in Africa.

Unlike Thai, Dominican or American men for example, most African men do not have one-time sex partners. As already noted, *most* African men are practicing A or B behaviors, and the trend is toward higher levels of both. It is true that some African men have more than one concurrent partner, whether in polygamous or monogamous unions. And this pattern unfortunately facilitates HIV transmission much more than serial monogamy, even if the total number of partners is the same as in a population that practices serial monogamy. But the point is one that condom social marketers know well: most men will not use condoms with their wives *or their long-term, enduring sex partners*. Perhaps they *should*, but they do not and this is unlikely to change easily or at all.

And Africans are not unique in this reluctance to use condoms in long-term relationships. Who does that leave as likely candidates to use condoms?

Sex workers and their clients are high on this list. However reliable data of this sort are, only 1.6 percent of Ugandan men reported paying for sex in the last year. There are also truck drivers and soldiers posted far from home. And there is evidence that these men, at least in Uganda, are quite likely to use condoms during one-time intercourse. But such experiences do not add up to a substantial condom market.

Westerners have criticized Africans for "just not getting" that they must use condoms in each any every sex act, "something very few people on the planet do," in the words of science journalist Helen Epstein. Yet we should look more carefully at the size and characteristics of the potential condom market before we criticize.

Does the ABC approach demand an unrealistic standard of behaviour?

Critics of the ABC approach often make statements such as: "The behavioral bias of the ABC approach is based on the assumption that individuals all have an innate and equal power to make perfectly correct decisions about every issue in their sexual and reproductive health lives," or, "We all know that abstinence and couples being mutually faithful would be great if they were applicable to everybody's lives, but they're not." Critics also argue African culture is polygamous, moreover A and B behaviors are constrained or precluded because of external factors, including poverty, displacement, illiteracy, disability, and gender disparities. Many factors can limit or take away a person's ability to practice abstinence, faithfulness, or consistent condom use. These factors can include poverty, illiteracy, instability and displacement, and gender disparity. Is the ABC approach still an effective strategy in such circumstances? In fact, some of the strongest evidence for an ABC approach comes from situations in which there were high levels of poverty, illiteracy, and instability.

When Uganda began to respond to HIV/AIDS in the late 1980s and early 1990s, it was just emerging from two decades of war and extreme civil unrest. Far from being passive victims of forces beyond their control, Ugandans mounted an effective response to HIV/AIDS in spite of the difficult situations in which they were living.

The same can be said of Senegal. But what about unrealistic standard of behaviour? Africans are often depicted as starting to engage in sex at a very early age and having numerous sexual partners. But the best biological and survey data do not support the popular image of the promiscuous African. According to UNAIDS, Sub-Saharan Africa now has an average HIV prevalence rate of 7.2 percent, down from 7.3 percent in 2004 and 7.5 percent a year earlier. This means that about 93 percent of Africans ages 15-49 are *not* HIV infected. Complementing these epidemiological data, DHS and other survey data show that the great majority of African women and men are already practicing B and A behaviors (in that order). Indeed, the trend in Africa is toward higher levels of monogamy, fidelity, and abstinence, and the trend in HIV prevalence is incrementally downward. These welcome trends have come about in spite of the paucity or complete absence of national programs aimed at promoting fidelity and abstinence.

The United States is the first major donor to include such programs in global AIDS prevention. This initiative should be supported and other major funding organizations should follow this example. By citing these figures, we are *not* saying we should shift attention and resources away from those at high risk, as discussed further in the Conclusion. In the few countries where abstinence and fidelity have been promoted at the national level and backed by resources, sexual behaviour has changed and rates of HIV and other STIs have decreased. Examples include Uganda, Senegal, Jamaica, Thailand, Zambia in the 1990s, Dominican Republic (after the mid-1990s), and Kenya (after the late 1990s). Data show that abstinence and faithfulness are realistic behaviors for most Africans.

Abstinence and fidelity may also have a higher chance of sustained success than condom use, which is often sporadic and inconsistent, and which may rely on availability more than resolve. More than half of African youth aged 15 to 19 years report abstaining from premarital sex in the previous year, according to DHS data For example, 64 percent of Zambian youth had no sex partner last year, 78 percent of Ugandan youth had no sex partner in the previous year, and in some countries an even higher proportion reported abstinence. Most sexually active adults, whether married or not, report having only one partner in the previous year. In Uganda, this figure was 93 percent. Condom adoption is sometimes assumed to be a simpler behaviour change to adopt than that of abstinence or faithfulness. Yet condom use, especially correct and consistent condom use, is also a difficult and demanding behaviour change. Part of the proof of this observation is the disappointingly low levels of consistent condom use after more than 20 years of condom promotion in the developing world.

Is the ABC Approach Unrealistic for Women?

The argument is often made that women do not have the choice to abstain or practice faithfulness. It is a tragic fact that women who have practiced premarital abstinence and marital fidelity have become infected by unfaithful partners. Some women and girls may be in situations where sex is coerced by various circumstances, such as poverty or a difficult marriage. Condoms are often proposed as the solution for these women, and the ABC approach supports condom use for those at risk of HIV transmission. Yet condom use can be difficult if not impossible to negotiate for a women in a coercive situation. As for married people, or others in regular sexual relationships, empirical data and anecdotal evidence show that condoms are rarely used by married couples. African women have more power than they are given credit for—power that must extend to being able to refuse unwanted sex and not just negotiating condom use. Between 75 percent and 92 percent of Ugandan women say they can refuse sex, or sex without a condom, for reasons such as suspecting that their husband has an STI or is unfaithful, according to the DHS. Although this is a greater percentage than in many other African countries, most women in other countries also report that they have the power to refuse sex with their husbands. For instance, 73 percent of women in Malawi, 87 percent in Rwanda, 82 percent in Tanzania, and 71 percent in Zimbabwe said that they could refuse sex with their husbands if they knew their husbands had STIs.

What is the solution for women who truly do lack the power to refuse unwanted—and often risky—sex? Women who do not have the power to say no to unwanted sex probably do not have the power to insist on condom use. While much attention has been given to developing products that women can control, female condoms cannot be used without the male partner's knowledge, and a safe and effective vaginal microbicide has yet to be developed. The best solution is for more men to be faithful and more women to be empowered to be able to refuse sex (or refuse sex without a condom). That is, the B of ABC is urgently needed. The B message must also address cross-generational sex, including the rape and seduction of minor girls by older men. Uganda provides evidence that far from being insensitive to the needs and status of women, an ABC approach can go hand in hand with raising the status of women and the social responsibility of men. Under Uganda's ABC approach, women were empowered to leave husbands and boyfriends who were unfaithful and were putting them at risk for infection. More women became economically independent, and more women and girls went further in their education. Uganda also targeted men and boys with abstinence and "zero grazing" messages, which is crucial to achieving behaviour change given prevailing power disparities between genders.

The official guidance provided by the Office of the Global AIDS Coordinator calls for communities to mobilize to reduce the vulnerability of women: Communities must mobilize to address the norms, attitudes, values, and behaviors that increase vulnerability to HIV, including the acceptance or tolerance of multiple casual sex partnerships, cross-generational and transactional sex, forced sex, the unequal status of women, and the sexual coercion and exploitation of young people. To stimulate such mobilization, there is an urgent need to help communities identify the ways in which they contribute to establishing and reinforcing norms that contribute to risk, vulnerability, and stigma, and to help communities identify interventions that can change norms, attitudes, values, and behaviors that increase vulnerability to HIV.

Do the ABCs consider local realities such as gender and social inequalities, poverty, and cultural impediments to behaviour change? The ABC approach focuses on what individuals can do to change (or maintain) behaviour, and thereby avoid or reduce risk of infection. Those who would put their AIDS prevention energies and resources into calling for structural changes such as eradicating poverty or civil unrest should consider whether these factors can be influenced, within a reasonable time frame, and within the budget of AIDS programs. In countries such as Uganda where an ABC approach has been successful, broader goals such as empowering women, increasing access to education, and decreasing poverty, were also pursued. Yet these broader societal and structural goals may not be fully achievable in the short or even medium-term. In Uganda, HIV prevention was successful even though these broader goals had not been fully met. As changing structural inequalities are usually outside one individual's control, the ABC approach focuses on what most individuals can change and control, in the short-term.

When it comes to practical, workable AIDS prevention, what kinds of messages are useful to individuals at risk of HIV? Clearly, we cannot ask an African villager to reduce poverty or change laws to empower women. These things are not within an individual's control. Behaviour change messages should focus on things that usually (but not always) *are* within such control, such as remaining monogamous or using a condom. It may also be feasible to begin changing sociocultural norms that can facilitate AIDS prevention and stigma reduction, starting with individual change. An example would be making it (more) socially disapproved and disparaged for adult men to entice and seduce school-age girls. On the intervention side, this process might involve participatory dramas and role plays, reinforced by posters and billboards. Broader, complementary structural changes may also be possible in the short-to medium-term.

For example, countries can enact "defilement laws" that make intercourse with a woman under age 18 a criminal offense, as was done in Uganda. Such laws can in turn be influential in changing social norms and lead indirectly to reduced HIV infection rates. Does the ABC approach contribute to the stigmatization and marginalization of PLWHAs? Many public health strategies promote healthy behaviors that not everyone in a population is capable of, or willing to, adopt. Although this may be felt to stigmatize and marginalize those who do not adopt those healthy behaviors, the benefit for those who do adopt healthy behaviors may outweigh the risks of stigmatizing some. Consider a parallel. While the best public health campaigns about the dangers of smoking may not persuade all smokers to stop smoking, and may in fact make some smokers feel stigmatized, anti-smoking campaigns have proven to be effective. It is widely believed that the health, economic and environmental benefits of decreased smoking justify some stigmatization of those who continue to smoke.

In fact, anti-smoking campaigns in the United States have been largely successful, and rates of lung cancer have fallen. In the face of the health crisis of HIV/AIDS, advocates of an ABC approach feel that it is justified to promote an approach that has been effective in changing sexual behaviour and saving lives. Some people may feel marginalised or stigmatized by an ABC approach, for example if one does or does not engage in A, B or C behaviors, there could be social disapproval by some. Yet to object to an ABC approach on these grounds ignores the great benefit of such an approach to most people in a population. Specifically, to object to the promotion of abstinence and faithfulness because some will not or cannot abstain or be faithful ignores the fact that this message is appropriate for most people.

These DHS survey findings appear greatly at variance with popular stereotypes of African sexual behaviour. Indeed, risk reduction programs are justified by the alleged "reality" that Africans have many sexual partners and women in particular can do nothing about this. DHS data show that only 3 percent of African women report multiple sex partners in the previous year, and this figure has been quietly decreasing in recent years, beneath the "radar screen" of public discourse about global AIDS.

Have the US Government imposed the ABC approach on people in the developing world?

The President's Emergency Plan for AIDS Relief has adopted an ABC approach for generalized HIV/AIDS epidemics, using Uganda's experience as a model. Some observers allege that the ABC approach is driven by the ideology of US conservatives, and that PEPFAR inappropriately imposed it on other countries. In fact, the ABC approach was developed and successfully implemented by Africans, without significant involvement of the US or other large donor organizations. Although Ugandans did not invent the ABC approach or necessarily use the term "ABC" in the beginning of the pandemic, Uganda's response was to promote abstinence, faithfulness, and later, condom use. Other countries in Africa have since adopted an ABC approach, but Uganda still provides the best example of a balanced and successful implementation of the approach.

Far from dictating prevention approaches to Africans, PEPFAR has learned from an indigenous African approach. Africans, and particularly Ugandans, should be given the credit for an approach that was culturally relevant, very low cost, and very successful.

Even if the ABC approach did work in Uganda, is there evidence that it could work in other countries? The ABC approach has been implemented to varying degrees in Senegal, Jamaica, Zambia, Kenya, and among Thailand's general population, and elsewhere, with varying degrees of positive results in at least the countries just named. In Zambia, there were significant declines in HIV among youth in the 1990s, but this was not sustained after about 1998. Kenya may provide the most recent example of a successful ABC approach. In Kenya, the major response to AIDS before 1999 was condom supply and promotion. There was little or no impact on the pandemic. Finally, the Kenyan government implemented an ABC approach. In addition, faith-based groups were mobilized. AIDS education was implemented in schools. Educators and officials emphasized the seriousness of the epidemic, and government officials were told that they must mention AIDS every time they had a public meeting.

There was a significant increase in proportion of unmarried people reporting no sex in the past year, and a roughly 50 percent decline in the proportion reporting more than two partners in past year, among both men and women. What impact did this have? Comparisons between population-based and antenatal clinic (ANC) surveys, using sophisticated statistical techniques, "suggest that the epidemic in Kenya peaked in the late 1990s with an overall prevalence of 10 percent in adults, and declined to 6.7 percent by 200322." And the B component is again looking like the crucial factor associated with national HIV prevalence decline, just as in Uganda. Those reporting two or more partners in the past year in the 2003 DHS were twice as likely to be HIV-infected as those reporting one partner.

National prevalence is now slightly lower than that of Uganda, which is estimated at 7 percent using the same population-based method. The fact that 80 percent of Kenyan men are circumcised likely contributes to lower infections rates in Kenya. Conclusion This paper has devoted much effort to explaining and defending the AB components of ABC because these components are the least understood and raise the most concerns – not necessarily among the public, but among those who work in key AIDS and reproductive health organizations, including the decision makers and program implementers. The major organizations and agencies working in AIDS, such as USAID, UNAIDS, the World Bank, the WHO, the EU, as well as implementers such as Family Health International and Population Services International, have several decades of experience in designing and implementing condom programs.

There is no such experience with AB programs. These key organizations have not put significant resources into abstinence or faithfulness interventions anywhere in the world, although this began to change in 2002-3 when USAID and PEPFAR adopted a Uganda-style ABC approach for countries with generalized epidemics.

Yet even within these agencies, there has been confusion, resistance, fear, rumour, political and ideological debate, misunderstanding and misrepresentation of the Uganda ABC approach, notably the new AB components. There has also been resistance to, and misinformation about, condoms. But condom opponents or doubters are not normally represented in the AIDS and reproductive health organizations. Those unwilling to promote condoms were simply excluded from work in AIDS prevention programs that benefited from funding from major donor organizations, at least before passage of a Congressional amendment in 2003. For example, Roman Catholic groups did not receive AIDS prevention funds.

Yet if the United States is following the Uganda approach, it should be realized that the Ugandan government funnelled foreign donor funds to local Catholic NGOs from very early in the epidemic, knowing that Catholics:

(1) represented nearly 40% of the population;
(2) were willing and able to promote effectively the AB components of AIDS prevention;
(3) were already major players in care and support of PLWHAs, orphans and vulnerable children, etc, as well as in the treatment of PLWHAs;
(4) would be less likely to oppose condom promotion if they were working collaboratively with major donors and NGOs in prevention.

We agree with the consensus statement published in the Lancet and endorsed by over 150 scientists, NGO AIDS workers, activists, and President

Museveni of Uganda, namely: All three elements of this approach are essential to reducing HIV incidence, although the emphasis placed on individual elements needs to vary according to the target population. Although the overall programmatic mix should include an appropriate balance of A,B, and C interventions, it is not essential that every organisation promote all three elements: each can focus on the parts they are most comfortable supporting. However, all people should have accurate and complete information about different prevention options, including all three elements of the ABC approach. Some observers have suggested that the AB components are no longer relevant in "mature epidemics," such as Uganda's. We have addressed this question above, and the most recent public statement from the Ugandan government—the lead author being the official who ran the Uganda's national AIDS Control program in the earliest years—is that ABC is needed even more in the era of antiretroviral treatment:

Abstinence, being faithful, and condom use are complementary, synergistic, and inseparable components in the country's HIV/AIDS national prevention and control programmes, and we need to roll out these prevention messages with extra urgency now, in the era of ART. Finally, we wish to stress that we are not arguing for shifting attention and resources away from those at special high risk, including the powerless, oppressed, exploited, raped and abused. We *are* saying that it is inaccurate to characterize (all) Africans this way, and that we can no longer base *all* our AIDS prevention resources to this minority target group. It is a tragedy that all-or-nothing thinking and polemics have dominated the AIDS debate to date, e.g., either one *cares* about the oppressed and therefore conducts AIDS prevention the risk-reduction way, or one is heartless and uncaring.

What has been missing in this bitter debate is a calm, even-handed, balanced viewpoint that recognizes that *some* resources clearly *must* be targeted to high-risk groups, while *some* resources must be directed to what survey and epidemiological evidence show are the *majority* of people – Africans, in the context of this review. To do only the former is to effectively ignore most Africans in prevention efforts. Meanwhile to do both need not result in diminished quality or even quantity of prevention resources going to either group, the minority or the majority. It is only catastrophist, polemical, all-or-nothing thinking that would have us believe otherwise. If Uganda, with very few resources in the early years of its response to AIDS could design and implement a *balanced and targeted* ABC program, surely the major donors with billions of dollars can do the same.

Condom Controversy

Father Michael Stogre S.J., in an article on AIDS in The Catholic Register, May 22, 2005, stated that "Currently, when a spouse has AIDS-the use of condoms to prevent transmission of the virus is more and more being seen not as a contraceptive measure, but as a justifiable medical intervention."

Support for the use of condoms to prevent the spread of HIV/AIDS has recently come from some surprising sources-cardinals, individual bishops and Catholic bishops' conferences. Since 2004, support has been expressed by the bishops' conferences of Spain, Mexico, and England and Wales (through its agency, the Catholic Agency for Overseas Development). The French bishops expressed their support in 1996. Supporting cardinals included Murhpy-O'Connor (Westminster England), Daneels (Brussels, Belgium), Barragan (President of the Pontifical Council for Health Care Workers), and Cottier (household theologian to Pope John Paul 11). The supporting bishops are Kevin Dowling (South Africa), and Fabian Marulauda (Colombia). The Spanish bishops' subsequent clarification said that responsible and moral sexual activity is the only "advisable" way to avoid disease. The statement stopped short of the Catholic teaching that sexual abstinence and faithfulness in marriage are the only morally permissible means of avoiding disease. One is forced to ask the question whether this clerical support is morally correct and based on sound medical science?

Catholic Moral Teaching

- The nature of an act (its object) determines its morality. Intercourse with a condom is intrinsically disordered, evil in and of itself.
- The intention of the acting person is important, but it cannot change the nature of the act of intercourse with a condom. It remains an intrinsic evil.
- The reason why a good intention is not in itself sufficient, but a correct choice of actions is needed, is that the human act depends on its object, whether that object is capable or not of being ordered to God-thus bringing about the perfection of the person. (Veritatis Splendor, n.80). "...reason attests that there are objects of the human act which are by their nature incapable of being ordered to God, because they radically contradict the good of the person made in his image. These are the acts which, in the Church's moral tradition, have been termed intrinsically evil' (intrinsece malum) on account of their very object, and quite apart from ulterior intentions of the one acting and the circumstances.".

- The law of "double effect" requires that if an action has two effects, the action itself must be morally good or indifferent. Since intercourse with a condom is intrinsically evil, the law of double effect does not apply.
- "Though it is true that sometimes it is lawful to tolerate a lesser evil to avoid a greater moral evil or in order to promote a greater moral good, it is never lawful, even for the gravest reasons, to do evil that good may come of it.". When comparing greater or lesser evils, the comparison must be between evils of a similar nature. Risk of disease is a physical and not a moral evil, whereas intercourse with a condom is a moral evil. Some theologians hold that the risk of HIV infection is more evil than the use of a condom to reduce that risk. This statement is not doctrinally sound.
- To advise or suggest evil is to induce evil and that is always a scandal. Msgr. Vincent Foy states that in considering the question of the lesser evil, some distinctions must be made between homosexual intercourse and heterosexual intercourse and also between intrinsic and extrinsic factors.

"Homosexual intercourse: It is true that, intrinsically, homosexual intercourse with or without a condom are equivalent moral evils, even though they are not precisely the same act. In both there is sodomitical intent.

"Extrinsically, sodomy with or without a condom is not a moral equivalent. A condom must be obtained and obtaining a condom for sex is a moral evil, both in itself and by support of the condom industry. Obtaining a condom may or may not give scandal.

Obtaining a condom makes the sin of sodomy more likely and its repetition more probable. Repetition can lead to a habit of perversion and greater likelihood of loss of faith and damnation. It also leads to greater danger of the physical evil called AIDS. When one is told that condom use is the lesser evil, the advice may be perceived as undue toleration of evil and neglect of proper spiritual direction.

"Heterosexual intercourse: In heterosexual intercourse, and that means 95% of intercourse, the moral evil of using a condom is greater both intrinsically and extrinsically.

"Intrinsically the act is transformed from a natural one to an unnatural one even when contraception does not take place. Even spouses who are sterile may not use a condom to protect themselves from infection because the inherent unity and procreative nature of the conjugal act is destroyed. It becomes and act of mutual self-abuse. Intrinsically, there is a greater moral evil when the condom acts as a contraceptive. Contraception is an intrinsic evil and immoral whether in or out of marriage.

"Extrinsically, condom use brings its own train of evils. There is the act of obtaining or receiving a condom. Condom possession may be a constant temptation to sin as well as an instrument of seduction. It may lead to a habit of fornication and a contraceptive mentality that may destroy a future marriage. Another extrinsic possibility is the multiplication of malefactors, not only condom manufacturers and vendors, but school boards, or trustees, or teachers, or counsellors, or chaplains, who advise condom use, or neglect the spiritual direction needed by the young. So in heterosexual intercourse, there are both intrinsic and extrinsic reasons to say that to use a condom is never the lesser sin." It is clear that support for the use of the condom to prevent spread of HIV is in contradiction to Church teaching.

5

NGO Activity: Positive and Negative Aspects

Environmentally sound decisions are reflected in legal actions adopted by state and local government bodies and constituent entities. Their execution has to do with individual sites and with the natural environment as a whole. The decisions must have an ecological basis and pass the environmental examination and public hearing process.

The following decisions on large-scale projects have been made by the Tomsk Oblast agencies taking into account public opinion:

- o Stoppage of gravel extraction from the Tom River bed. (A public organization, the Committee for Conservation of the Tom)
- o Ban on construction of a nutritional supplement biotechnology plant. (A public organization, the Ecological Initiative)
- o Removal from service three of five reactors of the Siberian Chemical Complex. (A public organization, the Ecological Initiative)
- o Ban on containers for storing fissile materials received from military units under the governmental decision on sharp reduction of nuclear warheads in Russia. (A public organization, the Ecological Initiative) The activity of NGOs made it possible to deepen public understanding of environmental problems and to exert pressure upon Tomsk Oblast agencies. One example is the public hearing held in September 2000 on the premises of the Tomsk Oblast Administration. The public hearing or, to be more precise, a discussion on construction of the Seversk Nuclear Power Station (NHS-500), took place due to inquiries of public organizations and citizens under the federal law "On Using Atomic Energy" (Articles 11 and 14). Effective actions that had been carried out by public organizations of Tomsk, Moscow, and other towns forced the Tomsk Oblast government to conclude that the designers of the

NHS-500 project must eliminate all shortcomings and violations of environmental legislation related to the project. The local authorities also decided that the NHS-500 project must be revised drastically in view of comments expressed at the public discussion.

The public discussion on construction of the Seversk Nuclear Power Station was the first large-scale public action in the region. All interested persons could take part. Those who were not able to make personal presentations could send their written proposals to the Tomsk Oblast government for consideration. Under the law, decisions of the government agencies must be officially published for the information of the general public, although this has not yet been done. A large number of Tomsk city and oblast public organizations and movements are involved in environmental problems. In 1999 there were more than ten public organizations working in the following areas:

- o Free expression of opinion
- o Participation in development of normative acts
- o Referenda on problems of environmental protection
- o Environmental examinations
- o Construction projects and selection of sites
- o Public environmental monitoring
- o Ecological education

Let us briefly summarize achievements of the main local public organizations. The Tomsk Environmental Student Inspection (TESI) is a public organization created in October 1999. It has more than 200 members, primarily students of Tomsk. Much attention was given to TESI by the local mass media in 1999. Forty- seven articles were published in the regional newspapers; the town and regional radio stations broadcast 51 reports; and four local TV channels devoted 11 reports to its work. TESI is a major organizer of environmental demonstrations. The Tomsk Oblast Council of the All-Russian Nature Protection Society was founded in 1992. One of the main tasks of the Council is a TV program, "The Ecology Club," devoted to the environmental problems of Tomsk Oblast. A distinctive feature of TESI is its corps of inspectors.

Members have the status of non-staff inspectors of the State Committee for Protection of the Natural Environment. Under the law "On Non-Staff Environmental Inspection," TESI has the right to conduct inspections of different enterprises and plants and to make claims against inappropriate use of the natural environment. In 1999, TESI members carried out 165 inspections in the industrial zones of Tomsk and the oblast. In the course of inspections they prepared 81 claims, and they imposed 73 fines totaling 7,130 rubles. In 1999, complex explorations of the Ob, the Tom, and the Ushaika rivers were conducted under the TESI environmental program "Clean Rivers." The Environmental Legal Center is a public organization founded in 1996 with the objectives of protecting citizens' rights to a safe environment and monitoring environmental legislation.

Its members are intellectuals, students of the Tomsk colleges, and farmers. The Center keeps in touch with prominent scientists. The Center deals with bans on environmentally hazardous activity and compensation for damage caused by abusing the right to a safe environment. The Center supports appeals against actions (or inactions) of state bodies violating citizens' non-property rights.

Recently the Supreme Court Judiciary Board overturned the Tomsk local court decision on a license for disposal of liquid radioactive wastes in the ground water areas of Seversk. The license was issued by the local administration to the Siberian Chemical Complex in 1996. The Environmental Initiative movement (EI) was founded in 1989 with the primary goal of providing a public focus for anti-nuclear activity. The main achievements are the following:

- A 1989 ban on construction of a nutrition supplement biotechnology plant.
- Support of the Krapivinsky water reservoir construction (1989-90).
- Obtaining about 100,000 signatures to ban storage containers for fissile materials received from military units.

EI's primary goal is to counteract the plans of the Ministry of Atomic Energy to start construction of a nuclear-powered heating plant (AST-500) attached to the Siberian Chemical Complex. The goal is to be achieved by dissemination of reliable information about the hazardous impact of the complex on the environment and on the health of the population. EI also tries to expose "the nuclear myths" about the illusory low-price, ecological safety, and harmlessness of nuclear energy. A Tomsk Oblast public organization, the Wind Rose, was founded in 1992 with the purpose of attracting local attention to environmental problems, to ecologically safe commercial activity, and to ecological education. It has 10 members.

The organization has developed the following actions and publications: a training program of continuous ecological education for schoolchildren, a textbook, Education in Nature Protection: Elementary Course, and a textbook on ecology, Changing the World. It set up an ecological club, The Road to the

Twenty-First Century, for pupils and students. It held an Internet conference, Environmental Security, and published materials of the conference.

A roundtable, The Tomsk Oblast's Pupils' and Students' Participation in Solving Regional Environment Problems, was held in November 1999. Teachers, lecturers, and local public organization representatives were among the participants. The subject was methods for informal ecological education such as tourism, clubs of ecologists, teenage environmental projects, Internet and e-mail, and cooperation with the mass media.

An ecological and ethnographical excursion called Elan was organized in September 1999. Twenty-four pupils and three teachers took part. A textbook on ecological-ethnographical excursions and games was developed. An information bulletin EKObanderol [ECO Mailbag] is being published. If necessary it can include urgent information, such as developments in Yugoslavia (NATO strikes and the environmental consequences). A youth organization, Siberian House, was created in 1974 on the base of the Explorer tourist brigade. The team includes 20 youngsters and five tutors. The main activities are regional ethnography studies, summer camps, and sporting contests. One goal is exploration of rare sites of nature with visits to 19 sites. To clarify the formal status and legal base of the sites, appropriate documentation has been submitted to the Oblast Administration.

The Nature House is a children's ecological and tourist organization and has created reasonable attitudes to nature protection. The Aliom Club is an environmental educational society created to popularize ecologically safe technologies. Scientists, managers, engineers, and technologists are among its members.

The Tomsk Oblast Scout Center is an organization related to tourism and ecological education. Its activity stretches over seven regions. The number of scouts is about 500. In Chainsk district a school scout team cooperates with the local forest management authorities in the village of Podgornoye.

The tourist club Odyssey is a public organization created to organize tourism and ecological education. The Strezhevoi Ecological-Biological Center (the township of Strezhevoi) is a public organization dealing with ecological education and fostering. Summing up, the above public organizations are of great benefit to the community as well as to the region as a whole. In conclusion, let us make some recommendations on increasing the role of nongovernmental organizations in the environmental decision-making process. Is it difficult for state bodies to coordinate the activity of the public environmental organizations? Among the different laws currently in force, there are inconsistencies in regulations relating to public participation in managing state affairs. However, public environmental organizations must be able to make their own contributions. Adoption of appropriate normative acts is the only way out of the situation. It is these acts that provide for comprehensive and adequate public participation in environmentally sound decision-making.

Also, it is necessary to carry out training courses on management and sustainable development for nongovernmental organizations. Problems of preventing environmental harm and compensation are of extreme concern for the population. However, the solution is being implemented by "residual financing." Financial sources and the measures to prevent and compensate environmental harm should be determined by law. Nowadays it may be worthwhile to combine all financial payments to the local budget for utilization of natural resources in a joint natural resources restoration fund. The fund could allow for local government bodies to focus financial means on strategic directions. Payments for utilization of subsurface resources could form the principal part of the fund. Use of the funds for improvement and restoration of water resources, biological resources, and wild nature sites.

INTERACTION OF NONGOVERNMENTAL ORGANIZATIONS AND REGIONAL AUTHORITIES IN SOLVING PROBLEMS OF THE LAKE BAIKAL REGION

The UN Conference on Environment and Development (Rio de Janeiro, 1992) has proclaimed the concept of sustainable development as a basis for a new paradigm of future development of our civilization and has adopted a program of actions when entering the twenty-first century (The Agenda for the Twenty-First Century). Principle 4 of the adopted Declaration states: "In order to achieve sustainable development, environmental protection shall constitute an integral part of the development process and cannot be considered in isolation from it." The Lake Baikal region is an example of a territory that has not only national, but also international importance. It has an eternal value not only for Russians, but also for the whole of mankind. Lake Baikal is the most ancient lake on the planet. Its age is about 25-30 million years. It is the deepest lake, with a depth of 1,637 meters. It contains a tremendous volume of water-23,000 cubic kilometers or 23 percent of the world's resources of pure fresh water. It is also one of the largest in areal expanse.

According to present-day data, the genetic diversity of Baikal includes 2,565 species and subspecies of aquatic fauna and 1,000 species and subspecies of aquatic plants, of which two-thirds are endemic, meaning they are found nowhere else. To this number one should add many hundreds of species of water and bottom micro- organisms as well as viruses and microbes that have been little investigated. Thus, the diversity of Baikal has no equal in the world, and Lake Baikal is included in the UNESCO World Nature Heritage List of 1996.

What is the Baikal region? This is a region directly connected with the internationally known Lake Baikal and located in the center of Asia on the territory of two states, Russia and Mongolia. The territory of the Baikal region stretches from south to north for 1300 km, and from west to east for 1,000 km. Its total area is 800,000 sq. km. The unique combination of various landscapes in the center of Asia-from mountain-tundra and mountain-taiga to steppe and semi-desert along with the largest and most ancient freshwater reservoir-is of special significance and value in the biosphere structure of the planet as a whole. The Baikal watershed occupies territory in the southeast of Siberia and the northern part of Mongolia.

The largest part is located in Russia, where it has been divided without taking into account the lake's area over several administrative and territorial entities of the Russian Federation: Republic of Buryatia-73 percent, Chita Oblast-21 percent, Irkutsk Oblast-6 percent. The Baikal ecosystem has become better known just as its protection and rational use have become more complicated. New territories located outside the bounds of the lake's watershed have been included in the Baikal region, including that part of Irkutsk Oblast that adjoins the northwest boundary of the Baikal watershed. It is up to 200 km. wide and regarded as a zone from which atmospheric emissions of industrial installations may reach the watershed.

At present in accordance with the Law of the Russian Federation "On Protection of Lake Baikal," the Baikal region is divided into three zones:

- o Central ecological zone ("the core")-territory that includes Lake Baikal and islands, a water protection zone adjacent to Lake Baikal, and protected natural territories adjacent to Lake Baikal;
- o Buffer ecological zone-territory outside the central ecological zone that includes the watershed of Lake Baikal within the bounds of the Russian Federation;
- o Ecological zone of atmospheric effect-territory outside the watershed of Lake Baikal within the bounds of the Russian Federation up to 200 km. wide to the north and northwest of the watershed where there are economic units with activity that has a negative influence on Lake Baikal. Such a division of the Baikal region is an important condition

for preservation of Baikal as a part of the World Nature Heritage. At the same time, the Baikal region is characterized by considerable development of industry and agriculture, which cannot avoid affecting the condition of the lake. Therefore, the question of a balanced solution of ecological and socio- economic problems is especially acute here.

The following ecological problems of the Baikal region are priority issues:

o The natural conditions of the geosystem components

o Preservation of a large amount of biological diversity

o Consequences of industrial and agricultural development

o Use of reliable ecological information

The natural conditions of the Baikal region require accurate methods of investigations for measuring the parameters of water and ground ecosystems and the air basin. For the most part the region is still not polluted. While solving the questions of environmental protection in the Baikal region, particular attention must be paid to preservation of biological diversity which means, according to the Convention on Biological Diversity, variability of living organisms from all sources including soil, sea, and other water ecosystems as well as ecological complexes including these components. For addressing the questions of preservation of the Baikal region, the normative-legal basis includes both international documents and the laws of the Russian Federation:

o Convention on Biological Diversity, Rio de Janeiro, 1992.

o Convention on Protection of the World Cultural and Natural Heritage, 1972.

o All-European Strategy of Preservation of Biological and Landscape Biodiversity, Sofia, 1995.

o Convention on Assessment of Environmental Effects in a Transboundary Context, 1991.

o Federal law "On Natural Environment Preservation," 1991.

o Federal law "On Ecological Examination," 1995.

o Federal law "On Especially Protected Territories," 1990.

o Federal law "On Protection of Lake Baikal," 1999.

o Water Code of the Russian Federation.

o Forest Code of the Russian Federation.

o "On State Strategy of the Russian Federation Regarding Environmental

Protection and Ensuring Sustainable Development," the Edict of the President of the Russian Federation of February 4, 1994, # 236.

o "Conception of Transition of the Russian Federation to Sustainable

Development," the Edict of the President of the Russian Federation of April 1, 1996, #440.

- o "National Plan of Action for Environmental Protection of the Russian Federation in 1999-2001." Approved at the meeting of the Government of the Russian Federation on November 12, 1998.
- o "Strategy of Sustainable Development of the Russian Federation." Approved at the meeting of the Government of the Russian Federation in December 1997.

Thus, in the Russian Federation there are a number of strategic planning documents in the field of environmental protection and Sustainable development that have not yet been put in a strict hierarchical order due to the fact that the legislation in this field is relatively new. However these documents can already be used as a legislative basis.

In the Baikal region a number of attempts have been made by state structures and public organizations to implement programs aimed at preservation. The state documents on Baikal preservation are as follows: o Resolution of the Central Committee of the Communist Party of the Soviet Union and the USSR Council of Ministers of April 13, 1987, # 434, "On Arrangements to Ensure Protection and Rational Use of Natural Resources of the Lake Baikal Basin in 1987-1995."

- o "Territorial Integrated Scheme of Protection of Nature in the Lake Baikal Basin," approved on April 14, 1990, by the Resolution of the Presidium of the Russian Federation Council of Ministers.
- o "Integrated Federal Program of Ensuring Lake Baikal Preservation and Rational Use of Natural Resources of Its Basin," 1994.

The role of nongovernmental public organizations in implementing the above decisions is difficult to overestimate. The destiny of "the sacred sea," as people living on the banks of Baikal call the lake, has worried both children and old people. This is evident from signatures for preservation of the unique Baikal, demonstrations, appearances on television, and unauthorized signs reading "Let us preserve Baikal" on the chimneys of the Baikal Pulp and Paper Plant. The most active supporters of environmental protection in the Baikal region are the following public organizations:

- o Baikal Ecological Wave, which has organized regular publication of the ecological magazine Wave.
- o Baikal Ecological Parliament, with prominent scientists from Irkutsk as its members.
- o Revival of the Land of Siberia.
- o Greenpeace.

The above public organizations are in continuous contact with local government institutions. They participate in all ecological decisions without exception. In particular, they put forward the idea of instituting Baikal Day, which since 1999 has been routinely conducted at the end of August-beginning of September in the form of various actions for the protection of the lake, thereby joining the efforts of local governing institutions and various ecological movements.

In March 1998, the Limnological Institute in Irkutsk and the Baikal Institute of Nature Management in Ulan-Ude, with the support of ecological organizations of Irkutsk Oblast and the Republic of Buryatia, started implementation of a TACIS project "Assistance in Gaining Ecological Information and Its Dissemination among the Population of the Baikal Region." The financial support was provided by the European Union and the technical support by the Society of Technical Assistance (Germany). The aim of the project is to distribute information among the population and organizations responsible for decision-making in the field of environmental protection. As a result of the joint work conducted by a large number of state and public ecological organization as well as institutions of basic and additional education, the Baikal Ecological Information Network has been established. Its participants are located in 12 towns of Irkutsk Oblast alone.

The inhabitants of the Baikal region realize that they are responsible to the whole of mankind and future generations for preservation of the world pearl, Lake Baikal. The ecological conditions in our region are very tense and complicated. Thus, realizing their personal responsibility, more and more people are standing up for environmental protection. People also realize that nothing will change if the way of thinking remains unchanged. But it can be changed only if there is reliable information. Ecological workers understand the importance and necessity of ecological education; but very often they have no possibility to obtain the information they need, even though such information is available at research institutes situated in the Baikal region. In Irkutsk alone there are nine institutes of the Russian Academy of Sciences conducting research on nature management. The organizers and those implementing the above mentioned project have identified the following problems:

- To collect and process ecological information and make it accessible to all those who need it.
- To establish a standing network of ecological organizations of Irkutsk Oblast and the Republic of Buryatia, including consumers and distributors of this information.

The project participants have defined the concept of providing the population of the Baikal region with information as a strategy of collecting, processing, and presenting data about natural resources of the territory based on the principles of integration and legal responsibility, using up-to-date information technologies to make well-grounded decisions regarding nature management in the region. Now the important tasks for teachers, ecologists, and progressive groups of the population are not only the ecological orientation of the public and providing the population with information, but also the task of promoting civic positions and stimulating social activities for democratization of ecological knowledge.

The implementation of this large-scale TACIS project has resulted in:

- o Establishing the Baikal Ecological Information Network.
- o Obtaining a large number of computers.
- o Establishing contacts with ecological organizations from other countries and regions (ISAR, Social Information Agency, the American organization Sacred Earth Network, and others).
- o Participating in preparation of the state report "On the Status of Environmental Conditions of Irkutsk Oblast," which says, "In arranging ecological education of the population there must be coordinated efforts of the government organs; environmental, educational, scientific, and public organizations; and the mass media."

The importance of continuous ecological education is clear to all the participants in the Baikal Ecological Information Network. Most of them have been closely cooperating with each other and with other organizations in this important task. Another example of cooperation between local autonomous bodies and public organizations is the Russian-Canadian project on cooperation in decision-making in the field of environmental protection and, in particular, the Irkutsk component, "Water Resources Management in the Angara River Basin." During the 1998-2000 period, the project organizers combined the efforts of state authorities and public organizations of Irkutsk Oblast in arriving at a "consensus" in decision-making in the field of environmental protection. Some of the project participants are:

- o State Committee on Environmental Protection
- o Committee on Natural Resources
- o Department of Nature Management, Irkutsk Oblast Administration
- o Angara-Baikal Basin Water Department
- o Irkutsk Territory Department of Hydrology, Meteorology, and Environmental Monitoring

- o Irkutsk Hydro-Electric Station Administration
- o Irkutskenergo Joint-Stock Company
- o Baikal-Angara Department of Waterways and Navigation
- o Committee on Nature Management Legislation and Ecology of the Irkutsk Oblast Legislative Assembly
- o Limnological Institute, Russian Academy of Sciences (RAS)
- o Institute of Geography, RAS
- o Energy Systems Institute, RAS
- o Institute of Geochemistry, RAS
- o Institute of the Earth's Crust, RAS
- o Institute of Plant Physiology and Biochemistry, RAS
- o Institute of Biological Research at Irkustk State University
- o Irkutsk Refrigeration Industrial Complex (state-owned enterprise)
- o Irkutsk Housing Design and Construction Administration
- o Science in Siberia (publication)
- o Academy of Water Industry
- o Children's Ecological Organization of the city of Angarsk
- o Baikal Ecological Education (public organization)
- o Regional Ecological Forecasting (research and production firm)
- o Baikal Ecological Wave (public organization)
- o Civic Informational Initiative (public organization)
- o Irkutsk Branch of the All-Russian Nature Protection Society
- o Mayor of the Usolye Administrative Region
- o Mayor of the town of Shelekhov.

In spite of the fact that the programs and governmental decisions regarding the Baikal region were only partially realized, progress has been made:

- o The Selenga Pulp and Paperboard Plant has converted to a closed-loop water consumption system.
- o Wood drift floating along Baikal's tributaries has been stopped.
- o Collection of waste water from boats in Lake Baikal has been put into practice.
- o Pollutant emissions to the atmosphere from the Baikal Pulp and Paper Plant have been reduced.
- o Hazardous substance discharges into Lake Baikal have been reduced.
- o Lake Baikal was put on the World Nature Heritage List by UNESCO.

- o The Law of the Russian Federation "On Lake Baikal Protection" was passed.
- o The Baikal state information system has been established.
- o Norms for permissible pollutant impact on the Baikal ecological system have been worked out, and a new ecological approach is under preparation.
- o Integrated ecological monitoring of the Baikal ecosystem is being conducted.
- o A new way of obtaining drinking water from the depths of Lake Bakial has been developed and patented, and production of bottled water has been organized as an alternative type of profitable production. At the same time, experience makes it possible to identify the reasons why environmental programs being realized by local government bodies in cooperation with public organizations and population are not completely effective.

They include:

- o Lack of a coordinated system of objectives and tasks being realized under various projects and programs.
- o Lack of an ecological basis in some programs.
- o Lack of economic, financial, and legal mechanisms due to budget constraints.
- o Methodological miscalculations, in particular, not taking into account the integrated ecological approach.
- o Unreasonable "centralization" and lack of orientation towards priorities of the concerned parties and users of the results of activities under the programs.

With regard to resource potential, this region has all the necessary qualities to be chosen as a "model" when elaborating the concept of sustainable development from the position of the Agenda for the Twenty-First Century. A rather well- preserved environment of the region, a huge resource potential, and a unique natural object-Lake Baikal with the surrounding landscapes-form a natural basis for the sustainable development process. On the other hand, the ecological fragility of the natural landscape system of the region, especially the ecosystem of Lake Baikal, will determine the high requirements for social and economic development processes, including the ethics and aesthetics of nature management oriented toward the future. Lake Baikal and the whole Baikal region should become an area for international cooperation of intellectual, financial, material, and human efforts aimed at solving the integrated problems of the survival of mankind and the preservation of the biosphere.

HIGHLIGHTS OF PRESENTATIONS

The list of organizations represented at this workshop provides a good overview of the types of environmental NGOs that are active in Russia and the United States. There are of course hundreds of others with special interests and unique approaches-at both the national and local levels. But in general, advocacy, analytical, and educational NGOs have been well represented. At the same time, the concept of NGOs is somewhat different in the two countries. An American environmental NGO is usually perceived as an organization established specifically to contribute to environmental improvement at the national or local level, or both. Professional societies (e.g., the American Chemical Society), nongovernmental laboratories supported by the federal government (e.g., Oak Ridge National Laboratory), and departments of universities, for example, are not usually considered to be environmental NGOs, even though Russian specialists might consider them to be an important form of NGOs.

In Russia there is a long history of many types of organizations outside the formal governmental structure participating in environmental protection activities that today are considered to be environmental NGOs. They include, for example, coordinating councils established by regional governments with common environmental interests, institutes of the Russian Academy of Sciences, government- sponsored citizen organizations, museums with environmental outreach programs, and societies that promote ecology programs for students. During the past decade, hundreds of western-style environmental NGOs have been established in Russia, many with strong international ties to western NGOs. Greenpeace is probably the leading example of this trend.

Several speakers have noted, however, that some of the new Russian NGOs, with far less stature than Greenpeace, are primarily interested not in championing environmental causes, but rather in serving as a vehicle for expressing dissent with broader governmental policies and in becoming conduits for western grants. Still, many new Russian NGOs are very vigorous advocates of greater attention to environmental concerns amidst the economic collapse in the country, and they certainly have carved out a permanent niche on the Russian landscape.

Some environmental NGOs in both countries are devoted to ensuring that decisions and policies taken by government, including the enforcement of environmental regulations, are in the best interests of the public. They use direct communications with governments, the power of the mass media, and the judicial system to achieve this goal. Others have assumed responsibilities not adequately handled by government agencies, such as packaging government information and data in a form that is understandable to both specialists and the public and in developing additional data relevant to governmental decisions. Others serve as rallying points for voices of the people or provide meeting grounds for polluters, the public, and government. Others direct their energies to education and training of both professionals and the public-offering courses, preparing educational literature, and generally supplementing activities of educational institutions by sharing experiences, developing new analytical techniques, and applying new methodological approaches. Still others serve as coordinating centers for governmental authorities and specialists from different regions of the country with common interests. Then there are hybrid organizations that assume several of these tasks and additional responsibilities as well.

The workshop addressed many environmental issues, with heavy reliance on case studies; and the discussions of immediate environmental problems placed the consideration of NGOs into a meaningful perspective. In the aggregate, NGOs are interested in all aspects of environmental protection. At the same time, several differences in the agendas of NGOs in Russia and the United States seemed apparent. Of course, the differences expressed at the workshop were somewhat influenced by the individual interests of the participants. The Russian emphasis on protection of forests and on the impacts of large-area radioactive contamination was understandable. The economic crisis has led to a deterioration of the technical and administrative capabilities to control pollution with the result that particulate and other common pollutants are of greater concern in Russia than in the United States.

Also, solid waste disposal is a serious problem in Russia, where segregation of wastes, recycling of wastes, and establishment of adequate landfills lag behind efforts in the United States. The U.S. effort, on the other hand, has increasingly focused on human health impacts of pollution. Control of toxic effluents and emissions is a high priority with risk assessment being an area of intensive development. Also, the United States is able to devote more resources to investigation and protection of biodiversity; and global environmental issues also receive increasing priority. In both countries, scientific research plays an important role in the work of NGOs. Many Russian presentations were by specialists of the institutes and centers of the Russian Academy of Sciences, clearly an important resource for NGOs. In the United

States, many NGOs now have internal scientific capabilities, which enhances their credibility in dealing with government agencies. In both countries, solid scientific data are important in convincing the government agencies, the legislative bodies, and the public to give greater priority to environmental concerns.

Turning to education and training, Russia has an impressive array of programs at both the high school and university levels. However, a recent law rescinds the long-standing requirement that an ecology component must be included in the mandatory-core high school curricula, leaving the decision on this matter up to local authorities when they prescribe the optional aspects of the curricula. Several universities have adopted "sustainable development" as a theme, and a number of NGOs work with the universities in this field. It is important that "sustainable" development not become "no" development, and the importance of economics in the work of the NGOs was recognized. One example of the tight linkage between NGOs and students is in the city of Tomsk, where students provide much of the core of the NGO movement.

The internet was repeatedly cited as an important tool for the NGOs. U.S. government agencies increasingly use the internet to disseminate important information related to their decisions; and this trend has been of considerable importance for NGOs. The role of e-mail in tightening the linkages among NGOs with common agendas is clear; but there are many uncertainties as to the environmental data that are disseminated on the internet, given the absence of good quality control mechanisms. Nevertheless, in the years ahead, internet communications and data transfer will be central to the activities of many NGOs. Several questions were not completely answered during the workshop, and they should help provide a framework for more focused workshops on the role of environmental NGOs that could be organized in the future.

- o What additional steps can the Russian Government take to facilitate the work of NGOs? The pending legislation to update the basic environment protection law addresses the role of NGOs, but will additional amendments be necessary? As the Ministry of Natural Resources absorbs its new responsibilities for protection of the environment and protection of forests, how will it ensure that NGOs continue to have access to governmental decision-making, how will it disseminate information to NGOs, and how will it support NGO activities at the local level?
- o Given the economic crisis, should Russian NGOs emphasize cooperation or confrontation with government agencies and with the polluters? Is the judicial system sufficiently responsive to environmental concerns

encapsulated in law suits to warrant greater efforts in the field of litigation- at the national and local levels? Are the councils supported by regional governments in the Urals and in Siberia useful models for replication in other areas? How can the Ministry of Defense and Ministry of Atomic Energy be encouraged to pay more attention to NGOs?

o What are the characteristics of successful NGOs? Is support by western grants an asset or a liability? Can the Russian Academy of Sciences' new committee on cooperation with environmental NGOs facilitate cooperation among the scientific community and environmental organizations in a manner that enhances the credibility and the impact of these organizations?

CLOSING REMARKS

This workshop was characterized by active participation of the attendees and proved of importance in further improving cooperation between ecological scientists and nongovernmental organizations. Reports of the Russian side showed that nongovernmental organizations have become real participants in dialogues during the decision-making process at local and regional levels all over the country from the Pacific Ocean to the Baltic and Barents Seas. The experience of the "Siberian Agreement" demonstrates the possibility of involving significant scientific centers for realization of large international projects.

The Kemerovo and Khabarovsk research centers of the Russian Academy of Sciences strongly contribute to establishing problem priorities, and they actively collaborate with social organizations in educational endeavors. The workshop agenda coincides with a priority set by Agenda 21, by other UN documents concerning sustainable development, and by instruction documents of UNESCO. All speakers and discussants especially stressed the importance of scientific education and help in interpretation of complex new interdisciplinary problems. We are very interested in the experience of the Hampshire Institute, a nongovernmental organization developing software for assessment of hazards due to different chemical pollutants in food and environment. Joint projects adapting this software for Russia can meet with support in our regions. Without doubt the experience of our American colleagues in database technologies would be very useful for us in making information available to everyone.

Reports devoted to interaction with the mass media, social organizations, and decision-makers were of significant mutual interest. Undoubtedly, the reports by Professors Kraft and Kokhanova and by Ms. O'Connell gave food for thought. These themes can serve also as research areas for joint projects.

All the participants came out in favor of continuation of such workshops. I expect the Cooperation Section of the Russian Academy of Sciences Scientific Council on Ecological Problems and Emergency Events will take into account these wishes in their planning for 2001.

In conclusion, I would like to turn to comments by Dr. Gibbons. He expressed his thought that the scientist's duty is to explain to the society outward phenomena, being based on the most advanced scientific concepts. It is a challenging task to help people make proper decisions in a condition of global indeterminacy and continuously changing environments. The coming millennium will be characterized by the increasing importance of quality of life, human health, and education. Natural resources are finite, but knowledge and development of human intelligence are infinite. Let me wish all colleagues every success in this important field.

SCIENTIFIC COUNCIL ON ECOLOGICAL PROBLEMS AND EMERGENCY EVENTS

The Scientific Council on Ecological Problems and Emergency Events (hereinafter called the Council) was established for general coordination and further development of basic and applied research activities of the Russian Academy of Sciences in ecology, environmental protection, and emergency events (natural and man-made catastrophic processes).

The Council is a coordination and consultative unit working on a voluntary basis and attached to the Presidium of the Russian Academy of Sciences.

The Council works in cooperation with the government and with other institutions of Russia, foreign countries, and international organizations dealing with scientific research in ecology, environmental protection, and emergency events. The main purposes of the Council are the following:

1. The general coordination of research carried out by the Russian Academy of Sciences on ecology, environmental protection, and emergency events.
2. Development of an electronic library based on research materials of the institutes of the Russian Academy of Sciences on ecology, environmental protection, and emergency events. The library should be of interest to users of Russian information networks and for connection to the Internet.
3. Analysis and synthesis of research results obtained by institutions of the Russian Academy of Sciences on environmental protection and natural and man-made catastrophic events.

4. Preparation of proposals and recommendations for the Presidium of the Russian Academy of Sciences concerning problems of ecology, environmental protection, and emergency events.
5. Preparation of materials concerning problems of ecology, environmental protection, and emergency events according to the needs of state agencies addressed to the Russian Academy of Sciences.
6. Promotion of ecological research including interdisciplinary research in the institutions of the Russian Academy of Sciences.
7. Promotion of ecological examination of projects and facilities of the state involving scientific institutions of the Russian Academy of Sciences.
8. Promotion of links of the scientific institutions of the Russian Academy of Sciences with governmental bodies, Russian ecological organizations, including public ones, and foreign organizations dealing with problems of ecology, environmental protection, and emergency events.
9. Promotion of links of the scientific institutions of the Russian Academy of Sciences, dealing with problems of ecology, environmental protection, and emergency events with the Russian and foreign mass media.
10. Participation in the organization of scientific meetings on the problems of ecology, environmental protection, and emergency events.
11. Cooperation with international scientific organizations, foreign scientific institutions, and individual foreign scientists on problems of the Council.
12. Promotion of joint activity of scientists from different departments by establishing interdepartmental and international research groups in ecology, environmental protection, and emergency events.

STAFF AND STRUCTURE OF THE COUNCIL

The main structural units of the Council are:

- The Bureau of the Council.
- Regional divisions of the Council on the problems of ecology, environmental protection, and emergency events in the Far East, Siberia, the Urals, and the European part of Russia.
- Sections on the following problems: catastrophic processes, ecological problems of the atmosphere, ecology and wildlife conservation, ecology of continental waters of Russia, ecology of the world ocean, ecology of the lithosphere and underground waters, information support for ecological research, ecological problems of education, interaction with nongovernmental and international ecological organizations, social and economic problems of ecology, and methods and technologies of ecological research.

LIMNOLOGICAL INSTITUTE, SIBERIAN BRANCH, RUSSIAN ACADEMY OF SCIENCES

1. The Baikal International Center for Ecological Research has been created. It allows increased scientific investigations of different integrated problems.
2. Ecological passports for different enterprises and institutions functioning in the Baikal region have been developed.
3. Norms of the allowed pollutant impact on the Lake Baikal ecosystem have been developed.
4. A draft of the Law on Lake Baikal has been worked out and submitted to the State Council.
5. The technical conditions for Baikal bottled drinking water have been developed, and a patent for its production has been obtained.
6. A draft of the Federal Target Program of the Baikal Pulp and Paper Plant that solves social problems of the town of Baikalsk has been developed.
7. Microbiological and hydrobiological monitoring of the Lake Baikal ecosystem and its main tributaries is being conducted.
8. Integrated research of biodiversity in the Lake Baikal ecosystem and in the water bodies of its basin has been considerably expanded.

PUBLIC PARTICIPATION IN ENVIRONMENTALLY SOUND DECISION-MAKING: LEGAL ASPECTS CONSTITUTIONAL AND LEGAL GUARANTEES

While speaking about guaranteeing the rights of citizens to participate in environmentally sound decision-making, one normally refers to Article 32 of the Constitution of the Russian Federation as the basic document. The article states, "Citizens of the Russian Federation have the right to participate in managing state affairs both directly and through their representatives." Moreover, Article 33 of the Constitution ensures the right of citizens "to appeal in person and make individual and collective appeals to state bodies and bodies of local government." Appropriate federal legislation has not been developed. It is uncertain whether it will ever be adopted, but existing legal provisions are insufficient.

Yet, the priority of human and civil rights as well as numerous guarantees of exercising these rights has already been guaranteed in the Russian Constitution and in some laws currently in force. To be sure, we should abandon a narrow academic approach to civil rights and start protecting them in practice. The Institute of Environmental Law, hereinafter called Ecojuris, is a professional human rights organization. Ecojuris was the first in our country to start protecting environmental rights of citizens and nongovernmental organizations in practice, including the right to participate in the decision-making process. It seeks to accomplish this role on the basis of the following basic principles:

1. The Constitution of the Russian Federation shall be used directly. Part 1 of Article 15 of the Constitution states that the Constitution "shall have supreme legal force and direct effect and shall be applicable on the entire territory of the Russian Federation."
2. Gaps, contradictions, and common and controversial points in the laws shall be interpreted in favor of the citizens. The heart of this principle is Article 2 and Article 18 of the Constitution. The first one proclaims: "Man and his rights and freedom shall be the supreme value." The second one says: "Human and civil rights and freedoms shall have direct force. They shall determine the meaning, content, and implementation of laws, they shall determine the functioning of legislative and executive authority and of local government, and they shall be guaranteed by law."
3. Environmental rights (like any other human and civil rights) shall be fundamental and of high priority. State and local government bodies shall only be able to establish procedural norms for their execution and protection. This principle is based on the following articles of the Constitution:
   - o Part 1 of Article 3: "The bearer of sovereignty and the sole source of power in the Russian Federation shall be its people of many nationalities."
   - o Part 2 of Article 17: "Basic human rights and freedoms shall be inalienable and shall be enjoyed by everyone from birth."
   - o The above cited Article 18.
4. The following principle is based on the very same articles of the Constitution: Opinions of the citizens on any activity to be carried out or on any object to be located on the territory where they live shall prevail and shall be disputed only in accordance with legal procedures.
5. The right to participate in decision-making shall be a part of the human right to a favorable environment, that, in turn, shall be an inalienable element of the right to life. This principle emerges from the following complex of articles of the Constitution and other laws:

- o Article 42: "Everyone shall have the right to a favorable environment..."
- o Part 1 of Article 20: "Everyone shall have the right to life."
- o Part 1 of Article 9: "Land and other natural resources shall be utilized and protected in the Russian Federation as the basis of life and activity of the people living on the concerned territory."
- o Article 92 of the Law "On Protection of the Natural Environment":
- " Everyone shall have the right to life in the most favorable environmental conditions."
- o Articles 12 and 13 of the above law, guaranteeing environmental rights of the public.

6. Information necessary for the exercise of citizens' environmental rights, including the right to participate in decision-making, shall be of public interest. Classifying this information as limited access information (that is, state secrets or confidential information) shall be prohibited (Article 10 of the Federal Law "On Information and Protection of Information," based on Part 4 of Article 29 and Article 42 of the Constitution).
7. Environmental rights of citizens and nongovernmental organizations shall be ensured and protected by the whole body of laws currently in force-civil, civil-procedural, investment, information, nuclear, environmental, natural resources, and so on. We are successfully using these principles to protect the environmental rights of citizens and nongovernment organizations as well as to protect rights in related fields, such as the right to information, to participation in managing state affairs, and to legal protection.

Ecojuris, in close cooperation with an organization it created, the Network of Russian Public Interest Environmental Lawyers, protects public interests, using the possibilities provided by the environmental legislation. These laws are rather progressive and, to some extent, pioneering in our country. Environmental lawyers- practitioners have made a substantial breakthrough in human and civil rights protection, adding environmental legislation with creative approaches to civil and civil-procedural law.

In addition to the above general principles, when protecting environmental rights we use more specific fundamental approaches and provisions of Russian legislation:

1. At the stage of obtaining preliminary agreement on location of a facility, bodies of local government shall be obliged to clarify the

opinion of the population by means of local referenda and citizen meetings. Citizens, public associations, and bodies of local government shall have the right to participate in considering issues pertaining to exemptions and allotments of land plots of interest to the population (Article 28 of the Russian Federation Land Code).

2. A scheduled economic or other activity that could be environmentally dangerous in the future shall be subject to mandatory state environmental examination (Article 3 of the Federal Law "On Environmental Examination").
3. As to an activity (regardless of the territory where it is carried out) that causes harm to the health or property of citizens, their households, or the environment, citizens or organizations may turn to the courts to stop environmentally harmful activity (Article 91 of the Law "On Protection of the Natural Environment").
4. The danger of causing harm in the future may be grounds for filing a lawsuit to prohibit an activity creating such danger (Article 1065 of the Civil Code of the Russian Federation).
5. Interests of citizens, nongovernmental organizations, and other persons may be represented in a court as well as in extra-juridical examinations of disputes by lawyers and other persons acting with a power of attorney in the traditional way (Chapter 5 of the Civil Procedural Code and Article 185 of the Russian Federation Civil Code). Besides, their interests may be represented in the above mentioned bodies on the basis of Chapter 50 of the Civil Code, "Actions without authority in the interest of another person." Conditions of actions in the interest of another person are determined by Part 1 of Article 980 of the Civil Code: "Actions without agency, other instructions, or the prior consent of the interested person for the purpose of preventing harm to his person...or in his lawful interests shall be carried out based on their benefit or usefulness..." Part 1 of Article 981 establishes an obligation to notify the interested person of action in his interest:

   "A person acting in the interest of another person is obligated at the first opportunity to inform the interested person of such action and wait for a reasonable period of time for his ratification or non-ratification of the action undertaken..."
6. Inasmuch as nature and its resources shall be the national property of the people of Russia as the natural basis of their social and economic development and well-being (Preamble of the Law "On Protection of the Natural Environment"), Article 980 of the Civil Code provides for

the possibility of protecting interests not only of living people, but also of future generations. This innovative approach is being successfully used by Ecojuris. It has found support among the representatives of the Office of the Prosecutor General and has not met opposition among judges of the Supreme Court of the Russian Federation.

The Civil Code does not establish definite forms of ratification of the actions undertaken in the interest of another person. So we have developed an application form (Table 1) for a person to implement the requirements of Article 981. This form can be used in case of representation of the interests of private citizens or groups of citizens. (Legal persons and nongovernmental organizations, in particular, fill out a similar application form, except the column on descendants.)

7. The right to participate in environmental decision-making along with other environmental rights pertains to personal non-property rights, that is to non- material values (Article 150 of the Civil Code). Therefore, in accordance with Article 208 of the above Code, legal limitations shall not be placed on the requirements of protecting these rights.
8. In 2000, a possibility of actions in the lawful interest of another person was secured in the procedural legislation, namely in new wording of Article 42 of the Civil Code.

Thus, in summary, rather vast legislation is currently in force in our country to be used in protecting public rights to participate in environmentally sound decision- making. Of course, one would like to have good special legislation concerning regulations under review. However, due to the poor quality of many new laws (issued by the "fluent pen" of the State Duma), serious anxiety exists that public rights would not be secured and extended but substantially limited.

A relatively fresh example from the environmental sphere can be presented. The new Federal Law "On Sanitary and Epidemiological Well-being" was adopted in 1999, replacing the previous one with the same title (1991). (The Code of Laws of the Russian Federation, No. 14, 1999, Art. 1650). The latter had been adopted at the height of perestroika and became the first Russian normative act to secure the citizen's right to a favorable environment as well as the right to participate in decision-making.

Part 4 of Article 5 of the law stipulated that citizens "shall have the right to participate both directly or through their representative or public associations in developing, discussing, and making decisions by state government and On Approval of Actions Undertaken by Ecojuris In accordance with the procedure established by Articles 980 and 981 of the Civil Code on protecting the lawful interest of another person (in case of appeal against the Government relating to transfer of the first group of forest lands into non- forest group lands for managing forests and using the forest fund, adopted in 1994- 1998). The public waited for the State Duma to update the wording of this provision and advance it in the spirit of the times. Instead, the provision was excluded in full from the law, and as a result the public received the toothless pre-perestroika right "to submit proposals."

It should be noted that for the last two or three years, attempts have been made by some groups of deputies and officials to submit new wording of the Federal Law "On Environmental Examination" to the State Duma for consideration, which has limited human and civil rights.

My long-standing human rights activity is evidence that our country has unfortunately remained a state not governed by laws. "Under-regulation" of some relations and incoherence of some legal norms sometimes are better from the human rights standpoint than excessive "over-regulation" undertaken by incompetent and dishonest lawmakers.

In spite of the absence of general unified mechanisms of participation in making decisions that can affect the environment and natural resources, citizens, nongovernmental organizations, and other strata of our society have "compensatory mechanisms" for such participation. This is public participation in evaluating the effect on the environment (EEE) in the environmental examination.

An EEE is a stage of environmentally sound decision-making to be carried out before the environmental examination. A new regulation on evaluation of the effect of economic and other activity on the environment was adopted in 2000 with direct participation of the author of this article (approved by the order of the State Committee on the Environment on May 16, 2000, No. 372, registered in the Ministry of Justice on July 4, 2000, No. 2302). A pioneering attempt was made in this document to regulate more carefully the procedure of public participation in decision-making. The document considers public participation to be not only the basic principle of EEE, but also an "inalienable part" of this procedure. Notification and participation of the public as well as due consideration of its opinion shall be binding at all stages of EEE, beginning with preparation of the EEE technical design (paragraphs 2.5, 4.1, and others).

In decision-making, public preferences must be revealed and taken into account. This shall be one of the results of EEE (paragraph 1.6). Part IV of the regulation is fully devoted to notification and participation of the public in the EEE procedure. It fixes the terms and order of notification, information content, and rules of collection and analysis of comments and proposals. Preliminary consultations, public discussions, and submissions of written comments shall be the main forms of citizen participation.

All these procedures are regulated in the document. For example, paragraph 4.9 stipulates that public hearings are to be arranged by local governments. All decisions related to public participation shall be documented.

The advocate of an action shall arrange public hearings on a planned activity and keep the record. The main issues of discussion as well as disputes between the public and the advocate (if any) shall be clearly fixed in the record. The record shall be signed by representatives of local government, citizens, public organizations (associations), and the advocate. The record of public hearings shall be included in the final set of documents on evaluating planned economic activity and the effect on the environment.

The new regulation, unlike the previous ones clearly stipulates the obligation to take into account information on comments and proposals of the public. A supplement of the regulation contains a list of documents to be included in the final set of EEE materials to prove the actual participation of the public in the decision- making process. All these materials shall be submitted for environmental examination (paragraphs 12.1-12.7). The following information shall be included in the materials of public hearings:

- Means of notification of the public on the place, time, and form of the public discussion.
- A list of public discussion participants, including names, and the names of organizations (if any), with their addresses and telephone numbers.
- A list of issues under consideration and abstracts of presentations, and records of public hearings (if any).
- All comments and proposals raised in the course of the public discussions, names of their authors, and materials of possible disputes between the public, local government, and advocate.
- Conclusions of the public discussion on the environmental aspects of a planned activity.
- A summary of public comments and proposals with the indication of those which have been or have not been taken into consideration and grounds for refusal.
- A mailing list of appropriate information to be sent out to the public at all stages of EEE.

The principle of public participation in the environmental examination has been secured in Article 3 of the Federal Law "On the Environmental Examination" mentioned above. According to this article, any project can be a subject of state environmental examination beginning with drafts and ending with documentation justifying the license, agreement on division of production, and so on, depending on the nature and importance of a project (Articles 11 and 12 of the above law). The state environmental examination is an obligatory measure to protect the natural environment. It should prevent economic decisions which can cause harm to the natural environment. A positive conclusion of the state environmental examination is necessary to finance and implement any project and programm (Parts 1 and 2 of Article 36 of the Russian Federation Law "On Protection of the Natural Environment"). The legal consequences of a negative result of the examination shall be a prohibition on implementing the project (Part 5 of Article 18 of the Law "On the State Environment Examination").

The right of public associations to carry out a public environmental examination of the same project before or at the time of the state environment examination is provided by Chapter 4 of the above law. Public examination findings shall reflect public opinion and shall be obligatory for consideration during the State decision on realization of the project. Of great importance for public rights is Article 14 of the Law "On the Environmental Examination" providing an obligatory submission of (1) EEE results and (2) results of citizen and public organization discussions organized by local government concerning the subject of the state environmental examination. In this case, the law considers the power of local government to organize public discussions, polls, and referenda among the population on economic activity as a power in the sphere of the environmental examination (Part 2 of Article 9). Thus, the above analysis of the federal law "On the Environmental Examination" and EEE Regulations clearly demonstrates (analysis of law and regulations) that a duplication, or "overdose," of public discussions takes place in these documents. But given the great number of human rights violations in our country, this is not bad. To exercise one's constitutional right to participate in managing state affairs (Part 1 of Article 32 of the Constitution), one must participate in decision-making at all stages of the process. If it doesn't work at one stage, it may at another. Consequently, Russian land and environmental legislation gives the public some possibilities to express views in favor of or against placing a facility or carrying out an activity on territory of their residence as follows:

- By means of a local referendum or meeting to be held by local government at a stage of preliminary planning.

- o By means of public hearings/discussions at the EEE stage organized by joint actions of local government and an investor on a federal, regional or local level according to the importance of the project.
- o By means of a public discussion, as an integral part of the environmental examination, organized by local government. Thus, in accordance with the Constitution's provisions, public opinion shall be decisive. State decisions that are inconsistent with residents' opinions or impede expressions of such opinions are violations of a number of constitutional rights that can be appealed to interstate bodies for the protection of human rights and freedoms, if all available internal means of legal protection have been exhausted (Article 46 of the Constitution).

EXPERIENCE IN DEFENDING THE ENVIRONMENTAL INTERESTS OF SOCIETY

Ecojuris is a nongovernmental organization seeking to execute public interest environmental law. The term "public interest environmental law" had not even existed in our country when we started our activity although some decades ago this term became popular in the United States, Canada, and other countries. Nevertheless, we succeeded in opening and introducing this direction in Russia. We began our work at the end of 1989 on the base of the Academy of Sciences' Institute of State and Law. At that time, illegal construction of the North Thermal Power Station was underway in Moscow, organized without appropriate environmental examination. Later a similar problem arose in Southern Butovo (a district of Moscow). Having realized that it was impossible to continue our work without pooling efforts of many people, we set up Ecojuris; and in 1991 it was registered as a nongovernmental organization. Since that time it has re-registered more than once because of changes in legislation and in membership.

As of now the name of our public organization is "The Institute of Environmental Law-Ecojuris." Our experts carry out consultative-judicial practice as well as research, legal drafting, education, seminars, and training not only in Moscow, but also in the regions. We hold training courses for environmental lawyers. We are currently carrying out a lawyers' training program on protecting national minorities' rights for traditional uses of natural resources. For the first few years, Ecojuris had been the only nongovernmental organization in the USSR and Russia to protect public environmental interests and civil environmental rights. But now, about ten such organizations exist in our country. Most have been created with our direct involvement. Lawyers work for environmental organizations, such as Karelia's Association of the

Greens and Kamchatka's League of Independent Experts. In 1994, it occurred to us that we should informally pool our efforts. Since that time we have been holding annual conferences of our organizations. To exchange experience and information, the informal Network of Russian Public Interest Environmental Lawyers was set up in 1997. It currently has more than forty members.

In 2000, representatives from five countries of the former Soviet Union took part in our Seventh Annual Public Interest Environmental Law Conference for the first time. In addition to the Russian network, we have established the Eurasian Public Interest Environmental Law Network to protect public environmental interests. Our colleagues from Azerbaijan, Moldova, Ukraine, Kazakhstan, Kyrgyzstan, and Uzbekistan have joined us. In each of these countries, there are one or two persons engaged in consulting, pleading cases, and other legal activities. Human rights lawyers from Belarus, Georgia, and Armenia have also expressed their wish to join the Network. Most of these countries have similar legislation and problems: the oil mafia, the fishing mafia, the timber mafia, and corruption, particularly among the highest and middle rank officials responsible for granting licenses and permissions to carry out different projects and use different kinds of resources.

Conduct of rank-and-file officials is not immaculate, yet they have a long way to go to reach the standards set by "the highest echelons." During all these years, we have been involved with law on behalf of the public. In the early 1990s, courts did not take environmental cases for examination at all. Judges did not know the environmental legislation. We brought them copies of appropriate normative acts. In such a manner, they learned about this information for the first time. To ensure that an original jurisdiction would take such a case for examination, we would sometimes have to appeal to the Supreme Court. We were the first who acquainted judges and other officials with the Constitutional right to a favorable environment and unlimited guarantee of protecting this right in court. What is more, they learned that a European Human Rights Court existed, and we could appeal to it. It was a revelation for them. Since the middle of the 1990s the judicial system has begun stirring. Judges and public prosecutors are displaying interest in our activity. They have started taking part in our seminars and delivering lectures for our trainees. Bodies dedicated to guaranteeing human rights have arisen. We won cases in Moscow and in the regions. To illustrate, in Chelyabinsk, a member of our Network in cooperation with Ecojuris has managed to gain psychological damage compensation for a child who is a third-generation radiation victim.

At present, Ecojuris has a rather complex structure. It includes a consultative center for citizens and public organizations. Muscovites and Moscow Oblast residents are able to consult the Center. People from other parts of the country can send us written inquiries. Verbal inquiries center largely around citizens' environmental rights in populated areas, including unlawful building, destruction of trees, infringement of sanitary and epidemiological norms, and neglect of environmental assessment and examination. Deforestation and unlawful construction in protected wetlands are common. It is these violations that upset people. In general, the inquiries show considerable variation, ranging from protection of domestic animals to complaints against housing quality to noise pollution.

Apart from consultative assistance, Ecojuris continues dealing with public interest environmental law. In Moscow, Moscow Oblast, and adjoining oblasts, the consultative center pleads different cases, including sanitary and epidemiological infringement, unlawful construction, and neglect of environmental impact examination on various projects. As a rule, about ten such small cases are under consideration by Ecojuris at any one time.

More complicated cases of interregional and even All-Russian interest are also being handled by Ecojuris. Considerable advances have been made on these levels. In 1998-1999, Ecojuris won two cases against the Government on the illegitimate reclassification of pristine forest lands as non-forest lands. In September 1999, we won a case against the Government on its unlawful granting of permits for the discharge of drilling wastes into the Far East seas. These cases have been won at the level of the Supreme Court. To be sure, failures also occur. We try to see that a lost case does not turn into a conspicuous failure. Each case, even a small one, is normally accompanied by a public campaign and mass media support. Letters and requests are sent to the state bodies, including the office of the Prosecutor General. Here are some concrete examples.

We actually lost the case on the St. Peterburg-Moscow high-speed railway project. The Supreme Court rejected our claim. But a large-scale mass media campaign was launched. More than three thousand supporters of our position were involved from different regions of the country. A great number of publications were issued. All TV channels broadcast reports on the matter, including on our lawsuit. We believe that this case made its contribution to stopping construction of this line. In our view, President B.N.Yeltsin reversed a substantial number of his decrees due to the threat presented by this very case. Though this case may have been lost in court, it should not be considered a failure. Ecojuris opposes President Putin's edict of May 17, 2000, on abolishment of the State Committee on Ecology and Ministry of Forest Management.

A great number of laws, from the Constitution to the environmental legislation, have been violated by this edict. The Presidential edict is a very important decision related to citizens' environmental and human rights to a favorable environment, to information, and to participation in managing State affairs. We believe the edict to be undeniably unlawful. There is not a general unified procedure for public participation in environmental decision-making in our country. Consequently, so- called "compensatory" mechanisms should have been put into operation. This would imply, that in accordance with the federal Law "On the Environmental Examination," the draft of this edict as well as the draft of the corresponding government decree adopted on the base of this edict should have undergone state examination with participation of the public. This procedure has not been observed. Therefore, we consider it to be a serious abuse of citizens' rights.

Nevertheless, the Supreme Court has ignored our claim, so we are now at the stage of appeal. We are currently developing a strategy of future actions, as we cannot let this case end without legal consequences.

6

International Human Rights Law and Role of NGOs

NON-GOVERNMENTAL ORGANIZATION

A non-governmental organization (NGO) is a legally constituted organization created by natural or legal persons that operates independently from any government. The term is usually used by governments to refer to entities that have no government status. In the cases in which NGOs are funded totally or partially by governments, the NGO maintains its non-governmental status by excluding government representatives from membership in the organization. The term is usually applied only to organizations that pursue some wider social aim that has political aspects, but that are not overtly political organizations such as political parties. Unlike the term "intergovernmental organization", the term "non-governmental organization" has no generally agreed legal definition. In many jurisdictions, these types of organization are called "civil society organizations" or referred to by other names.

The number of internationally operating NGOs is estimated at 40,000. National numbers are even higher: Russia has 277,000 NGOs; India is estimated to have around 3.3 million NGOs in year 2009 that is one NGO for less than 400 Indians, and many times the number of primary schools and primary health centres in India.

DEFINITION OF NGO

NGOs are difficult to define and classify due to the term's inconsistent use. NGO, nonprofit organization (NPO) and private voluntary organization (PVO) are the most used terms and are used interchangeably despite differing definitions. Classifying non-governmental organizations within defined boundaries excludes NGOs that fall outside each specific boundary. Additionally, it is beneficial for NGO networks to create a classification that allows similar organizations to exchange information more easily. To attempt a classification of NGO's requires a framework, that includes the orientation and the organization's level of operation. An NGO's orientation refers to the type of activities an organization takes on. These activities might include environmental, development, or advocacy work. An NGO's level of operation indicates the scale at which an organization works on, like the difference in work between an international NGO and community or national NGO.

One of the earliest mentions of the term "NGO" was in 1945 when the UN was created. The UN introduced the term "NGO," to distinguish between the participation of international private organizations and intergovernmental specialized agencies. According to the UN, all kinds of private organizations that are independent from government control can be recognized as "NGOs." "NGOs" cannot seek to diminish a nation's government in the shape of an opposing political party; NGOs also need to be non-criminal and nonprofit. Professor Peter Willets, from the City University of London, argues the definition of NGOs can be interpreted differently by various organizations and depending on a situation's context. He defines an NGO as "an independent voluntary association of people acting together on a continuous basis for some common purpose other than achieving government office, making money or illegal activities." In this view, two main types of NGOs are recognized according to the activities they pursue: operational and campaigning NGO's. Although, Willets proposes the operational and campaigning NGO's as a tool to differentiate the main activities of these organizations, he also explains that they have more similarities than differences. Their activities are unrestricted; thus operational NGOs may need to campaign and campaigning NGO's may need to take on structural projects.

NGO consultative status with ECOSOC: A consultative status for an NGO is the right to participate in resolutions and deliberations within the ECOSOC, which is the Economic and Social Council in the United Nations.

In order to be eligible for a consultative status, an NGO must have at least two years of existence, which requires to have been properly registered with the respective authorities and government. The organizations must have a democratic constitution, representative authority, stablished headquarters, accountability for transparent and democratic decision-making and be independent from government control.

NGOs are defined by the World Bank as "private organizations that pursue activities to relieve suffering, promote the interests of the poor, protect the environment, provide basic social services, or undertake community development".

NPOs and NGOs

Common usage varies between countries-for example NGO is commonly used for domestic organizations in Australia that would be referred to as non-profit organizations in the United States. Such organizations that operate on the international level are fairly consistently referred to as "non-governmental organizations", in the United States and elsewhere.

There is a growing movement within the non-profit organization/non-government sector to define itself in a more constructive, accurate way. The "non-profit" designation is seen to be particularly disfunctional for at least three reasons: 1) It says nothing about the purpose of the organization, only what it is not; 2) It focuses the mind on "profit" as being the opposite of the organization's purpose; 3) It implies that the organization has few financial resources and may run out of money before completing its mission. Instead of being defined by "non-" words, organizations are suggesting new terminology to describe the sector. The term "social benefit organization" (SBO) is being adopted by some organizations. This defines them in terms of their positive mission. The term "civil society organization" (CSO) has also been used by a growing number of organizations, such as the Center for the Study of Global Governance. The term "citizen sector organization" (CSO) has also been advocated to describe the sector — as one of citizens, for citizens. These labels, SBO and CSO, position the sector as its own entity, without relying on language used for the government or business sectors. However, some have argued that *CSO* is not particularly helpful, given that most NGOs are in fact funded by governments and/or profit-driven businesses and that some NGOs are clearly hostile to independently organized people's organizations. The term "social benefit organization" seems to avoid that problem, since it does not assume any particular structure, but rather focuses on the organization's mission.

History

International non-governmental organizations have a history dating back to at least 1839. It has been estimated that by 1914 there were 1083 NGOs. International NGOs were important in the anti-slavery movement and the movement for women's suffrage, and reached a peak at the time of the World

Disarmament Conference. However, the phrase "non-governmental organization" only came into popular use with the establishment of the United Nations Organization in 1945 with provisions in Article 71 of Chapter 10 of the United Nations Charter for a consultative role for organizations which are neither governments nor member states—see Consultative Status. The definition of "international NGO" (INGO) is first given in resolution 288 (X) of ECOSOC on February 27, 1950: it is defined as "any international organization that is not founded by an international treaty". The vital role of NGOs and other "major groups" in sustainable development was recognized in Chapter 27 of Agenda 21, leading to intense arrangements for a consultative relationship between the United Nations and non-governmental organizations.

Rapid development of the non-governmental sector occurred in western countries as a result of the processes of restructuring of the welfare state. Further globalization of that process occurred after the fall of the communist system and was an important part of the Washington consensus.

Globalization during the 20th century gave rise to the importance of NGOs. Many problems could not be solved within a nation. International treaties and international organizations such as the World Trade Organization were centred mainly on the interests of capitalist enterprises. In an attempt to counterbalance this trend, NGOs have developed to emphasize humanitarian issues, developmental aid and sustainable development. A prominent example of this is the World Social Forum, which is a rival convention to the World Economic Forum held annually in January in Davos, Switzerland. The fifth World Social Forum in Porto Alegre, Brazil, in January 2005 was attended by representatives from more than 1,000 NGOs. Some have argued that in forums like these, NGOs take the place of what should belong to popular movements of the poor. Others argue that NGOs are often imperialist in nature, that they sometimes operate in a racialized manner in third world countries, and that they fulfil a similar function to that of the clergy during the high colonial era. The philosopher Peter Hallward argues that they are an aristocratic form of politics. Whatever the case, NGO transnational networking is now extensive.

SOURCES OF THE GUARANTEE

Global and regional human rights instruments contain a number of general guarantees of freedom of association which are addressed to persons forming bodies with all the concerns already mentioned-and many more besides-and the protection provided by the provisions concerned is reinforced in a number of other undertakings directed to associations with a particular type of membership or objective. The principal general guarantees are found in Article 20 of the Universal Declaration of Human Rights, Article 22 of the International Covenant on Civil and Political Rights, Article 10 of the African Charter on Human and Peoples' Rights, Article 16 of the American Convention on Human Rights, Article 11 of the European Convention on Human Rights and an undertaking made by States belonging to the Organisation for Security and Cooperation in Europe.

These guarantees are supplemented by provisions in the same instruments requiring that they be secured without any distinction such as race, colour, sex, language, religion, political or other opinion, national or social origin, property, birth or other status, as well as by specific guarantees against discrimination in the case of race, colour, descent, national or ethnic origin and gender that are to be found in the International Convention on the Elimination of All Forms of Racial Discrimination and the Convention on the Elimination of All Forms of Discrimination against Women.

Apart from the Universal Declaration, the African Charter and the American Convention, all of the general guarantees make specific mention of the freedom applying to the formation of trade unions. However, the references to unions in these guarantees are intended only to clarify the position rather than to limit their scope in some way. There are, however, several guarantees of freedom of association specifically directed to trade unions, notably Article 8 of the International Covenant on Economic, Social and Cultural Rights, Article 5 of the European Social Charter and the Convention Concerning Freedom of Association and Protection of the Right to Organise of the International Labour Organization, as well as an undertaking given by members of the OSCE. Furthermore there are a number of other guarantees concerned with the enjoyment of freedom of association by particular sectors in a society, namely, children, environmental campaigners, human rights defenders, judges, members of national minorities, migrant workers, refugees and stateless persons, as well as for non-governmental bodies of an international character. Moreover the guarantee-in Article 15 of the International Covenant on Economic, Social and Cultural Rights-of the right to take part in cultural life undoubtedly includes the possibility of forming associations for this purpose. In addition, although not formally a guarantee, it should be noted that the Council of Europe has also articulated some Fundamental Principles on the Legal Status of Non-governmental Organisations in Europe ('Fundamental Principles').

Some of the specific guarantees, particularly those relating to trade unions, undoubtedly require recognition of certain rights over and above those to be enjoyed by associations generally and it is with the latter that this chapter is especially concerned. Furthermore not all of the guarantees entail legal obligations but treaties such as the two International Covenants and those adopted by regional organisations are binding under international law on the States that are parties to them.

Nevertheless the other instruments not only reinforce the significance of the political commitment to secure freedom of association but can also help to elucidate how it should be implemented in particular contexts. However, given the lack of specificity in the language used in most of the guarantees, the most helpful source of guidance in determining the scope of the general freedom of association is to be derived from the case law generated under those instruments which enable individual or collective claims to be brought. Of all of those instruments, it is only in respect of the Convention Concerning Freedom of Association and Protection of the Right to Organise and the European Convention that there is at present a significant body of case law. Although the approach in both of them is broadly the same, this chapter will focus mainly on that relating to the latter instrument in order to ensure that there is no confusion between the general obligations and those of concern only with the treatment of trade unions. Nevertheless it also needs to be kept in mind that this case law, notwithstanding the considerable benefit to be derived from it in understanding what freedom of association entails, addresses only those issues which have already been brought before the various tribunals. Although these are undoubtedly important ones, this does not mean that the full extent of the protection which States are legally obliged to afford to associations has yet been fully clarified. Indeed it remains the case that provisions such as Article 11 of the European Convention have not received the same degree of attention from international and regional tribunals as have many other rights and freedoms. The fact that this has begun to change in recent years means that the main elements of this freedom can now be readily discerned but this should not encourage a reluctance to draw upon other potentially useful sources of guidance as to how to interpret and apply the general guarantees.

Moreover it should not be overlooked that one possible explanation for the relative dearth of applications involving Article 11 of the European Convention may well be the limited controls applied in many European countries with respect to this freedom and that this is something that should be more generally emulated. It should also be recalled that interference with the activities of associations may well engage other legally binding rights and freedoms-notably, rights to a fair hearing and peaceful enjoyment of possessions and freedom of assembly, conscience, correspondence and expression-and appropriate account is taken of these in the discussion below.

CONCEPT OF ASSOCIATION

Although the role of non-governmental organisations has been, and continues to be, important for the elaboration, implementation and protection of human rights, specific reference to them is not frequently found in human rights treaties. Indeed this term is only used in two of them and then only with regard to the procedural competence to submit applications or petitions in respect of alleged violations of the substantive rights. The failure to recognise them may have implications not only for their ability to complain to some supervisory bodies but also to rely on the substantive rights afforded by some treaties. Nevertheless the ability of most non-governmental organisations to exist and to operate is generally well-secured by the extensive guarantees of freedom of association.

As with all terms found in international human rights instruments, the concept of 'association' is something that has to be accorded an autonomous meaning; national provisions cannot, therefore, be conclusive in determining whether something is or is not an association for the purpose of guarantees such as that in Article 11 of the European Convention. This not only means that it is inappropriate to attach too much significance to the language used in particular laws when trying to ascertain whether the exercise of freedom of association is involved but also that the conditions which laws may impose before something will be regarded as an association will not necessarily be regarded as acceptable from the international perspective. Certainly a very inclusive approach is taken at the international level to the sort of gatherings of persons that are protected by freedom of association guarantees. However, in order for those guarantees to become applicable, it would have to be demonstrated that the grouping concerned is something more than a body of persons who have a common objective since it has already been established that Article 11 does not seek to protect a mere gathering of people desirous of sharing each other's company and a different approach is unlikely to be taken to the interpretation of other guarantees. Furthermore some forms of protest action such as demonstrations and public meetings, albeit gatherings of a more organised character, would still not be an exercise of freedom of association because of their essentially transient nature; they would, however, be regarded as activities coming under the protection of freedom of assembly, the second limb of that provision. What is thus required is that the gathering not only have been formed with the object of pursuing certain aims but also that it has a degree of stability as regards its existence and thus have some kind of institutional (albeit not formal) structure to which the persons comprising it can really be regarded as belonging.

In many instances associations will be bodies with a formal status-namely, legal personality-and this will also be what the founders of most of them want. Nevertheless the international guarantees are not limited to such bodies but also apply to groupings of an informal character so long as they have, or are meant to have, more than a fleeting existence. This is a necessary consequence of the general freedom of those associating to determine the basis on which they do so. The fact that some protection is available to the latter bodies will, of course, be particularly significant where a formal status has been improperly denied to persons who have formed an association but it will also be important where it is not considered necessary by those establishing certain groupings that they should also have a formal legal character. It is thus not open to a State to require that freedom of association only be exercised by the establishment of an entity with legal personality.

Apart from the unacceptability of common objectives that are unconstitutional or illegal, the only qualification on what might be the aim of a grouping in order for this to be accepted as an exercise of freedom of association is that it is either intended not to be a profitmaking body or, where trading activities are undertaken, any profits accruing are ploughed back into the pursuit of the common objectives rather than distributed to its membership. This is because this freedom is essentially a civil and political right rather than an economic one. Nevertheless this does not mean that an association cannot exist to advance the interests of its members; the specific inclusion of the formation of trade unions within the scope of the guarantee is the clearest indication that the securing of benefits for those who belong to an association is a legitimate objective and these benefits can be economic as much as moral, physical, social or spiritual.

However, if the principal objective is trading or some other form of business activity then protection for the interests of those belonging to the body concerned should be sought in guarantees such as the right to property rather than freedom of association. The fact that express reference is only made in general guarantees such as Article 11 of the European Convention to only one form of association, namely, trade unions, might lead to the conclusion that these either enjoyed a privileged position or that this provisions was not intended to cover all other forms of association. However, as the European Court first made clear in United Communist Party of Turkey and Others v Turkey, the special mention of them is no more than a reminder that they are within the definition of associations; the conjunction 'including' in Article 11 'clearly shows that trade unions are but one example among others of the form in which the right to freedom of association may be exercised'. This conclusion was reinforced in the context of that case, which concerned the dissolution of a political party, by the incontestable view that political parties were 'essential to the proper functioning of democracy in the Convention system' and they could thus not be excluded from the scope of Article 11. Nevertheless it is evident that no category of association is a priori denied the protection afforded by the general guarantees.

Some entities that may be treated as associations under domestic law will not, however, generally be so regarded for the purpose of Article 11 or other freedom of association guarantees. These are the many bodies which are established by law and to which doctors, lawyers, architects and other members of professions are often required to join. The European Court has regarded these as being public law bodies designed to regulate a particular profession and, as such, they will not normally attract the protection of Article 11 or other freedom of association guarantees. A similar view has also been taken of bodies such as works councils which may be required under employment legislation to be established to secure staff participation in the management at a particular work place; this is the sole basis on which the 'members' are brought together and the compulsion in their formation is sufficient to preclude such councils from being associations.

The fact that groupings are established pursuant to a legislative requirement does not, however, necessarily mean that they will not be treated as associations for the purpose of international guarantees. Thus in Chassagnou and Others v France the Court had no hesitation in regarding as associations those bodies which had been established for the purpose of organising hunting where these were 'composed of hunters or owners of land or hunting rights, and therefore, of private individuals, all of whom, a priori, wish to pool their land for the purpose of hunting.' It did not matter that the way in which these associations operated was subject to the supervisory power of the prefect as this was not in itself sufficient for them to be integrated into the structures of the State. It was, however, significant that these bodies did not enjoy. Attempts to exclude a particular body from the scope of the freedom of association guarantee by stipulating, as in this case, that it is 'public' or 'para-administrative' will thus not be effective if that is not actually an accurate reflection of its essential character.

The compulsion to belong to bodies such as professional associations and works councils can have the potential to encroach upon this freedom-as well as others such as conscience and expression-because of the constraint that might be imposed upon the manifestation of beliefs and opinions by their members. Nevertheless such a problem does not tend to arise in practice because the bodies involved are primarily concerned with regulatory issues and do not have any monopoly over representing the interests and views of their members. It should also be noted that voluntary groupings established within these bodies-such as a bar association's human rights committee-could be regarded as an association enjoying the protection of Article 11 and other freedom of association guarantees. This is because they will be concerned with promoting the objectives of those belonging to it rather than with the regulation of their professional conduct.

THE RIGHT TO FOUND AND TO BELONG

The ability to form and join associations is something that the general guarantees all provide as being open to 'everyone' within a State's jurisdiction and the scope for imposing limitations on this capacity is quite limited. 'Everyone' certainly means legal as well as natural persons as association is not one of the rights or freedoms that are capable of being exercised only by human beings. The only exception in this regard would be public bodies since these are a part of the State which is bound to secure freedom of association rather than beneficiaries of this right.

The unqualified nature of the formulation in all instruments means that the freedom should be exercisable by children as much as by adults, without needing to rely on the specific guarantees in respect of the former in the Convention on the Rights of the Child and the African Charter on the Rights and Welfare of the Child. Nevertheless this would not preclude the adoption of protective measures to ensure that they are not exploited or exposed to moral and related dangers, so long as the total exclusion of the ability to associate did not result. Such measures, insofar as they are proportionate and meet the requirements of legal certainty, could be justified as a restriction on their freedom pursuant to provisions such as Article 11(2). However, in judging the appropriateness of any such measures account would have to be taken of the need stipulated by the Convention on the Rights of the Child to respect 'the evolving capacities of the child' which would mean that the effect of any restrictions that might be adopted would undoubtedly have to be diminished as those affected grow older.

The inclusive nature of 'everyone' would also mean that freedom of association can, in principle, be exercised by people who are not actually citizens of the country concerned (whether they are citizens of another country or stateless persons). Article 16 of the European Convention does accept the possibility of some restrictions being imposed on the political activity of those who are not citizens and this is defined to cover freedom of association. However, in order to be acceptable, such restrictions ought to be compatible with the Convention's overall objectives of political democracy, freedom and the rule of law and they ought not to be disproportionate. It might, therefore, be possible to justify the exclusion of persons who are not citizens from membership of national political parties but it would certainly be harder to do so where the body was concerned only with local or non-party issues, particularly if those affected were established residents there.

There is also likely to be a reluctance to accept restrictions as being justified under Article 16 where they relate to persons from a country with which the one imposing them has close political and institutional links. Moreover restrictions on non-citizens forming or joining associations with no political objectives-such as those concerned with sport and culture-could hardly be defended by invoking Article 1667.

There is no comparable restriction to Article 16 in the other general guarantees of freedom of association but the International Convention on the Elimination of All Forms of Racial Discrimination does exclude differential treatment between citizens and non-citizens from its definition of discrimination, those concerned with refugees and stateless persons sets the freedom enjoyed by certain foreign nationals as regards 'non-political and non-profit-making associations and trade unions' as the standard to be met and the right accorded by the International Convention on the Protection of the Rights of All Migrant Workers and Members of their Families is limited to trade unions and certain forms of associations and not all migrant workers can form (as opposed to join) them. It is thus unlikely that some restriction on the political aspect of associational activity in respect of noncitizens might not be considered compatible with the freedom accorded by the other, ostensibly unrestricted, general guarantees but it seems improbable that anything going beyond the approach suggested appropriate for Article 16 of the European Convention would be considered acceptable.

Freedom of association entails the ability both to form associations with others and to seek to join existing ones. However, the latter freedom amounts only to a restriction on the power of the State to impose unjustified restrictions on the ability of persons-as defined above-to seek membership of an association; it is improbable that the guarantee would be construed as conferring any general right on them to join one against the wishes of its members. The matter has so far not been directly addressed by the European Court but this seems to be the inevitable conclusion of existing case law restricting the circumstances in which someone can be required to belong to an association; compulsion to admit members would effectively amount to the same thing since it would be denying those who already belong to an association the freedom to choose with whom they wish to associate. Nevertheless there would be good justification for constraining the freedom of existing members of an association to determine whom to admit as new members where this was done in order to fulfil obligations to prevent discrimination on any inadmissible ground and thereby protect the rights of others, as permitted by the second paragraph of Article 1175.

A person's imprisonment is likely to be a constraint on his or her ability to take a full part in the activities of an association but this should not otherwise be an obstacle to his or her continued membership of it and involvement in its affairs; it would be very difficult to demonstrate that a restriction on freedom of association which went beyond the inevitable impracticality of attending meetings was something really needed for the purposes of confinement and that is the test by which the impact of a deprivation of liberty on other human rights must be judged. Nevertheless it is possible that some limits could be imposed on a person's exercise of freedom of association as a penalty for certain conduct, provided that a legitimate aim for them could be demonstrated and that they were sufficiently carefully drawn to avoid being challenged for a lack of proportionality. Thus one of the penalties imposed on a Belgian newspaper editor who had collaborated with the German occupying authorities during the Second World War was a prohibition for life on involvement in the administration, management or direction of a professional or non-profit making association or the leadership of a political association.

The principle of such a penalty was not specifically dealt with by the European Commission in De Becker v Belgium but it did consider other such indefinite restrictions affecting the applicant's freedom of expression could not be justified in so far as they covered non-political matters; the scope of the restriction was simply too broad.

The issue never went before the European Court as the applicant applied to have the case struck off after the restrictions on his civil and political rights had been withdrawn and the law permitting such penalties had been modified so that they would apply only for fixed periods determined according to the seriousness of the offence.

In these circumstances it was not surprising that the Commission did not object to the case being struck off. However, it is evident that the Court will require very cogent justification for such restrictions on the exercise of freedom of association and it is unlikely that they would be seen as acceptable where their scope did not correspond to the nature of the offence giving rise to them or they lasted for an undue length of time.

There is no indication in case law or other practice in respect of treaties guaranteeing freedom of association as to the acceptability of imposing a minimum number of founders before an association can established. However, the Council of Europe's Fundamental Principles, while stating that 'Two or more persons should be able to establish a membership-based NGO', does accept the possibility that a higher number might be required 'where legal personality is to be acquired, but this number should not be set at a level that discourages the establishment of an NGO'. This qualification took account of the fact that higher numbers were in fact required in the law of some of the States involved in the adoption of the Fundamental Principles. However, while a certain threshold might be appropriate where the entity then became eligible for certain exceptional benefits, it seems questionable whether a requirement of more than two-even where legal personality is being acquired-is a restriction that is really compatible with freedom of association, especially since incorporation in a commercial context can often be undertaken by an individual and no particular case other than control has been identified as the rationale for insisting upon it. Although in practice most of the associations which are formed or joined are likely to be in the State where the persons concerned reside or are present, the freedom guaranteed by Article 11 would also extend to the creation and membership of associations in other countries and this could be restricted by reference only to the same considerations that govern regulation.

OBJECTIVES

Apart from the instruments concerned with trade unions or devoted to particular groups of person, no substantive limitations are expressly placed on the type of objectives that might be pursued by associations. However, while none of the guarantees are framed in absolute terms, neither the requirement to abide by law found in the African Charter nor the broad grounds of limitations found in instruments such as the International Covenant, the Convention on the Rights of the Child, the American Convention and the European Convention actually afford much indication as to what precisely will be regarded as objectionable.

This is a matter of concern for those who would associate-particularly where a formal process of approval or registration must be followed in order to establish an association as a legal entity-but it has also proved problematic for States in Europe on a number of occasions as the European Court has found restrictions imposed by them on the objectives of associations to be excessive and thus a violation of Article 11 of the European Convention. Nevertheless the jurisprudence which has emerged from the challenge to these restrictions now affords considerable guidance both as to what can legitimately be treated as unacceptable-with particular emphasis being placed on respect for the principles of legality and democracy-and as to the equally important basis on which any assessment of objectives for this purpose should be carried out.

LEGALITY

The starting point with respect to objectives is actually quite clear; an association should be able to pursue any activity which individuals alone are able to pursue since a grouping of individuals with the same objective does not thereby make that objective inherently objectionable. Indeed to accept the latter view would be to negate the very concept of freedom of association as a means for like-minded persons to come together. So it follows from this that, so long as the activities or objects are lawful, then it should be possible for an association to be formed to undertake or pursue them. Although an association cannot be formed to pursue specifically unlawful objectives, it should be borne in mind, when determining what conduct is unlawful in this context, that the permitted restrictions on internationally guaranteed rights and freedoms must also not be exceeded and thus make it impossible for an association to be established to pursue objects that are entirely legitimate. No blank cheque is thus given to States that would allow them to make unlawful anything to which they object.

Even where a particular activity is rendered unlawful without meeting the objection that this is through an improper use of State power, this status does not necessarily mean that the activity cannot still in some way shape the objectives of a would-be association. Certainly it is, in principle, perfectly proper for a body to be established to pursue a change in the law, so long as the intention is to do this only by lawful means. Recognition of this can be seen in X v United Kingdom in which it was found that the scope of certain offences concerned with homosexual relations was not such as to prevent the advocacy of reform of the criminal law. On the other hand, the fact that the applicant's object in Lavisse v France did not appear to be confined to such advocacy meant that no objection was raised to the refusal of the registration of an association to promote surrogate motherhood; the endorsement of surrogacy could be regarded as inciting the commission of the offence of abandoning children. Nevertheless the European Commission in that case regarded it as significant that this refusal-which meant that the association could not acquire legal personality-did not prevent the body from promoting a change in the law on this matter; it is thus implicit in the ruling that a refusal of registration to an association which merely sought to promote such a change would be incompatible with Article 1194. Similar objections that an association would cross the line between promoting a change in the law and promoting a breach of it were raised with respect to an association which wanted to promote the use of cannabis in Finland where such use was at the time a crime; in many respects the association concerned could be regarded as amounting to no more than a conspiracy to commit this very crime and thus could be seen as going well beyond advocacy of change.

The protection for the ability to propose changes in the established position can even extend to, and include, the very nature of the existing constitutional structure of a State. Thus in the European Court was not prepared simply to accept that objection could be taken to the applicant party's proposal for a federal system-in which Turks and Kurds would be represented on an equal footing and on a voluntary basis-because this would change the existing constitutional arrangements. Its reluctance to find such an objective inadmissible stemmed from the importance to be attached to political pluralism in applying the European Convention (and indeed other international human rights guarantees). On this basis it concluded that the fact that It is thus generally impossible to immunise matters from change through according them constitutional status.

DEMOCRATIC MEANS AND OUTCOME

However, there is an important qualification on the freedom to campaign for change in the legal and constitutional basis of the State at the end of the European Court's conclusion in the judgment just cited, namely, that the proposed change must not actually be anti-democratic. This qualification is both a corollary of the requirement that restrictions on freedoms such as that of association must be necessary in a democratic society and a reflection of the unambiguous stipulation in Article 17 of the European Convention that nothing in that instrument is to be interpreted as implying 'any right to engage in any activity or perform any act aimed at the destruction of any of the rights and freedoms' set forth in it. The qualification on the freedom to advocate change has subsequently been given some elaboration by the European Court in Refah Partisi (The Welfare Party) and Others v Turkey, demonstrating that it is in fact comprised of two elements, namely, that firstly the means used to that end must in every respect be legal and democratic; secondly the change proposed must itself be compatible with fundamental democratic principles.

Nevertheless it is a qualification that should not be taken entirely at face value. In the first place, although the insistence on the means being democratic rightly entails a process that respects political pluralism, the requirement of lawfulness must still be read subject to the need for any restrictions that ought to be observed being themselves compatible with international human rights standards; it is certainly conceivable that the means which have been rendered unlawful are in fact well-established elements of Convention rights or freedoms and this cannot be an acceptable constraint on the freedom to advocate change. Moreover the qualification in a concurring opinion by Judges Ress and Rozakis ought also to be noted, namely, that insufficient account is taken in the Court's formulation of the scale of the violation of the law. Certainly this must be correct as far as the sanction of dissolution is applied for the occurrence of such violations that are minor since otherwise the well-established principle of proportionality would not be respected. Nevertheless this does not affect the general inadmissibility of an association seeking to use unlawful means to achieve its objectives.

There should also be some concern about the way in which the second aspect of the qualification on the freedom to advocate change is applied, even though there is no basis for disputing the European Court's view that: a political party whose leaders incite recourse to violence or put forward a policy which fails to respect democracy or which is aimed at the destruction of democracy and the flouting of the rights and freedoms recognised in a democracy cannot lay claim to the Convention's protection against penalties imposed on those grounds.

The need for concern arises from the fact that it is not generally going to be self-evident that the objectives of an association are necessarily anti-democratic or violent and thus inherently objectionable. It is true that there were some early cases in which it was accepted that a State could, without further justification, object to bodies that had as their aim the promotion of fascist or communist ideology because these were organisations that were automatically to be regarded as being against the constitution and democratic values but the rulings in them now have to be approached with some care as more recent decisions demonstrate that over-simplistic conclusions can be drawn too readily about the possible threat posed by an association's stated objectives, especially where the latter use terms or concepts which are open to a pejorative construction but that is not their only possible meaning.

Thus in Vogt v Germany the European Court took into account the fact that the communist party had not actually been banned in the course of finding that the applicant's dismissal as a schoolteacher because of her membership of, and active role within, that party could not be necessary in a democratic society. It accepted that the dismissal was an act motivated by the legitimate aim of protecting constitutional democracy but the Court emphasised, that in determining the justifiability of such a step, the focus had to be on individual conduct and not abstract aims. In examining the former, it was evident not only that the applicant in this case had never confused her political and working lives-by using the classroom to promote party ideas-but also that she had asserted her belief in the German constitutional order.

Furthermore the absence of a formal ban on the party made it even harder to conclude that there was any danger being posed to that constitutional order by the employment as a teacher of someone who belonged to that party. The Court in that case was not actually concerned with whether it would have been acceptable then in Germany to have banned the party but the importance that was attached to what it did, rather than conclusions to be drawn from its general objectives, would certainly have made it very unlikely that a cogent case could have been made for the imposition of a ban; whatever suppositions there might have been about the nature of the communist party's objectives, it would at that time have been scarcely credible, given the way it actually operated, to regard it as being anti-constitutional in practice.

Similarly, while in Refah Partisi (The Welfare Party) and Others v Turkey it was generally accepted that preserving secularism was necessary for the protection of the democratic system in Turkey, it was only in the particular context of remarks showing a wish to bring into being an order based on religious rules that the advocacy of changes in the law to take account of certain religious concerns-such as with respect to the wearing of Islamic headscarves and the organisation of working hours in the public sector to accommodate prayers-would necessarily be regarded as threatening secularism and thus be objectionable.

HUMAN RIGHTS AND INTERNATIONAL HUMANITARIAN LAW

International humanitarian law is the law of armed conflict or law of war and their effects. The goal of international humanitarian law is to limit the effects of war on people and property and to protect particularly vulnerable persons. States have always been limited in the ways in which they conduct armed conflicts, from the adherence to national laws and bilateral treaties, to the observance of time-honoured customary rules. However, throughout history these limitations on warfare varied greatly among conflicts and were ultimately dependant on time, place, and the countries involved. Not until the 19th century was there a successfully effort to create a set of internationally recognized laws governing the conduct and treatment of persons in warfare. In the mid-1850s, Henri Dunant-founder of the International Red Cross-helped champion the first universally applicable codification of international humanitarian law: the Geneva Convention of 1864. From these roots, international humanitarian law evolved over the course of a century and a half. The Hague Conventions of 1899 and 1904 limited the means by which belligerent states could conduct warfare.

Many of the international treaties on armed conflict were made in response to the many new methods of warfare. World War I (1914-1918) witnessed the first large-scale use of poison, aerial bombardments and capture of prisoners of war. World War II (1939-1945) saw civilians and military personnel killed in equal numbers. The Charter of the United Nations (1945) stipulates that the threat or use of force against other states is unlawful, except in the case of self-defence. Following World War II, the Geneva Conventions of 1949, as well as its two Additional Protocols of 1977, further limited the means of warfare and provided protections to non-combatants civilians, and prisoners of war. In the aftermath of the atrocities of the Holocaust, the Genocide Convention of 1948 outlawed acts that were carried out with the intention of destroying a particular group. In addition to these conventions, international humanitarian law has been developed and refined through several statutes and precedents laid down by international tribunals set up to try war criminals, as well as advisory opinions the International Court of Justice.

Rights at Stake

Humanitarian law is the branch of public international law that comprises the rules, which, in times of armed conflict, seek to (i) protect persons who are not or are no longer taking part in the hostilities, (ii) restrict the methods and means of warfare employed, and (iii) resolve matters of humanitarian concern resulting from war. The term "humanitarian" is often used in everyday language in a very broad sense, and can be confused with the term "human rights." Although both are concerned with the protection of the individual, the two bodies of law apply to different circumstances and possess slightly different objectives. The main distinction between the two bodies of law is that humanitarian law applies to situations of armed conflict, while human rights protect the individual in times of both war and peace. Humanitarian law aims to limit the suffering caused by war by regulating the way in which military operations are conducted.

FUNDAMENTAL PRINCIPLES OF HUMANITARIAN LAW

International humanitarian law aims to limit the suffering caused by war by forcing parties engaged in a conflict to:

- engage in limited methods and means of warfare;
- differentiate between civilian population and combatants, and work to spare civilian population and property;
- abstain from harming or killing an adversary who surrenders or who can no longer take part in the fighting;
- abstain from physically or mentally torturing or performing cruel punishments on adversaries.

TYPES OF ARMED CONFLICT

International armed conflicts are conflicts between states. The four 1949 Geneva Conventions and Protocol I deal extensively with the humanitarian issues raised by such conflicts. The whole body of law on prisoners of war, their status and their treatment is geared to wars between States (Third Convention). The Fourth Convention states inter alia the rights and duties of an occupying power, i.e. a state whose armed forces control part or all of the territory of another state. Protocol I deals exclusively with international armed conflicts.

Under Protocol I of 8 June 1977, *wars of national liberation* must also be treated as conflicts of an international character. A war of national liberation is a conflict in which a people is fighting against a colonial power, in the exercise of its right of self-determination. Whereas the concept of the right of self-determination is today well accepted by the international community, the conclusions to be drawn from that right for the purposes of humanitarian law and, in particular, its application to specific conflict situations are still somewhat controversial.

The majority of today's armed conflicts take place within the territory of a state: they are conflicts of a non-international character. A common feature of many such internal armed conflicts is the intervention of armed forces of another state, supporting the government or the insurgents.

The substantive rules of humanitarian law governing *non-international armed conflicts* are much simpler than their counterparts governing international conflicts. They are derived from one main source, namely article 3 common to the four Geneva Conventions of 1949, which obliges the parties to an internal conflict to respect some basic principles of humanitarian behaviour already mentioned above.

Article 3 is binding not only on governments but also on insurgents, without, however, conferring any special status upon them.

Additional Protocol II of 1977 supplements Article 3 common to the Geneva Conventions with a number of more specific provisions. This is a welcome contribution to the strengthening of humanitarian protection in situations of internal armed conflict. Protocol II has, however, a narrower scope of application than common Article 3. It applies only if the insurgent party controls part of the national territory.

INTERNATIONAL AND REGIONAL INSTRUMENTS FOR PROTECTION

International legal instruments take the form of a *treaty* (also called agreement, convention, protocol) which may be binding on the contracting states. When negotiations are completed, the text of a treaty is established as authentic and definitive and is "signed" to that effect by the representatives of states. There are various means by which a state expresses its consent to be bound by a treaty. The most common are ratification or accession. A new treaty is "ratified" by those states who have negotiated the instrument. A state which has not participated in the negotiations may, at a later stage, "accede" to the treaty. The treaty *enters into force* when a pre-determined number of states have ratified or acceded to the treaty.

When a state ratifies or accedes to a treaty, that state may make *reservations* to one or more articles of the treaty, unless reservations are prohibited by the treaty. Reservations may normally be withdrawn at any time. In some countries, international treaties take precedence over national law; in others, a specific law may be required to give an international treaty, although ratified or acceded to, the force of a national law. Practically all states that have ratified or acceded to an international treaty must issue decrees, amend existing laws or introduce new legislation in order for the treaty to be fully effective on the national territory.

Many international treaties have a mechanism to monitor the implementation of the treaty.

Many provisions of the four Geneva Conventions, the two Protocols, and the Hague Conventions of 1899 and 1907 are broadly accepted as restating customary international humanitarian law applicable to all countries. Humanitarian law applies specifically to armed conflict situations, which would ordinarily qualify as "public emergencies". (Weissbrodt)

Unlike human rights treaties, which often have a monitoring body to which individuals and states can submit complaints, humanitarian law relies much more on informal procedures. The Geneva Conventions and the Additional Protocols require the States party to adopt a number of measures in order to assure compliance with these treaties. Some of these measures have to be taken in peacetime, others in the course of an armed conflict. In this short overview, only three such obligations will be mentioned, as examples:

Instructions to and training of the armed forces: the complex set of obligations arising out of the Conventions and the Protocols must be translated into a language which is clearly understandable to those who have to comply with the rules, in particular the members of armed forces, according to their ranks and their functions. Good manuals on humanitarian law play a decisive part in effectively spreading knowledge of that law among military personnel. Rules which are not understood by or remain unknown to those who have to respect them will not have much effect.

Domestic legislation on implementation: Many provisions of the Geneva Conventions and of their Additional Protocols imperatively require each State Party to enact laws and issue other regulations to guarantee full implementation of its international obligations. This holds particularly true for the obligation to make grave breaches of international humanitarian law (commonly called "war crimes") crimes under domestic law. In the same way, misuse of the red cross or the red crescent distinctive emblem must be prosecuted under domestic law.

Prosecution of persons who have committed grave breaches of international humanitarian law: Such persons must be prosecuted by any State party under whose authority they find themselves. That State may, however, extradite the suspect to another State Party which is willing to prosecute him. Individuals accused of violating humanitarian law may also be tried by an international criminal court. The United Nations Security Council has established two such courts: the Tribunals for the former Yugoslavia and for Rwanda. On 17 July 1998, a Diplomatic Conference convened by the United Nations in Rome adopted the Statute of the International Criminal Court.

Geneva Convention relative to the Protection of Civilian Persons in Time of War (1949) (article 44, 70).

This treaty protects refugees during war. Refugees cannot be treated as "enemy aliens".

Protocol Additional to the Geneva Conventions of 12 August 1949, and relating to the Protection of Victims of International Armed Conflicts (Protocol 1) (1977) (article 73).

"Persons who, before the beginning of hostilities, were considered as stateless persons or refugees... shall be protected persons..., in all circumstances and without any adverse distinction."

HUMAN RIGHTS AND LAWS REGARDING RIGHTS OF SELF-DETERMINATION

Self-determination is the free choice of one's own acts without external compulsion. In politics it is seen as the freedom of the people of a given territory or national grouping to determine their own political status and how they will be governed without undue influence from any other country. There are conflicting definitions and legal criteria for determining which groups may legitimately claim the right to self-determination.

HISTORY

Pre-20th Century

Origins: Just as colonisation and colonialism have been practiced throughout recorded history, political self-determination, on an individual level, has been documented similarly and cherished highly by collective peoples despite them; ancient Mesopotamia and the later Greek city-states are early examples of its practice. The employment of imperialism, through the expansion of empires, and the concept of political sovereignty, as developed after the Treaty of Westphalia, also explain the emergence of self determination during the Modern Era. During, and after, the Industrial Revolution many groups of people recognized their shared history, geography, language, and customs. Nationalism emerged as a uniting ideology not only between competing powers, but also for groups that felt subordinated or disenfranchised inside larger states, in this situation self determination can be seen as a reaction to imperialism. Such groups often pursued independence and sovereignty over territory, but sometimes a different sense of autonomy has been pursued or achieved.

Empires

The world possessed several traditional, continental empires such as the Ottoman, Russian, Austrian or Hapsburg, and the Qing Empire. Political scientists often define competition in Europe during the Modern Era as a balance of power struggle, which also induced various European states to pursue colonial empires, beginning with the Spanish and Portuguese, and later including the British, French, Dutch, and German.

During the early 1800s, competition in Europe produced multiple wars, most notably the Napoleonic Wars. After this conflict, the British Empire became dominant and entered its "imperial century", while nationalism became a powerful political ideology in Europe. Later, after the Franco-Prussian War in 1870, "New Imperialism" was unleashed with France and later Germany establishing colonies in Asia, the Pacific, and Africa. Japan also emerged as a new power. Multiple theaters of competition developed across the world:

- Africa: multiple European states competed for colonies in the "Scramble for Africa";
- Central Asia: Russia and Britain competed for domination in the "Great Game", while the Qing Empire attempted to convert western areas of Mongolia, Xinjiang and Tibet into sovereign territories;
- Eastern Asia: colonies and various spheres of influence were established, largely to the detriment of the Qing Empire.

The Ottoman Empire, Austrian Empire, Russian Empire, Qing Empire and the new Empire of Japan maintained themselves, often expanding or contracting at the expense of another empire. All ignored notions of self-determination for those governed.

Rebellions and Emergence of Nationalism

The revolt of New World British colonists in North America, during the mid-1770s, has been seen as the first assertion of the right of national and democratic self-determination, because of the explicit invocation of natural law, the natural rights of man, as well as the consent of, and sovereignty by, the people governed; these ideas were inspired particularly by John Locke's enlightened writings of the previous century.

Thomas Jefferson further promoted the notion that the will of the people was supreme, especially through authorship of the Declaration of Independence which inspired Europeans throughout the 19th century. The French Revolution was motivated similarly and legitimatized the ideas of self-determination on that Old World continent.

Within the New World during the early 1800s, most of the nations of Spanish America achieved independence from Spain. The United States supported that status, as policy in the hemisphere relative to European colonialism, with the Monroe Doctrine.

The American public, organized associated groups, and even Congressional resolutions, often supported such movements, particularly the Greek War of Independence (1821–29) and the demands of Hungarian revolutionaries in 1848. Such support, however, never became official government policy, due to balancing of other national interests.

After the American Civil War and with increasing capability, the United States government did not accept self-determination as a basis during its Purchase of Alaska and attempted purchase of the West Indian islands of Saint Thomas and Saint John in 1860s, or its growing influence in the Hawaiian Islands, that led to annexation in 1898.

With its victory in the Spanish-American War in 1899 and its growing stature in the world, the United States supported annexation of the former Spanish colonies of Guam, Puerto Rico and the Philippines, without the consent of their peoples, and it retained "quasi-suzerainty" over Cuba, as well.

WORLD WAR I AND II

Europe, Asia and Africa

Woodrow Wilson revived the American commitment to self-determination, at least for European states, during World War I. When the Bolsheviks came to power in Russia in November 1917, they called for Russia's immediate withdrawal as a member of the Allies of World War I. They also supported the right of all nations, including colonies, to self-determination." The 1918 Constitution of the Soviet Union acknowledged the right of secession for its constituent republics.

This presented a challenge to Wilson's more limited demands. In January 1918 Wilson issued his Fourteen Points of January 1918 which, among other things, called for adjustment of colonial claims, as long as the interests of colonial powers had equal weight with the claims of subject peoples. The Treaty of Brest-Litovsk in March 1918 led to Russia's exit from the war and the independence of Finland, Estonia, Latvia, Ukraine, Lithuania and Poland.

The end of the war led to the dissolution of the defeated Austro-Hungarian Empire and the creation by the Allies of Czechoslovakia and the union of the State of Slovenes, Croats and Serbs and the Kingdom of Serbia as new states.

However, this imposition of states where some nationalities (especially Poles, Czechs, and Serbs and Romanians) were given power over nationalities who disliked and distrusted them eventually helped lead to World War II. The defeated Ottoman empire was dissolved into the Republic of Turkey and several smaller nations, including Yemen, plus the new Middle east Allied "mandates" of Syria and Lebanon (future Syria, Lebanon and Hatay State), Palestine (future Transjordan and Israel), Mesopotamia (future Iraq). The League of Nations was proposed as much as a means of consolidating these new states, as a path to peace. During the 1920s and 1930s there were some successful movements for self-determination in the beginnings of the process of decolonization.

In the Statute of Westminster the United Kingdom granted independence to Canada, New Zealand, Newfoundland, the Irish Free State, the Commonwealth of Australia, and the Union of South Africa after the British parliament declared itself as incapable of passing laws over them without their consent.

Egypt, Afghanistan and Iraq also achieved independence from Britain and Lebanon from France. Other efforts were unsuccessful, like the Indian independence movement.

And Italy, Japan and Germany all initiated new efforts to bring certain territories under their control, leading to World War II. In Asia, Japan became a rising power and gained more respect from Western powers after its victory in the Russo-Japanese War.

Japan joined the Allied Powers in World War I and attacked German colonial possessions in the Far East, adding former German possessions to its own empire. In the 1930s, Japan gained significant influence in Inner Mongolia and Manchuria after it invaded Manchuria.

It established Manchukuo, a puppet state in Manchuria and eastern Inner Mongolia. This was essentially the model Japan followed as it invaded other areas in Asia and established the Greater East Asia Co-Prosperity Sphere. In 1912, the Republic of China officially succeeded the Qing Dynasty, while Outer Mongolia, Tibet and Tuva proclaimed their independence. Independence was not accepted by the government of China. In 1915 treaty of Kyakhta Outer Mongolia recognized China's sovereignty. However, the Soviet threat of seizing parts of Inner Mongolia induced China to recognize Outer Mongolia's independence, provided that a referendum was held. The referendum took place on October 20, 1945, with (according to official numbers) 100% of the electorate voting for independence.

Many of Eastern Asia's current disputes to sovereignty and self-determination stem from unresolved disputes from World War II. After its fall, the Empire of Japan it renounced control over many of its former possessions including Korea, Sakhalin Island, and Taiwan. In none of these areas were the opinions of affected people consulted, or given significant priority. Korea was specifically granted independence but the receiver of various other areas was not stated in the Treaty of San Francisco, giving Taiwan de facto independence although its political status continues to be ambiguous.

THE COLD WAR WORLD

The UN Charter

In 1941 Allies of World War II signed the Atlantic Charter and accepted the principle of self-determination. In January 1942 twenty-six states signed the Declaration by United Nations, which accepted those principles. The ratification of the United Nations Charter in 1945 at then end of World War II placed the right of self-determination into the framework of international law and diplomacy.

- Chapter 1, Article 1, part 2 states that purpose of the UN Charter is: "To develop friendly relations among nations based on respect for the principle of equal rights and self-determination of peoples, and to take other appropriate measures to strengthen universal peace."
- Article 1 in both the International Covenant on Civil and Political Rights (ICCPR) and the International Covenant on Economic, Social and Cultural Rights (ICESCR). Both read: "All peoples have the right of self-determination. By virtue of that right they freely determine their political status and freely pursue their economic, social and cultural development."
- The United Nations Universal Declaration of Human Rights article 15 states that everyone has the right to a nationality and that no one should be arbitrarily deprived of a nationality or denied the right to change nationality.

However, the charter and other resolutions did not insist on full independence as the best way of obtaining self-government, nor did they include an enforcement mechanism. Moreover, new states were recognized by the legal doctrine of uti possidetis juris, meaning that old administrative boundaries would become international boundaries upon independence, even if they had little relevance to linguistic, ethnic, and cultural boundaries.

Nevertheless, justified by the language of self-determination, between 1946 and 1960, the peoples of thirty-seven new nations freed themselves from colonial status in Asia, Africa, and the Middle East. The territoriality issue inevitably would lead to more conflicts and independence movements within many states and challenges to the assumption that territorial integrity is as important as self-determination.

THE COMMUNIST VERSUS DEMOCRATIC WORLD

Decolonization in the world was contrasted by the Soviet Union's successful post-war expansionism. Tuva and several regional states in Eastern Europe, the Baltic, and Central Asia had been fully annexed by the Soviet Union during World War II.

Now, it extended its influence by establishing satellite states in Eastern Germany and the countries of Eastern Europe, along with support for revolutionary movements in China and North Korea. Although satellite states were independent and possessed sovereignty, the Soviet Union often violated principles of self-determination by suppressing the Hungarian revolution of 1956 and the Prague Spring Czechoslovak reforms of 1968. It invaded Afghanistan to support an increasingly unpopular communist government assailed by local tribal groups.

Soviet actions were countered by the United States which saw communism as a world threat. The United States often supported other nations, regardless of their nature, as long as they remained anti-communist.

In spite of this, communism was seen in a different way by many Third World countries, where it sometimes became an ideology that united groups to oppose imperialism or colonization.

Consequently, many self-determination movements, which spurned some type of authoritarian government, were accused of being communist-inspired or controlled. Thus the United States entered into a 10 year war in Vietnam, taking over from French colonialists and supported Portugal in its attempts to hold on to Angola.

Asia

In Asia, the Soviet Union had already converted Mongolia into a satellite state, but abandoned its assistance to the Second East Turkestan Republic and gave up its Manchurian claims to China. With the world focused on the Korean War in late 1950, Communist China entered the conflict in support of North Korea while it simultaneously invaded Tibet. Tibet failed to gather support from appeals to Western states and the United Nations because Tibet's proclaimed independence was not accepted by the government of China, nor did Tibet receive foreign diplomatic recognition.

After its appeals for help were ignored or rebuffed, it submitted to the People's Liberation Army, and was granted a special status under the Seventeen Point Agreement. This relationship came under stress during the 1950s and was ultimately negated when China fully incorporated Tibet after the 1959 Tibetan uprising.

The conflict in Korea ended with a split of the country into two states. After attempts to annex the Republic of China (ROC), PRC failed and turned its attention to other issues. For various reasons, China under Mao Zedong became bitterly divided with the Soviet Union and developed an adversarial relationship during the Sino Soviet Split.

In Taiwan, the Guomindang established a one-party state that brought significant economic reform, but also created bitter political identity tension between mainland Chinese immigrants and earlier Taiwanese residents.

In 1947, India gained independence from The British Empire. Great Britain's empire was in decline but it adapted to these circumstanced by creating the British Commonwealth—since 1949 the Commonwealth of Nations—which is a free association of equal states.

As India obtained its independence, multiple ethnic conflicts emerged in relation to the formation of a statehood during the Partition of India which resulted in Muslim Pakistan and Hindu India. Before the advent of the British no empire based in mainland India had controlled any part of what now makes up the country's Northeast and there is ongoing Insurgency in Northeast India.

In 1971 Bangladesh obtained independence from the eastern half of Pakistan. Burma also gained independence from the British Empire, but declined membership in the Commonwealth. Ethnic conflicts that challenge the ruling government persist.

When the British began their exit from British Malaya, they sought to consolidate several of the previous ruled entities. This also sparked a war with Indonesia which did not want the consolidated state.

Indonesia gained independence from the Netherlands in 1949 after the Dutch failed to restore colonial control. As mentioned above, Indonesia also wanted a powerful position in the region that could be lessened by the creation of united Malaysia. The Netherlands retained Dutch New Guinea, but Indonesia threatened to invade and annex it. A vote was allegedly taken under the UN sponsored Act of Free Choice to allow West New Guineans to decide their fate, although many dispute its veracity. Later, Portugal relinquished control over East Timor in 1975, at which time Indonesia promptly invaded and annexed it.

Post Cold War

The Cold War began to wind down after Mikhail Gorbachev assumed power in March 1985. With the cooperation of U.S. president Ronald Reagan, Gorbachev wound down the size of the Soviet Armed Forces and reduced nuclear arms in Europe, while liberalizing the economy.

In 1989-90, the communist regimes of Soviet satellite states collapsed in rapid succession in Poland, Hungary, Czechoslovakia, East Germany, Bulgaria, Romania, and Mongolia. East and West Germany united, Czechoslovakia peacefully split into Czech Republic and Slovakia, while in 1990 Yugoslavia began a violent break up into its former 6 sub-unit republics.

Kosovo, which was previously an autonomous unit of Serbia declared independence in 2008, but has received less international recognition. In December 1991, Gorbachev resigned as president and the Soviet Union dissolved relatively peacefully into fifteen sovereign republics, all of which rejected communism and most of which adopted democratic reforms and free-market economies. Inside those new republics, four major areas have claimed their own independence, but not received widespread international recognition.

After decades of civil war, Indonesia recognized the independence of East Timor in 2002. In 1949 the communists won the civil war and established the People's Republic of China in mainland China. The KMT-led Republic of China government retreated to Taipei, its jurisdiction now limited to Taiwan and several outlying islands. Since then, the PRC has been involved in disputes with the ROC over issues of sovereignty and the political status of Taiwan.

As noted, self determination movements remain strong in some areas of the world. Some areas possess de facto independence, such as Taiwan, North Cyprus, Kosovo, and South Ossetia, but their independence is disputed one or more major states. Significant movements for self-determination also persist for locations that lack de facto independence, such as Tibet, Kurdistan Region, Chechnya, and Palestine.

Current Issues

Since the early 1990s, the legitimatization of the principle of national self-determination has led to an increase in the number of conflicts within states, as sub-groups seek greater self-determination and even full secession, and as their conflicts for leadership within groups and with other groups and with the dominant state become violent. The international reaction to these new movements has been uneven and often dictated more by politics than principle. The year 2000 United Nations Millennium Declaration failed to deal with these new demands, mentioning only "the right to self-determination of peoples which remain under colonial domination and foreign occupation."

In an issue of Macquarie University Law Journal Associate professor Aleksandar Pavkovic and Senior Lecturer Peter Radan outlined current legal and political issues in self-determination. These include:

Defining "Peoples"

There is not yet a recognized legal definition of "peoples" in international law. Vita Gudeleviciute of Vytautas Magnus University Law School, reviewing international law and UN resolutions, finds in cases of non-self-governing peoples (colonized and/or indigenous) and foreign military occupation "a people" is the entire population of the occupied territorial unit, no matter their other differences.

In cases where people lack representation by a state's government, the unrepresented become a separate people. Present international law does not recognize ethnic and other minorities as separate peoples.

Other definitions offered are "peoples" being self-evident (from ethnicity, language, history, etc.), or defined by "ties of mutual affection or sentiment," i.e. "loyalty," or by mutual obligations among peoples. Or the definition may be simply that a people is a group of individuals who unanimously choose a separate state.

If the "people" are unanimous in their desire for self-determination, it strengthens their claim. For example, the populations of federal units of the Yugoslav federation were considered a people in the breakup of Yugoslavia, even though some of those units had very diverse populations.

Libertarians who argue for self-determination distinguish between the voluntary nation (the land, the culture, the terrain, the people) and the state, the coercive apparatus, which they have a right to choose or self-determine.

Self-determination Versus Territorial Integrity

National self-determination challenges the principle of territorial integrity (or sovereignty) of states because it is the will of the people that makes a state legitimate. This implies a people should be free to choose their own state and its territorial boundaries. However, there are far more self-identified nations than there are existing states and there is no legal process to redraw state boundaries according to the will of these peoples.

Pavkovic and Radan describe three theories of international relations relevant to self-determination.

- The realist theory of international relations insists that territorial sovereignty is more important than national self-determination. This policy was pursued by the major powers during the Cold War.
- Liberal internationalism has become an alternative since that time. It promotes the abolition of war among states as well as increased individual liberty within states, and holds the expansion of global markets and cross-border cooperation diminishes the significance of territorial integrity, allowing for somewhat greater recognition of greater self-determination of peoples.
- Cosmopolitan liberalism calls for political power to shift to a world government which would make secession and change of boundaries a relatively easy administrative matter. However, also would mean the de facto end of self-determination of national groups.

Allen Buchanan, author of seven books on self-determination and secession, supports territorial integrity as a moral and legal aspect of constitutional democracy.

However, he also advances a "Remedial Rights Only Theory" where a group has "a general right to secede if and only if it has suffered certain injustices, for which secession is the appropriate remedy of last resort." He also would recognize secession if the state grants, or the constitution includes, a right to secede.

Vita Gudeleviciute holds that in cases of non-self-governing peoples and foreign military occupation the principle of self-determination trumps that of territorial integrity. In cases where people lack representation by a state's government, they also may be considered a separate people, but under current law cannot claim the right to self-determination.

On the other hand, she finds that secession within a single state is a domestic matter not covered by international law. Thus there are no on what groups may constitute a seceding people.

Methods of Increasing Minority Rights

In order to accommodate demands for minority rights and avoid secession and the creation of a separate new state, many states decentralize or devolve greater decision-making power to new or existing subunits or even autonomous areas. More limited measures might include restricting demands to the maintenance of national cultures or granting non-territorial autonomy in the form of national associations which would assume control over cultural matters.

This would be available only to groups that abandoned secessionist demands and the territorial state would retain political and judicial control, but only if would remain with the territorially organized state.

Self-determination Versus Majority Rule/Equal Rights

Pavkoviæ explores how national self-determination, in the form of creation of a new state through secession, could override the principles of majority rule and of equal rights, which are primary liberal principles.

This includes the question of how an unwanted state can be imposed upon a minority.

He explores five contemporary theories of secession. In "anarcho-capitalist" theory only landowners have the right to secede.

In communitarian theory, only those groups that desire direct or greater political participation have the right, including groups deprived of rights, per Allen Buchanan. In two nationalist theories, only national cultural groups have a right to secede. Australian professor Harry Beran's democratic theory endorses the equality of the right of secession to all types of groups. Unilateral secession against majority rule is justified if the group allows secession of any other group within its territory.

Constitutional Law

Most sovereign states do not recognize the right to self-determination through secession in their constitutions. Many expressly forbid it. However, there are several existing models of self-determination through greater autonomy and through secession.

In liberal constitutional democracies the principle of majority rule has dictated whether a minority can secede.

In the United States Abraham Lincoln acknowledged that secession might be possible through amending the United States Constitution. The Supreme Court in Texas v White, held secession could occur "through revolution, or through consent of the States." The British Parliament in 1933 held that Western Australia only could secede from Australia upon vote of a majority of the country as a whole; the previous two-thirds majority vote for secession via referendum in Western Australia was insufficient.

The Chinese Communist Party followed the Soviet Union in including the right of secession in its 1931 constitution in order to entice ethnic nationalities and Tibet into joining.

However, the Party eliminated the right to secession in later years, and had anti-secession clause written into the Constitution before and after the founding the People's Republic of China.

The 1947 Constitution of the Union of Burma contained an express state right to secede from the union under a number of procedural conditions. It was eliminated in the 1974 constitution of the Socialist Republic of the Union of Burma (officially the "Union of Myanmar"). Burma still allows "local autonomy under central leadership."

As of 1996 the constitutions of Austria, Ethiopia, France, Singapore, Saint Kitts and Nevis Republics have express or implied rights to secession. Switzerland allows for the secession from current and the creation of new cantons. In the case of proposed Quebec separation from Canada the Supreme Court of Canada in 1998 ruled that only both a clear majority of the province and a constitutional amendment confirmed by all participants in the Canadian federation could allow secession.

The 2003 draft of the European Union Constitution allowed for the voluntary withdrawal of member states from the union. There was much discussion about such self-determination by minorities before the final document underwent the unsuccessful ratification process in 2005.

Drawing New Borders

Once groups exercise self-determination through secession, the issue of the proposed borders may prove more controversial than the fact of secession. The bloody Yugoslav wars in the 1990s were related mostly to borders issues because the international community applied a version of uti possidetis juris in transforming existing internal borders of the various Yugoslav republics into international borders, despite the conflicts of ethnic groups within those boundaries.

The northern two-thirds of Quebec already has made it clear it will resist by force being incorporated into a Quebec nation.

The border between Northern Ireland and the Irish Free State was based on the borders of existing counties and did not include all of historic Ulster.

A Boundary Commission was established to consider re-drawing it. Its proposals, which amounted to a small net transfer to Northern Ireland, were leaked to the press and then not acted upon.

In December 1925, the governments of the Irish Free State, Northern Ireland, and the United Kingdom agreed to accept the existing border. Most Irish Nationalists and Irish Republicans claim all of Northern Ireland and are not particularly interested in new borders.

CURRENT MOVEMENTS

Australia

Recently (2003 onwards), self-determination has become the topic of some debate in Australia in relation to Aborigines (indigenous Australians). In the 1970s, the Aboriginal community approached the Federal Government and requested the right to administer their own communities. This encompassed basic local government functions, ranging from land dealings and management of community centres to road maintenance and garbage collection, as well as setting education programmes and standards in their local schools.

Balochistan Province

Since 1948, Baloch nationalists in Pakistan, Iran, and Afghanistan have been seeking independence as a separate state for the Baloch people from elements outside the country. The movement has culminated in several armed uprisings in both Pakistan and Iran, that have been crushed, especially during the 1970s. The movement is strongest in Balochistan (Pakistan), where it is led by the Balochistan Liberation Army and the Baloch Students Organization.

Basque Country

The Basque Country as a cultural region (not to be confused with the homonym Autonomous Community of the Basque country) is a European region in the western Pyrenees that spans the border between France and Spain, on the Atlantic coast. It comprises the autonomous communities of the Basque Country and Navarre in Spain and the Northern Basque Country in France.

Since the 19th century, Basque nationalism has demanded the right of some kind of self-determination. This desire for independence is particularly stressed among leftist Basque nationalists. The right of self-determination was asserted by the Basque Parliament in 1990, 2002 and 2006. Since self-determination is not recognized in the Spanish Constitution of 1978, some Basques abstained and some even voted against it in the referendum of December 6 of that year.

However, it was approved by a clear majority at the Spanish level, and with 74,6% of the votes in the Basque Country. The derived autonomous regimes for the BAC was approved in later referendum but the autonomy of Navarre (*amejoramiento del fuero*: "improvement of the charter") was never subject to referendum but just approved by the Navarrese Cortes (parliament).

There are not many sources on the issue for the French Basque country. *Euskadi Ta Askatasuna* (ETA) Euskadi Ta Askatasuna or ETA is an armed Basque nationalist and separatist organization. Founded in 1959, it evolved from a group advocating traditional cultural ways to a paramilitary group with the goal of Basque independence. Its ideology is Marxist-Leninist.

Biafra

Biafra Republic was first declared in 1967 by Lt. Col Chukwuemeka Odumegwu Ojukwu but the state could only survive for 30 months during which Nigerian government fought the break-away republic to annex it. Over 3 million Igbos lost their lives in the ensuing war. In 1999, a new group of activists formed an organization Movement for the Actualization of the Sovereign Republic of Biafra (MASSOB). Various other other groups have been formed with similar agenda.

Catalan Countries

Paisos Catalans (in catalan, often literally translated into English as *Catalan Countries*) refers to the territories where Catalan language was historically spoken. These correspond with some parts of the medieval Crown of Aragon (concretely Catalonia, Balearic Islands, Valencia and La Franja in Spain, Northern Catalonia in France, the city of Alghero in Italy, and Andorra). Nowadays there are movements which support the independence of Catalan Countries from Spain and France, but they only get significant support in Catalonia. Some of the parties of Catalonia, Valencian community, and Balear islands that follow this idea are Republican Left of Catalonia and Republican Left of the Valencian Country, Estat Catala, Partit Republica Catala, Popular Unity Candidates, Valencian Nationalist Bloc, Bloc per Mallorca, etc. Furthermore, there are some other Catalan groups and movements that want the independence of Catalan Countries, such as: Sobirania i Progres, Deu Mil per l'autodeterminacio, Catalunya Estat Lliure, Sobirania Valenciana, etc. All these political parties and movements follow a non-violence way to express their ideas.

Recently, there have been some series of non-binding and unofficial referenda "popular votes" (consultes populars, in catalan) held in municipalities around Catalonia, in which voters indicate whether they support Catalan independence from Spain.

Chechnya

Under Dzhokkar Dudayev, Chechnya declared independence as the Chechen Republic of Ichkeria, using self-determination, Russia's history of bad treatment of Chechens, and a history of independence before invasion by Russia as main motives. Russia has restored control over Chechnya, but the separatist government functions still in exile, though it has been split into two entities: the Ahmed Zakayev-run pro-Russian Chechen Republic (based in Poland, the UK and the US), and the Islamic Caucasus Emirate.

Germany

Under conditions of peace and in democratic state the focus of German public addresses weaker topics, as especially the *Rights of informational self determination*. This is a new topic in the context of surveillance of public areas and surveillance at work.

Israel and Palestine

The right to self-determination as outlined in public international law is often referenced by both sides in the ongoing Israel-Palestinian conflict.

Jammu and Kashmir

United Nations Security Council Resolution 47, adopted in 1948, called for a plebiscite to decide the fate of Kashmir. The All Parties Hurriyat Conference (APHC), an alliance of 26 organizations in Kashmir seeks self-determination according to the UN resolution. Some groups have suggested that a third option of Independence be added to the resolutions two options of union with India or union with Pakistan. According to the above-mentioned resolution, Paksitan was being directed by the UNO to withdraw its forces and civilians from Gilgit-Baltistan and refrain from any interference in the issue. Today, still after 63 years of signing of covenant resolution, Pakistan occupies Gilgit-Baltistan region of J&K and refuses to comply with UNO resolutions on Kashmir. This has literally stalled the peace process.

HUMAN RIGHTS AND DEVELOPMENT: THE LEGAL (HI)STORY

The human rights community possesses an elaborate set of principles and norms that relate to the practice of development. The intellectual and operational focus of the human rights community, however, has rested almost exclusive upon a sub-set of civil and political rights in isolation from their economic context and broader struggles of social and economic change . No major human rights watchdog organizations exist for economic, social, and cultural rights, which are generally relegated to obscure UN sub-committees whose work never becomes newspaper headlines. Beyond routine declarations about the indivisibility of all rights, for all intents and purposes, most economic, social and cultural rights have not been part of human rights practice for most of the last half century.

Why were these rights so neglected? It seems there are two major reasons. The first is political: the economic rights agenda is more deeply connected to interventionist, non-liberal, and possibly even anti-individualist approaches to social change.

This approach was, and remains uncomfortable to many powerful people and governments in the West (Scott 1999: 644). This tension was reinforced by the Cold War politics, when ESC rights –and *all* human rights, really— became deeply politicized.

Economic, social and cultural rights were championed by communist and many Third World countries, who used them as weapons in the fight for a New International Economic Order and against US/Western hegemony. Western countries, in the meantime, focused exclusively on civil and political rights . For many politicians in the West, the entire body of law related to economic rights and the "right to development" was synonymous with cynical attempts to wiggle out of civil and political human rights obligations and destroy free markets worldwide.

The end of the Cold War profoundly changed the nature of the competing blocs and the strength of their ideological discourses, and as a result this vehemently partisan and partial interpretation of human rights has lost its sway. Indeed, the "universality, indivisibility, interdependence and interrelationship of all human rights" –in the language of the 1993 Vienna declaration— are now only rarely explicitly challenged, except by a handful of Asian countries . Yet, another major barrier against the mainstreaming of ESC rights remains.

There is a sense within the human rights community that the very nature of economic, social and cultural rights is fundamentally different from, and more difficult to implement than, civil and political rights. The latter, it was argued, are "negative" rights, meaning that governments need to abstain from certain behaviors (arbitrary imprisonment, torture, etc.), whereas the former are "positive" rights, often involving costly action. As such, many organizations have found it easier to push for the former. At the conceptual level, this separation has been broken down over the last two decades, and human rights declarations nowadays always refer to the indivisibility and complementariness of the two categories of human rights if not to their mutually reinforcing nature. In practice, however, the separation is still deeply alive.

The reason for this separation may be that it is not immediately clear what the Convention on Economic, Social and Cultural Rights obliges signatories to do. As article 2 states:

"Each party undertakes to *take steps* individually and through international assistance and cooperation, especially economic and technical, *to the maximum of its available resources*, with a view to *achieving progressively* the full realization of rights recognized in the covenant, by all *appropriate means*, including particularly the adoption of legislative measures."

With rights so vague and full of escape clauses, who could not forgive human rights advocates for their focus on monitoring and exposing the much clearer civil and political rights?

It is only in 1994 that the Committee on Economic, Social and Cultural Rights finally clarified these vague terms more stringently, giving them some intellectual and practical bite. According to the so-called Maastricht principles, the "maximum of available resources" clause, which had been interpreted as removing pressures from Third World countries on the grounds of their general state of poverty and budgetary limitations, has been interpreted to mean that a *minimum core obligation* exists to ensure the satisfaction of the minimum essential levels of rights, and that states must demonstrate that every effort has been made to use the resources at their disposition in an effort to satisfy, as a matter of priority, these minimum obligations.

Similarly, the "achieve progressively" wording, usually interpreted so to allow indefinite postponement of state obligations, has been defined to mean a) that states must move as expeditiously as possible; and b) that retrogressive measures are not permissible, not even if justified by progress on the realization of other rights (CESR 1994).

Note also that the Convention on ESC rights contains two rights whose obligations are unconditional, *i.e.*, not subject to progressive realization. These are the right to primary education and the freedom to establish trade unions (de Feyter 2001: 264).

In addition, the human rights community has come to define the nature of state obligations regarding economic, social and cultural rights along a continuum that blurs the distinction between commission and omission. These include the obligation to *respect* (i.e., states ought not take any measures that deprive people from a right they already enjoy); the obligation to *protect* (i.e., states must provide protection against deprivation by a third party); and the obligation to *provide* or *fulfill* (i.e., states have to progressively ensure that everyone on their territory enjoys the full rights). These three categories then, as applied to each individual right, can be the basis of a human rights analysis and for the development of subsequent strategies to address concrete rights issues. The categories can also provide the means to develop indicators, measure outcomes, and develop strategies – the kind of stuff development actors desperately need.

The right to development

Development as a concept first entered the human rights edifice through the debate on the "right to development." The idea was launched by the Senegalese jurist M'Baye in 1972, during a period of radical reform for the New International Economic Order (NIEO) and the Charter on the Economic Rights and Duties of States.

This was a period, beginning in late 1972, during which many Third World countries used their numerical majority in the UN to negotiate reforms in the global political economy of trade, finance, investment, aid, and information flows. This effort was led by well-known nationalist Third World statesmen, who were emboldened by the success of the OPEC embargo, which was widely perceived to have been a victory of the Third World over rich countries, and which many thought reshuffled the world's economic cards.

The notion of a right to development fitted well within this struggle, providing a legal and ethical authority to the Third World's request for international resource re-distribution. In addition, it acted as a counter-argument against rich countries' exclusive insistence on enforcement of political and civil human rights, with the argument essentially resting on the maxim that 'there are other rights that for the people of the Third World are more of a priority than Western civil rights, and you all ought to contribute to their realization rather than continuing to bother us about civil and political rights' (Rosas 1995: 248-5; Development gap paper 340).

Acrimonious discussions about the NIEO persisted for years, but led to no concrete results, apart from the signing of a few international commodity agreements. By the early 1980s, these negotiations, and any thought of a new international economic order, were unceremoniously terminated after the election of Ronald Reagan, Margaret Thatcher, and Helmut Kohl and the simultaneous weakening of OPEC and the outbreak of the Third World debt crisis. The intellectual and political pendulum swung dramatically rightwards, and structural adjustment replaced international reform.

Surprisingly, though, the notion of a right to development did not die altogether – partly because the developing countries learned that, in the words of Ian Brownlie, "it had become evident that the political futures market was in the area of human rights and it was therefore prudent to pursue policy goals under that banner."

After much legal wrangling, in 1986 the right to development was finally adopted as a UNGA resolution, stating that "the right to development is an inalienable human right by virtue of which every human person and all peoples are entitled to participate in, contribute to, and enjoy economic, social, cultural and political development, in which all human rights and fundamental freedoms can be fully realized."

This was the kind of rhetorical victory that diplomats cherish: the Third World got its right to development, while the First World ensured that the right could never be interpreted as more of a priority than political and civil rights, and that it carried no resource transfer obligations. On a less cynical level, the declaration does present a holistic approach, forcefully affirming the indivisibility of all human rights, putting the economic, social, and cultural rights on par with the civil and political ones – an important step in the development of the human rights edifice.

Demonstrating the extent to which rich countries found even this non-binding and emasculated compromise unacceptable, the U.S. voted against the resolution while 10 or so other OECD member states abstained.

Hence, even in its watered-down form, the right to development amounted to a rich country vs. poor country debate, as it had been from the beginning. In addition, according to most legal scholars, it was bad law: vague, internally contradictory, duplicative of other already clear codified rights, and devoid of identifiable parties bearing clear obligations.

What it really said is that all rights are important – period. Article 6 of the resolution, for example, states "All human rights and fundamental freedoms are indivisible and interdependent; equal attention and urgent consideration should be given to the implementation, promotion and protection of civil, political, economic, social and cultural rights."

While conceptually correct in affirming the indivisibility of human rights, the new supposed right to development does not provide any means for implementation. As law, it remains soft, declaratory, and deliberately emasculated.

Human rights, once set down on paper, never die, even though no one may care much about their survival. Rather, they mutate into working groups, commissions, and expert panels, each of which produces reports that are occasionally the subject of discussions in low-level meetings.

Sometimes, however, out of this patient work, contested or marginal rights obtain a second lease on life, which is what happened to the right to development. At the 1993 World Conference on Human Rights in Vienna, the right to development was re-adopted, this time with unanimity, as part of the broader Vienna Declaration and Program of Action. The relevant article 10 reads:

"The World Conference on human rights reaffirms the right to development, as established in the Declaration on the Right to Development, as a universal and inalienable right and an integral part of fundamental human rights. ... While development facilitates the enjoyment of all human rights, the lack of development may not be invoked to justify the abridgment of internationally recognized human rights."

Note that, as in the General Assembly Declaration on the Right to Development, the latter sentence was inserted at the insistence of the Western countries. Still, the Vienna Declaration was adopted with unanimity, and it can thus be claimed that the right to development now reflects a global legal consensus, and as such represents a significant victory for its advocates, Pyrrhic as it may be.

Following this promotion, in 1997 the right to development was honored with its very own "independent expert," whose mandate was (barely) renewed by the UN Human Rights Commission in late 2000. The expert has by now produced four annual reports, followed by annual discussions in the appropriate sub-Committee of the Human Rights Commission.

In retrospect, the right to development remains contested, and has had little if any impact . If, on the one hand, one believes that it affirms a claim by people to a form of economic growth that is distributed fairly over the inhabitants of a country and supported by international resource transfers, then one has to confront the opposition of most rich countries and the apathy of most poor countries –as well as the fact that there is nothing in international law generally that would even remotely support such a claim.

If, on the other hand, one believes it affirms that all people have the right to development, which consists of, and is realized through, the realization of every existing category of human rights, and which all people, states, and organizations ought to respect, then one essentially is in the presence of a correct, beautifully worded, operationally meaningless, and duplicative assertion.

The latter is clearly what the right to development amounts to, and the kind of meaningless statements it leads to are nicely exemplified in the following quote form the UN Working Group on the Right to Development, describing the right as being "multidimensional, integrated, dynamic and progressive. Its realization observes the full observance of economic, social, cultural, civil, and political rights. It further embraces the different concepts of development of all development sectors, namely sustainable development, human development, and the concept of indivisibility, interdependence, and universality of all human rights" .

Perhaps recognizing the difficulty of defining the right in abstract legal terms, the Independent Expert, Arjun Sengupta, has tried to better define the concrete substance of a right to development. Given the fact that, ultimately, very few people care what he does with his mandate, he has been able to go remarkably far in this work, thinking rather interestingly about a number of the conceptual issues related to development, to which we will come back later. Some of these points go far beyond the right to development, but relate to what can be called the international law of development. In this work, he oscillates between a very strong defense of the liberal mantra –no development without free markets, free trade, free flows of investment, and free elections – and an equally strong acceptance of a deep interventionist role for national and international governments in the promotion of development. In short, his policy prescriptions are inconsistent, contradictory, vague, and economically weak. These words may sound like a mean-spirited attack on the personality or competency of Mr. Sengupta, but they are truly not meant to convey that. He is a lawyer, after all, and has sure done more of an effort to get a grasp of his economics than most economists ever do with the law. More importantly, he works in a field of total absence of criteria or structures for judging effectiveness: as said above, as good as nobody cares about what he writes n any case, and the human rights edifice hardly provides him with a tool to challenge the dominance of economic thinking as the sole way of thinking about development. Hence, he must improvise, stumbling on, like a person in the dark, hands stretched out, trying to break nothing too expensive and still get somewhere...

The International Law of Development (ILD)

From a legal perspective, the "right to development" debate is not the end of, or synonymous with, concerns for economic rights and matters of development. If one moves beyond the specific and limited "right to development" debate one observe a growing body of international law, standards, and principles by which states and even non-state actors ought to behave so as to promote development worldwide. This body is not strictly spoken part of human rights law, but rather of the broader area of international economic law. It has been called the international law of development, although there is generally recognition that it does not (yet) exist as a formal, widely accepted body of law.

According to other sympathetic observers, the emerging law of development includes:

- the acceptance of "positive discrimination" in favor of developing states (Slinn 1999: 305; 314; Bunn 2000: 1447 ff.);
- the notion of differentiated rights, duties and responsibilities ;
- the notion that concerns for good governance and accountability shall be mainstreamed (Slinn 1999: 311; Bunn 2000: 1451 ff.; Paul 1997: passim; McAuslan, 1996);
- the right to participation by those concerned in the programs that affect them (Paul 1997; Bunn 2000: 1444 ff. ; Sengupta 1999: par. 36 ff.)
- and the necessity to eliminate all forms of discrimination against women, protect and rehabilitate environments, respect and protect cultures and cultural diversity

The international law of development is broader than human rights law, for it is about the responsibilities of and relations between those actors who engage in international economic relations –countries as well as corporations. The overall aim is to rethink and reorient the dynamics of international economic governance towards its impact on development – to add "development" as part of a "quality assurance" mechanism for the global governance system (Slinn 1999: 317).

At the same time, the ILD is narrower than human rights law, for its reach is less wide and much less codified than human rights law. Its relevance for the traditional development enterprise is rather low, and we will hence not come back to it until the very end of this chapter, when we go beyond the development paradigm and development assistance.

Paul also observes, in a nice understatement, that "while there now exists a rather comprehensive body of basic substantive principles, there is clearly a compelling need to develop additional principles that focus more closely on the procedural and institutional changes needed to implement these principles at state levels."

In other words, we can argue that there exists such a law in theory, but practically it is meaningless.

Priorities and conflicts among human rights

Another major criticism of the human rights edifice is that it provides no tools for making choices or setting priorities. This is especially visible in the case of ESC rights. Every specialist on some right, and every committee devoted to some right – be it the right to food, to education, to water, to a clean environment – essentially attempts to "prove" that the right needs to be respected, protected, and provided and leaves it at that. Every specialist will also tell you that all rights are indivisible, equally important, and mutually reinforcing. However, as development specialists know from practical experience, there is no way that most countries in the world can achieve all of these in an "indivisible" and "simultaneous" manner, even if they sincerely wished to do so, and as a result, the formulaic repetition of the indivisibility of all rights seems increasingly like empty sloganeering. Scott lays the problem out best:

the 1993 Vienna Declaration on Human Rights states: 'All human rights are universal, indivisible and interdependent and interrelated.' This trend is, on the whole, to be welcomed for its potential to promote less legalistic and category-dominated interdependence analysis. There are dangers, however, to keep in mind. One such danger is that the Vienna Declaration expresses the interconnection of human rights in so many abstract ways that it risks conveying the impression of meaningless sloganeering and thereby undermines attempts at more serious invocations of the ideas of interdependence and indivisibility. Another danger is of a flattening effect created by undifferentiated references to 'all' human rights. While it is true that the interdependence of overarching, grand categories of human rights speaks to the equal importance of those broad categories for human dignity, all legally recognized human rights cannot be of equal importance. This is especially true in concrete contexts where (hopefully principled) trade-offs among human rights are sometimes necessary. Rights advocates and defenders must encourage the idea of interdependence but not to the point that it helps to promote a discourse where all human rights, and thus all human rights violations, are treated as legally indistinguishable.

This debate is of great importance to the development community, which constantly faces the need to make tough choices about priorities and trade-offs . Note that, on conflict resolution, the need for trade-offs and prioritization is likely to be even more acute in post-conflict situations (Uvin 2001).

There can be many instances requiring certain human rights not to be acted upon. One, as said above, involves the necessity to make priorities, as resources and administrative capacity – for both developing country governments and development aid agencies – are insufficient to make significant progress on all human rights simultaneously. Another concerns the need to make choices between human rights as they conflict in particular instances. Cases of such conflicts, involving the rights to free speech versus the right to peace, or the rights to participation in cultural life versus gender rights, abound. As Klare correctly writes:

"Many of the most important rights are formulated at an exceedingly high level of abstraction... Thus rights concepts are sufficiently elastic so that they can mean different things to different people. But there is an even deeper problem. Even those who would consistently invoke rights in the service of self-determination, autonomy and equality find that rights concepts are internally contradictory.

This is because, like all of legal discourse, rights theory is an arena of conflicting conceptions of justice and human freedom... Thus choices must be made in elaborating any structure of human rights guarantees... The problem is that rights discourse itself does not provide neutral decision procedures with which to make choices..." .

Governments may need to curb the enjoyment of particular rights for in order to secure a different important right; they may need to sacrifice enjoyment of certain rights in the short term in order to enjoy them later; or they may need to curtain the enjoyment of certain rights in order to retain the same right for a separate group of people.

In other words, there may be conflicts between rights, or between the long term and the short term, or the group and its constituent elements. It is only if one were to argue that none of the above problems ever occurs in the real world –a blatantly false proposition — that the issue of prioritization and choice merits no explicit attention.

On what grounds ought choices about these matters to be made? As Klare says, merely invoking rights does not provide us with a means to decide between competing rights, especially as there is no legal mechanism in any human rights document that explicitly addresses the issue of choices and trade-offs.

And, maybe even more importantly, by whom should such choices be made? These are questions the human rights community has hardly addressed – they are heretical questions, for they cast into doubt the basis upon which the entire rights edifice is built: indivisibility. Each right is as important as all the others, as necessary, as untouchable. Fundamentally, then, the human rights community does not like to address the issue of choice and priority, for it takes the certainty out of the religion.. Human rights advocates, just like development practitioners, like to come down the mountain like Moses, bearing the stone plates of progress, safe in their knowledge that they occupy the high moral ground, relaying a revealed wisdom which is sacred and beyond human doubt.

Perhaps this is overstating things a bit. In fact, the legal community *has* developed some answers to the choices issue, though they are mostly limited and excessively formulistic. It is possible, for example, to distinguish a certain hierarchy of rights, based on their significance and solidity in international law.

The criteria to make that determination include the number of states that are parties to the instruments that provide for the right in question; whether states that are parties to the conventions are allowed to derogate from the protection of the right; whether the right is construed as a peremptory norm; whether the violation of the right is characterized as an international crime; or whether the right is considered *jus cogens* (Yasuaki 199: 117; Meron 1986). In addition, as was already noted above, article 4 of both the 1996 Covenants allows for temporary derogations of certain rights due to a state of emergency.

The suspensions ought to be limited in time and subject to some process of control, and they ought to be proportionate to the challenge faced. Some rights, however, are explicitly prohibited from suspension, even in times of emergency. One can thus suppose that these rights are more prioritary, more inviolable, more sacred, than the others.

While the principles governing emergency-justified suspensions are certainly of broader relevance and should be kept in mind as we continue our discussion, article 4 of the CCPR does not serve the development practitioner very well. It deals only with one possible instance, namely public emergencies, and focuses on only one actor, namely the state.

All this may be of some relevance to development practitioners as they decide whether they can ethically or legally work with a certain state that is violating human rights. It does not help them make concrete choices in the many much more ordinary, routine cases where conflicts or priorities among human rights (or development aims) exist. Art. 4 of the Convention on ESC rights is more related to the kind of issues the development practitioner typically deals with, allowing for limitations on the enjoyment of rights "for the purpose of promoting welfare in a democratic society." However, apart from telling us that such matters can at least be considered, this article to tells us nothing about how to implement any of this. Thus, the question remains: how should and human rights and development practitioners approach the matter of choices and trade-offs among human rights?

Before we present a few possible paths to solve this problem, one general remark is necessary. First, for human rights scholars, any trade-offs, to the extent that they can be justified, are bound to be temporary; they "cannot represent an inherently desirable form of government. Such sacrifices ought to be a matter of profound regret and discomfort" . This is evident. After all, fundamentally, the human rights mantra is that all rights are essential, universal, mutually reinforcing, and non-derogable; they are a package deal that cannot be unbundled.

Four solutions to the trade-off/priority problem can be distinguished in the human rights literature: the first is denial, the second and third involve empirically and theoretically grounded criteria for making decisions, and the fourth uses a participatory method to elicit the opinions of those concerned. To some extent, these strategies, outlined below, mirror those discussed earlier when we analyzed human rights responses to charges of Euro-centrism.

Denial

Denial is not really a solution, but it may well be the most popular way of addressing the issue of prioritization and trade-offs in the legal literature. It essentially consists of denying the relevance and even existence of the problem by minimizing or trivializing it. Arjun Sengupta, the special rapporteur for the right to development, argues that:

the problem [of prioritization] should not be blown out of proportion or used as a pretext for avoiding action.[This is because] many of the activities needed to fulfill these rights do not need many financial resources. They may require more input of administrative or organizational resources whose supplies are relatively elastic, depending on political will rather than on finance or physical infrastructure. Similarly, the resources requested may not be limited to national availability but also can be complemented by international supply."

Quite some work by the Committee on ESCR Rights displays the same categorical optimism.

While it is true that developing countries possess significant resources – especially if we add the resources currently allocated for military expenditures – and could spend more of these resources on guaranteeing basic human rights, it is equally true that merely asserting this fact does nothing to alter the existence of the problem. No state in the world, including the rich countries, has ever spent *all* of its resources on guaranteeing the basic rights of the poor. None of them have ever been willing to forego military spending for that goal, or, for that matter, much any other goal. None of them will make major progress in the direction of better resource allocation overnight. Hence, in the real world, the problem of scarcity and the need for prioritization does pose itself, and simply defining it away is nonsense. This is the typical castle-in-the-sky approach that has made so much human rights writing (especially regarding ESC rights) irrelevant and easy to dismiss. Resources are indeed no problem in a world where every government is suddenly and exclusively committed to the realization of basic human rights for all to the exclusion of all other concerns, knows how to achieve this goal efficiently and is fully supported by the international community and international organizations. Unfortunately, this world does not exist and no amount of legal proselytizing will bring it into being. Resource and priority questions, therefore, are bound to be crucial for all people seeking social change, whether within their own communities or across borders.

Empirical reasoning: the priority of economic growth

The second solution is to engage in empirically based reasoning, seeking to assess on the basis of case-specific evidence to what extent claims for trade-offs or priorities are justified, and what kind of choices and temporary derogations are allowable. As it stands, such empirical analysis is entirely missing from the human rights literature . One possible method for such an empirical approach could be anthropological, with decisions about priorities being made on the basis of a deep factual understanding of specific local cultural and religious norms and practices.

In practice in the development community, however, the most common empirical approach has been of an economic nature. The yardstick, then, is efficiency: experts seek to determine, based on economic data and theory, which rights have the highest pay-off or which ones will bring about the highest rate of economic growth, on the basis of the argument that this in turn will facilitate the achievement of other rights . QUOTE HADDAD 1999. The advantages of this empirical approach are many. It is scientific, building on the foundations of the most quantitatively rigorous of all social sciences. It employs the language of economics, which is a politically powerful one that has dominated development thinking for decades. Finally, it holds the promise of constant improvement: chose this option and not only can you make scientifically based choices about priorities right now, but in addition your need to make such choices will automatically decrease as economic growth increases the size of the resource pie. The resource optimism of economists –every pie can grow forever, and when it grows, everyone's piece will be bigger and tastier — is very appealing. There are, however, a number of problems with this strategy.

The first is most evident and simply empirical as well: economic growth does not automatically lead to improvements in human rights or well-being for all, and significant progress can be made at very different levels of national income. It may well be the case that the extent to which economic growth produces benefits for all, instead of for a small minority, depends on the degree of popular participation, democracy, accountability, and lack of repression that exist within the polity – in other words, that the realization of at least some human rights precedes any such empirical economic calculation.

Still, it seems likely that with economic growth the chance increases of countries being able to protect and promote a larger range of rights for a larger number of people. In addition, the opposite is certainly true, e.g., there is overwhelming evidence that, in the absence of economic growth, poverty and inequality always increase, and with them the enjoyment of rights falls. Hence, at the very least one could make the point that, all things being equal, if trade-offs or prioritizations among human rights are required, those choices that do not retard economic growth should be privileged.

But even this does not solve the matter, though, for two very fundamental reasons. One is that, usually, all things are *not* equal and determining priorities and trade-offs in function of their likely economic impact may amount to a very sub-optimal rights strategy. As Sengupta correctly observes, "those rights that require least expenditures of the resources which are most binding or in short supply will tend to be realized first. There is a risk that this may, as a result, fail to bring about the social change that is the ultimate objective of following the rights approach to development." In addition, once we get to these choices, we enter squarely into the domain of uncertainty, for opinions clearly differ dramatically on the best way to achieve growth, the best ways to deal with the efficiency-equity trade-off – or even the exact nature of that trade-off.

In addition, this strategy insufficiently addresses (pre)-existing inequalities in resource endowments. It takes the present as a given, as a fixed matter beyond human judgment – some countries and individuals are poor, while others are rich, period – without making judgments as to the historical processes that led to this situation. If past human rights violations – from colonialism to internationally supported post-independence exclusionary policies to corporate monopoly practices – are co-responsible for much of today's poverty, inequality and lack human rights fulfillment, does there exist an *a priori* obligation to redress these, before concerns of efficiency are even considered?

It is true that no question about priorization can be separated from questions about resource distribution, and the historical paths that have led to the current state of affairs. What seemed to be a rather technical matter at first – given that my aid agency's budget, or my government's budget, is limited, what to spend the scarce resources on first? – soon becomes a deeply political matter: why is my aid agency's budget as small as it is? What can be done to increase it?

Once one begins envisaging significant reform in the current national and international distribution and use of wealth – redistribution of assets or incomes, mechanisms for social security, etc – many (but not all!) of the painful choices and trade-offs would indeed disappear. Hence, much of the "tough choices" debate is indeed predicated on accepting the current patterns of spending and power in the world.

The empirical-economic method refuses to deal with this sort of issues: it has no tools, nor, typically, any inclination, to address such questions. It seems, thus, a rather inappropriate methodology for dealing with the 'tough choices' conundrum.

A human rights approach politicizes resource constraints (and the past processes by which these constraints have come to take the form they take), and provides an overall framework for judging alternative uses of resources. The human rights language, however, does possess little in the ways of concrete tools to make the choices that still do remain necessary. There exist two more paths out of the conundrum, however.

Theoretical Reasoning: Basic Rights

The third solution has been developed by Henry Shue in his seminal 1982 book, *Basic Rights*. It defines a sub-set of rights that can be seen as taking priority over others. His is an attempt to reason through the issue, rather than to empirically induce it. He defines basic rights as those required for the enjoyment of all other rights, *i.e.*, those without which no other right could be meaningfully said to exist. These rights are subsistence or minimal economic security; physical security (i.e., "not to be subjected to murder, torture, mayhem, rape, or assault"), and liberty. They constitute "everyone's minimum reasonable demands upon the rest of humanity".

Shue explicitly allows for the fact that "if a right is basic, other, non-basic rights may be sacrificed, if necessary, in order to secure the basic right." (ibid.) He thus offers us a compelling criterion for priorization and making trade-off. Note that Shue takes great care to argue that these basic rights are not more valuable or more satisfying or somehow morally superior than the other human rights; their priorization is merely functional and operational — a matter of sequencing, not of assigning valuing.

However, Shue does not even attempt to tackle the extraordinarily difficult task of specifying the concrete and complete list of basic rights, and, as Donnelly demonstrates, once one actually attempts to do so in a logically and ethically consistent manner, it is not clear if it can be done with total clarity and logic –or with any kind of brevity.

On the other hand, while theoretically subject to debate, a basic rights approach allows non-specialist practitioner organizations to define a minimum core rights about which there can be no doubt – rights that cannot be traded off, or made secondary to other concerns. This is an appealing idea, as clarity and brevity often can be.

Participatory methods

Both the previous solutions – the economist's one of selecting the right with the greatest pay-off in terms of growth, or Shue's method of defining a sub-set of basic rights that need to be satisfied before all others – are expert-based solutions, in which outsiders develop the tools allowing them to make tough choices. Much of the work of social change is of that nature. The fourth solution differs from the two previous ones in this respect.

The final solution is participatory, consisting of the development of mechanisms that allow those most concerned to play an active role in the prioritization or trade-off of rights. This strategy follows from the human rights approach itself, which strongly stresses participation and democracy . We have discussed it already supra, and will do so again, at some length, infra –testimony to the centrality of participation in the human rights approach to development. Suffice it here to say that, both ethically and legally, it makes evident sense that, if aid agencies need to make tough choices in how they spend their resources in a given community, it makes intuitive sense that a key criterion ought to be the opinion of the people concerned themselves.

Bibliography

Adrian Burgess: *Psychological Medicine of HIV Infection,* Oxford, New York, Oxford University Press, 1995.

David Hulme: *Beyond the Magic Bullet: NGO performance and accountability in the post-cold war world,* West Hartford, Kumarian Press, 1996.

Forsythe, David P.: *Human Rights and World Politics.* Second Edition. Lincoln: University of Nebraska Press, 1989.

Fozzard, S.: *Surviving Violence: A Recovery Program for Children and Families,* Geneva, International Catholic child Bureau, 1995.

Friedmann, J.: *Empowerment: The Politics of Alternative Development,* Oxford, Blackwell, 1992.

Gabriel, Marie Cruz: *Children of the street,* New York, Penguin Books, 1994.

Ghadially, Rehana: *Women in Indian Society,* New Delhi. Sage Publication, 1988.

Gies, Frances and Joseph: *Women in the Middle Ages.* New Jersey: Barnes and Noble, 1978.

Hannum, Hurst: *Autonomy, Sovereignty, and Self - Determination: The Accommodation of Conflicting Rights.* Philadelphia: University of Pennsylvania Press, 1990.

Harry J. Steiner: *Diverse Partners: non-governmental organizations in the human rights movement,* Cambridge, Harvard Law School and Human Rights Internet, 1990.

Jacobson, David : *Rights Across Borders: Immigration and the Decline of Citizenship.* Baltimore and London: The Johns Hopkins University Press, 1997.

John Boli and George Thomas: *Constructing World Culture: International Nongovernmental Organizations Since 1875,* Stanford, Stanford University Press, 1999.

John Clayton Thomas: *Public Participation in Public Decision: New Skills and Strategies for Public Managers,* San Francisco, Jossey-Bass Publishers, 1995.

John Ehrenberg: *Civil Society: The Critical History of an Idea,* New York, New York University Press, 1998.

Johnston, Barbara Rose: *Life and Death Matters: Human Rights and the Environment at the End of the Millennium.* Walnut Creek, California: AltaMira, 1997.

Jonathan A. Fox and L. David Brown: *The Struggle for Accountability: The World Bank, NGOs, and Grassroots Movements,* Cambridge, Mass.: MIT Press, 1998.

Kees Biekart: *The Politics of Civil Society Building: European Private Aid Agencies and Democratic Transitions in Central America,* Utrecht, International Books, 1999.

Kimlycka, Will: *The Rights of Minority Cultures.* Oxford and New York: Oxford University Press, 1995.

Lauren, Paul Gordon: *The Evolution of International Human Rights*: Visions Seen. Philadelphia: University of Pennsylvania Press, 1998.

Leon Gordenker: *NGOs, the UN & Global Governance,* Boulder, Lynne Riener, 1996.

Marcos Arruda: *NGOs and the World Bank: Is It Possible to Collaborate Critically?,* Rio de Janeiro: PACS, 1995.

Matthias Finger: *Environmental NGOs in World Politics,* London, Routledge, 1994.

Mayer, Ann E.: *Islam and Human Rights: Tradition and Politics.* Oxford and Boulder: Westview Press, 1999.

Mittal, Anuradha and Peter Rosset: *America Needs Human Rights.* Oakland, California: Food First Books, 1999.

Monshipouri, Mahmood: *Democratization, Liberalization, and Human Rights in the Third World,* Boulder, Colorado: Lynne Reinner Publishers, 1995.

Musgrave, Thomas D.: *Self-Determination and National Minorities.* Oxford: Clarendon Press, 1997.

Paul J. Nelson: *The World Bank and NGOs: The Limits of Apolitical Development,* New York, St. Martin's Press, 1995.

Paul Wapner: *Environmental Activism and World Civic Politics,* Albany, SUNY Press, 1996.

Peter Willetts: *Pressure Groups in the Global System,* London, Francis Pinter, 1982

Rehman, Javaid: *The Weaknesses in the International Protection of Minority Rights.* The Hague, The Netherlands: Kluwer Law International, 2000.

Thomas Carroll: *Intermediary NGOs: the supporting link in grassroots development,* West Hartford, CT: Kumarian Press, 1992.

Thomas Princen and Matthias Finger: *Environmental NGOs in World Politics,* London, Routledge, 1994.

Wei Jingsheng; Kristina M. Torgeson: *The Courage to Stand Alone: Letters from Prison and Other Writings,* New York: Viking, 1997.

Index

❑❑❑